Reaffirming Higher Education

Reaffirming Higher Education

Jacob Neusner &
Noam M. M. Neusner

with an epilogue by William Scott Green

Transaction Publishers
New Brunswick (U.S.A.) and London (U.K.)

Library of Congress Catalog Number: 99-14816
ISBN: 1-56000-425-8
Printed in the United States of America

Library of Congress Cataloging-in-Publication Data

Neusner, Jacob, 1932–
    Reaffirming higher education / Jacob Neusner and Noam M.M. Neusner; with an epilogue by William Scott Green.
        p. cm.
    Includes bibliographical references (p.   ) and index.
    ISBN 1-56000-425-8 (alk. paper)
    1. Education, Higher—Aims and objectives—United States. 2. Universities and colleges—United States.   I. Neusner, Noam M. M. (Noam Mordecai Menahem) III. Title
LA227.4.N47   1999
378.73—dc21   99-14816
                                                                    CIP

To

William Safire

Contents

Preface

In universities (1)who teaches?, (2) what?, (3) to whom?, and (4) why?: These are the four questions addressed in these pages. The answer, neither conservative nor liberal in the conventional sense of the words, will show how American higher education is different from higher education everywhere else and in all other forms. And we note how our country uniquely benefits because of the difference. The specific context in which we ask these questions finds its form in a much-debated issue: How should universities balance the requirements of teaching with those of scholarship? The received consensus that scholarship counts first and teaching comes second, has lost its hold. For in an academic world in which few publish — 95 percent of publication comes from 5 percent of the professors, and two-thirds of the professorate have never published a line! -- insisting on the priority of scholarship rings hollow. Few publish, fewer perish. Those who do perish do so at the hands of their colleagues, not for failing to publish, but for publishing too much.

The American college and university today has to assess what difference scholarship makes to teaching, and what teaching means to scholarship. Many assume the best scholars cannot teach, and the best teachers do not produce published contributions to learning or keep up with those of others. We argue that professors who do not publish should perish, and publishing scholars who disdain teaching should perish with them. What makes the American university unique is its insistence that scholars teach, that education counts, and that the task of the academy is defined by sharing what we learn. Colleges that tolerate a faculty lacking all scholarly ambition and universities that treat students as impediments to the calling of research -- both fail.

Ours is a program of reform and renewal, defending classical convictions about scholarship and teaching mounted in the center of the academic consensus. Ours is a position in the middle of the road, which —

alas! -- is never crowded.

Because we deal here with publishing, teaching, and scholarship, the shank of the book is devoted to the importance of the individual professor. Were we to limit our account to that one character, we would leave the impression that we think only isolated efforts by individuals can make a difference. Yet individuals can only survive. Only communities prosper. Universities flourish when professors work together and teach one another along with their students. The only truly consequential universities are also the largest and best-organized ones, the ones that take pride in their work and take their work seriously because they are answerable to large constituencies. So we mean to describe a labor of reform and renewal for both the institutional and personal dimensions that would encompass the ideal of the university and the academic ethic.

We therefore seek the connection between the individual and the institution: for the faculty, the academic department, and for the student, the academic major. There, we propose, the work of rebuilding begins. On that account we include an epilogue by Dean William Scott Green, founding chairman of the department of religious studies at the University of Rochester. As the creative force for the nation's most successful Department of Religious Studies, and as guiding spirit of his university's revolutionary curriculum, Green places into perspective everything that we wish to say about higher education. He shows why we can speak of "we" and not merely "I" in our program for the academic renewal of classical ideals in the American academy. At many points we allude to ideals he describes in his epilogue, so the argument is meant to form a virtuous circle.

Green speaks out of his own record of remarkable success. By the criteria of student enrollments, faculty achievement, and, above all, the intellectual vitality and cogency of the department's major, the Rochester model is not only a paradigm for what an effective department can accomplish, but also a rare example where the academic study of religion flourishes at all. Perhaps because the discipline of the academic study of religion (as distinct from the academic study of theology or of the social scientific study of religion) is new, Green, as one of its more ambitious representatives, undertakes serious reflection on its purpose and structure, where it succeeds, where it does not. But the main thrust of the book—an individual can do much in the academy, even under current conditions — is demonstrated best in Green's account of what he himself has created. That is why we decided to give him the last word. He shows what can be done.

A peculiarity of the book should be noted. Since it is jointly authored, we speak of "we" throughout. We mean to present a seamless narrative, but the tasks of each author are distinct. Some sections of the book refer to events in the career of the senior author. Rather than tell the story by shifting to "I," which would prove disruptive, we have chosen to speak at that point in the name of "the senior author." The junior author, whose eye is trained for a dispassionate rendering of events, has not participated in the fray of academic debates. The combined perspectives, we hope, describe as well as prescribe.

This book benefits from the senior author's experience in both types of institutions that comprise academic higher education in this country: the small, elite liberal arts college, and the massive, mass-enrollment, urban, commuter university. Each typifies the best in the remarkably diverse range of schools that comprise American higher education. As Professor of Religion at Bard College and Distinguished Research Professor of Religious Studies at the University of South Florida, the senior author is fortunate enough to enjoy two very different settings for teaching, both of which have shaped his view of how the problems addressed here should be considered. Each institution offers its own challenges, and makes life interesting.

One is huge, public, and populist in its admissions, the other is tiny, private, and elitist. And what they have in common is truly excellent, productive, and intellectually stimulating departments of religious studies and faculties encompassing academic superstars. And each in its way enjoys the leadership of thoroughly professional academic administrators, who demonstrate every day that higher education under both public and private auspices is led by responsible and effective people who facilitate the work of teacher-scholars, in libraries, laboratories, and classrooms. As Green describes the promise of how departmental organization can shape higher education, so too, do the deans, provosts, presidents, and other staff at Bard and USF show that the academy can perform its business with professionalism and pride.

The senior author expresses thanks to the University of South Florida and to Bard College for ongoing research support.

The junior author of this book has studied the results of America's system of higher education up close, at its pinnacle at The Johns Hopkins University and in the trenches, in America's economy. He gives thanks to his professors, especially Kyle McCarter, Stephen Dixon, Hugh Kenner, and Bill Freehling, who each in his own way, demanded more from this student than he was inclined to give. And thanks, too, to the editors and colleagues who, even without Ph.D.'s, give daily lessons in clear thinking: Adam Levy, Kevin Shinkle, John McCorry, Galen Meyer, Rebecca Cox, Steve Matthews, Mike Frankel, Mathew Horridge, C.T. Bowen, Phil Jacobs, Chuck Hawkins, John Cranford, Caitlin Hendel, and Steve Proctor. Thanks, too, for research assistance to Buddy Jaudon at the *Tampa Tribune*. And, of course, thanks to my wife Andrea and daughter Emma, who inspire me every day.

This book is aimed at both those who both strive to make universities better, and those who find in colleges only disappointment.

Jacob Neusner
Distinguished Research Professor of Religious Studies
University of South Florida, Tampa
and
Professor of Religion
Bard College
Annandale-on-Hudson, New York
jneusner@luna.cas.usf.edu

Noam M. M. Neusner
Reporter
Bloomberg News
Bethesda, Maryland

1

Who Should Teach in a University?

The Difference Professors Make

Why is a college or university different from all other forms of education and transmission of knowledge? Because professors teach, and by definition, they do a different job from all other teachers. They qualify to teach because they have made themselves scholars — people who not only communicate what they learn, but also test what they think they know. What marks the university professor as special is the power to infuse learning with a critical spirit in response to the call of curiosity. Professors alone make the difference — and only then the right kind of professors.

What ingredient separates a university from a CD-ROM, taped televised lecture, a high school advanced-placement curriculum, or an encyclopedia? All four convey useful knowledge. Then how do we know what makes the university unique among media for disseminating learning?

This is the question that should shape the future of higher education because universities are no longer the main producers of knowledge and never were the only way to seek illumination. To be sure, Americans will continue to attend colleges and universities, assuring that many of those institutions will not fail financially in wide numbers. But now and still more in the future, many Americans pursue learning through new media, correspondence courses, distance-learning arrangements, trade schools, or computer tutorials or audiotapes that can be played on the daily commute. Today, far more than in the past, colleges and universities compete for students with quite different modes of conveying higher education — and different theories of the definition of higher education. That is why the character of the American campus as the institutional medium for teaching, learning, and the pursuit of knowledge today determines its own fate. But that is as it should be, for character alone will differentiate one university from another.

Computer technology, which once served to create and manage information, now transmits it. Most information found in university libraries is as accessible in the Vaasa, Finland, or Dunedin, New Zealand, as it is in Cambridge, Massachusetts. If books and other amassed information are all that matter, then what makes one university superior to another? The Internet affords access to the bibliographical resources of the whole world. Interlibrary loans, state university library networks, and regional consortia supply to outlying academies the resources of internationally famous collections. Along these same lines, technical schools, computer-assisted learning and branch campuses organized ad hoc for businesses who request them — these tear down the walls that situate universities in some one place. If universities function largely as a training ground for people to use technology or to supply immediately saleable skills for future employees, then they cost too much. Those skills can be and are taught better elsewhere. But can they make the claim that they offer a different kind of learning altogether, one to which society should assign scarce resources?

We ask a simple question, and seek to answer it by breaking it into its components: Why do we learn? How should we learn? To whom we should teach? What should be the stuff of learning? In short, who teaches what to whom and why? The last question, that pertaining to curriculum, is an enigma until the first three can be answered. The "why" enters when we ask whether the task of education is to inform or to change minds. The "how" requires attention when we wonder whether the lecture system serves any useful educational purpose. The "to whom" demands that we reconsider the prevailing opinion that pretty much every high school graduate who wishes to and who can afford it should go to college, without regard to the relevance of a college education to that student's goals, if any. The "what" focuses our attention on those components of the curriculum that concern these writers in particular: the character and consequence of the humanities, particularly those humanities that have entered the curriculum in the past quarter-century.[1]

Conventional wisdom dictates that as goes the curriculum, so goes the university. That explains why Yale University in 1995 refused to accept a $20 million grant to establish a stronger presence in the study of "Western civilization." To Yale, the donors, and those who followed the controversy, which unfolded in painful detail before angry alumni, the university's refusal to accept the gift was a curricular one, about the priorities of teaching one subject over another. And so it happens, that whenever universities debate their futures, they often focus on what they teach, which then answers all the other questions in this book. Curriculum, in this manner, makes clear the purposes of learning (experience the values of the West or of a wider variety of cultures), who should be the teachers (those who have studied classic works of thought or those who have studied or experienced more exotic cultures), and who should be learning (the most qualified or a diversity of students, talented or not).

But if curriculum dictates all that follows, then it leaves wide open the question of how university instruction is different from any other. Content, now widely available both to the college educated and everyone else, cannot justify the huge expense of attending and supporting universities. If higher education is merely a more advanced version of high school, a more expensive form of an encyclopaedia, or a more personal form of CD-ROM, it will ultimately be surpassed by any of the three institutions, or many others that will one day emerge. Even now instruction by e-mail and by interactive television competes with the classroom and offers to many more people, at much lower unit-cost, the information that comprises education in most classrooms. After all, in each of those formats, there is a source of information, and someone seeking it. Each system of instruction expresses information in a unique way, peculiar to its medium.

So if not curriculum, what makes the university different, especially from other forms of content-based instruction? It is not a simple question to answer. That is because the university is a teaching institution like a high school, an accumulation of facts like an encyclopedia, and a repository of new forms or media of learning like a CD-ROM. It is at once different and the same, treated as a unique species while performing the same tasks as ordinary ones. So the distinctions are not clear. And that leaves American higher education open to criticism that it is unable or unwilling to rebut, because in many ways, those in universities themselves cannot make the distinctions between what goes on in their own institutions and that which goes on in so many others. Understandably, universities point to the prestige they confer, and the lack of such prestige in, say, the correspondence course. But conviction flags, and the question remains: Why does a university education cost so much if the information is available elsewhere at pennies on the dollar?

The confusion begins with teaching. On the campus, among professors, teaching simply never means the same thing. From the definitions of teaching that we now survey, professors must somehow choose for themselves a purpose higher than the display of erudition, although many settle for that alone. They must define the purpose of teaching — its content and its character — and make sense of what is clearly a debate with many angles and many pitfalls. A style that befits one professor does not treat another so kindly. But eventually, whether by choice or by habit, professors do choose. And that choice often yields their personal answer to the question that answers so many others: What makes college so special?

Information-Mongering vs. Tradition-Inculcating?

Some define teaching as transmitting information, others as inculcating tradition. Is teaching, as technophiles would have us believe, only or mainly the transmission of information, for the purpose of understanding subsequently more difficult information? In the sciences, knowledge often is built upon knowledge, yielding still more questions and mysteries that the next stage is expected to answer. Increasingly, the working world employs this teaching model, where skills are added as the need arises. Someone unschooled in computers will have the capability of mastering the software he needs to know, but no more. That may leave someone who can use four or five programs on a personal computer, but not understand how the whole machine works. Similarly, someone who has mastered organic chemistry is ready for molecular cell biology, which ultimately helps build towards an understanding of the organism. This understanding later allows a student to be considered for medical school application; thus demonstrating how in medicine in particular, knowledge not only builds on itself, but must be mastered before integrated fields of information, like pharmacology or neural medicine, can be understood.

The building blocks of education in this model usually follow a logical pattern of smaller to bigger, and this model yields a teaching pattern that tends to emphasize information. It is driven by exams, which permit a professor to do one of two things: see how well the class is understanding the material, or rate the class against a predetermined statistical law that predicts the likelihood of success in a group. Called a bell curve, it is employed chiefly for large groups, and it predicts a distribution of success in any task — with most students completing the exam with "average" results. Thus students may perform very well and be regarded as having performed according to the average; or a student could do poorly, along with his peers, and earn a passing grade, undermining the theory behind the building-block model. The student has learned enough information to compare favorably to other students, not the capacity to move on to the next level of knowledge.

Notwithstanding this contradiction, this building-block model of teaching enjoys support largely from a group we call traditionalists. In the humanities, they argue that a education of quality can only be judged by exposure to a certain canon – a collection of building blocks. Led by the National Association of Scholars, this group of traditionalists emphasizes subject matter that should be at the core of classroom instruction as they define it. Certain books, certain authors, certain languages take precedence over all others, with a full complement of certain history, certain philosophy, and certain science. The traditionalist view also values literacy and its demonstration, and tends to rail against any efforts to remove standards from admissions. A college education without Shakespeare, they argue, cheats students of access to all that has stood the test of time, with solid reason. But that raises the basic issue: What separates college from high school? Is it the subject matter? Is it the quality of the students? The traditionalists make their case on the issue of curriculum, but they do not appear to give much thought to the transmission of it. To be sure, they don't look at teaching as a faceless art where the textbook alone matters. But they also place subject matter ahead of all other issues. So they leave themselves exposed to the criticism that they are no different from a meddling school board, eager to prescribe subject matter, but no particular method with which to teach it. They have established an expectation of a curriculum and an academic methodology that extends out the high school experience four years. In addition, they look backwards for the standards worth upholding. Where English composition, mathematics, and foreign languages were once required course work for baccalaureate degrees at the nation's finest colleges, those requirements are now routinely waived or watered down. The traditionalists like to point out that knowledge was once sequential, that students once had to do much more before reaching certain plateaus of an education. NAS research shows that the average elite college in 1964 offered

127 courses without prerequisites; by 1993, that average number had surged to 582.[2] With budgets driven by enrollment, what choice faced professors but to dumb down the curriculum? But matters present more than a single face. Prerequisites in the humanities rarely set the norm for the curriculum, other than the major. Professors in the humanities rarely set their courses in sequential order, with subject B naturally flowing from subject A, which happened to be given last semester. That means every course is introductory, and, in the nature of things, surveys a mass of data.

With statistics showing the multiplication of introductory courses, it is no wonder that the traditionalists favor teaching that is self-referential and closely linked to a common canon. A "Great Books" curriculum, for instance, seeks to identify and teach those works that determined the essential challenges of entire academic fields and ways of thought. Grouping subjects together in survey, or core, classes has the appeal of insuring that every student will get a certain dose of information, just as the hors d'oeuvres act before a fancy meal. A little taste of everything will suffice to give a happy diner all that they need to know.

But as William Green argues in the epilogue, a generalized approach to teaching obscures the problem of expertise: "General learning is not learned generalization, and being able to generalize does not mean being a generalist." Those who have expertise don't want to leave students ignorant of the deepest mysteries of their subjects; those who don't have expertise are no better at imparting wisdom than a textbook. Which is to say, not any different and therefore undeserving of the responsibility for teaching a survey of information.

Notwithstanding the NAS's interest in the issue, the survey course died in the 1960s. By then, professors in most subjects had achieved a level of specialization that made coordination with other fields difficult, if not impossible. There are a number of colleges — St. John's College, Columbia College — that have used the generalist model of teaching. But in certain subjects, especially the sciences, generalism is viewed with concealed disdain by leading professors. Why, they ask, teach Darwin when the most exciting work is being done in microbiology?

But definitions of good teaching do not always rest with curriculum. The live interaction between teacher and student is taken to define the sole venue of teaching. Indeed, some argue that teaching is a by-product of time. In time-focused teaching, a professor is teaching best when he is in front of a classroom or talking to students. This time-oriented model assumes that learning occurs most often when professors are in the presence of students, transmitting some kind of information or wisdom. In its most limited sense, the time-model asks of the professors that they devote themselves to their students. Small colleges, for instance, New College of the University of South Florida, want their professors to spend nearly all of their time with students. What such universities sell is personal encounter. Whether their professors read books and write books interests them not at all. Then what the professors teach, in this model of a college (never a university) education, is simply what they learned before they began to teach. No wonder the Mr. Chipps model runs out of steam, and, in the classic formulation of an ideal education — Mark Hopkins on one end of a log, the student on the other — the tutorial turns into a transaction of personal, not intellectual, exchange. That may have its merits, and clearly no university can be sustained without students talking to professors. More on that later.

But academia is a bureaucracy, and therefore those who propose such an ideology must enforce it with rules about credit hours, committee service, office hours, and other duties. So the premise that learning occurs when professors spend time with students exacts the charge of professional incompetence. To Mr. Chipps we offer this caveat: You can stand before an amphitheater of students and teach but say nothing; you can run a seminar with no focus or purpose; you can meet with students and discuss anything but course work. The senior author of this book counted as colleagues (but never as friends) more than a few who spent their days mostly chatting with undergraduates. Perpetual accessibility, for personal as much as educational matters, turns professors into unpaid therapists and hand-holders. Even so, but, among students, parents, and alumni, this model of teaching enjoys wide support. It also persuades legislators to evaluate professors by the number of courses they teach, the number of hours they spend with students. They cannot understand the wage scale of professors who teach no more than ten hours a week. What else do they do?

This raises another issue. Should teaching be student-oriented? Does the truest teaching occur when a professor stops to consider a student's point of view? In the view of some, this is the only form of teaching that matters. It is a vision of teaching fed by scorn for cattle calls where thousands of students pack an amphitheater to hear a professor give canned lectures. This is a legitimate gripe, one that can be voiced on private campuses as well as large state schools, because professors have managed to distance themselves from undergraduates. Ohio, for example, passed in mostly symbolic legislation, a law requiring professors to spend 10 percent more time with students in classrooms.[3] The Florida Legislature passed a law requiring "twelve contact hours" weekly. Quite what the well-meaning legislators meant no one knew. What information is going back and forth, and what exchange takes place? There is a distinction between spending time with students and engaging them in real learning. One is friendship; the other, discourse.

Research without Students?

In the another model of teaching, students learn only from professors who are specialists engaged in highly developed academic fields. This, for definition's sake, is hyperscholarship, where professors teach each other and allow students to witness but not participate. Hyperscholarship traces its roots to the invention of a the modern university, when teaching became an act of discovery and not recapitulation. It occurred first in the sciences and medicine, and liberated from erudites the humanities. It created the social sciences. Hyperscholarship, in its rudimentary form, is what differentiates college from high school: Professors must do original research in their field, high school teachers do not.

But hyperscholarship — research without students — has its share of critics, and both authors take their places among them. Excluding students from the academy, except as necessary, makes hyperscholarship intensely specific, ultimately inaccessible to anyone without particular skills. It is also lucrative, since hyperscholarship most often occurs in the sciences, where applications of knowledge have the potential to make money, which explains the self-interest in the critics of hyperscholarship; they either do not understand or envy the particular skills of specialized professors. Nevertheless, they do have a point. Hyperscholarship occurs only when professors are freed from the responsibilities of teaching students, and thus evades for our purposes a lowest common definition of what teaching is all about. It is therefore easy prey for muckrakers such as Charles Sykes and Roger Kimball, who — with plenty of good reason and ample evidence — have pilloried professors in the general press.

Hyperscholarship has also encouraged professors who are not really specialists to adopt the trappings of specialization: jargon, aloofness, rejection of any critic who is not a full participant in the field, and castigation of any critic within it. Such methods, employed by professors in the humanities bent on propagating an ideology instead of inquiring into the basis of one, make for even easier targets than scientists working on complicated problems. Perhaps the demise of departments of English brought about by "lit crit" and the jargon of postmodernism represents an extreme, and the collapse of the structures of anthropology and sociology under the weight of politically correct ideology yet another. Professors who espouse Marxism or Marxist causes as a substitute for scholarship are ridiculed by conservatives and moderates alike for circling the wagons when criticized — they do not argue in the name of ideology, choosing instead to couch their defense in the language of hyperscholarship. To their critics and many disinterested observers, their defense makes no sense. After all, what kind of theory can't be criticized in a university, of all places?

To the defense of hyperscholarship come many different types of teachers, and not merely leftists. But most of its defenders, particularly defenders of what now pass for the social sciences, literary criticism and ethnic studies, come from the left. They latch onto a general theory of relativity of knowledge — all learning and all knowledge are matters of identity. Therefore any challenges to the validity of one fact, one field, one theory can be rebuffed by a torrent of nonsense that makes sense only to the true believers. In this world, journals are read by perhaps dozens, lectures understood by perhaps a few handful is, and whole fields — literary criticism a most definite example — are written off entirely. Author John Ellis notes that "lit crit" lectures, once widely attended, now are ignored. The languages of whole fields of learning have become self-celebratory and unintelligible to outsiders: "Those who don't speak the latest arcane language are dismissed as lacking sophistication ....[Yet] if these professors are so confident about their ideas, why don't they try harder to explain themselves to the reading public? The answer may lie in the fact that they are not really confident at all, and with good reason. Their vaunted ideas are in fact a self-contradictory muddle."[4] Needless to say, critics of academia don't have to struggle to find examples of such addlebrained thinking. The problem for professors — both good and bad — is when those critics take on the one institution which permits professors to justify all forms of inquiry as a university-protected goal: Tenure. To be sure, hyperscholarship is an outgrowth of the ideals of academia: Professors freely engaged in the creation of knowledge. It also encourages cliques of likeminded ignoramuses to protect their corners of the academy by barring lifetime employment to anyone who might challenge the status quo, since after all, tenure is a variation on peer review. Tenure is intended to protect the good, not the bad, but in fact sustains both. Tenure allows professors to meet minimal standards for labor, relying on past achievement of much more substantial requirements. Among the minority of professors who have published at all, the vast majority publish one book and fall silent. And it is not as though the one book they do publish marks the climax of years of effort; it ordinarily turns out to be their doctoral dissertation, which, having been mined for nine articles, soldiers on in yet another campaign. Tenure permits some professors to take advantage of pursuing scholarship above all else. It also permits professors to pursue nothing, whether scholarship or teaching. These professors often serve as case studies of why tenure should be dismantled, but what they prove is how easily tenure was granted in their time — and today. And since professors make comparatively little money by comparison with their researcher counterparts in industry, tenure is taken as a fringe benefit akin to lifetime job security. To be sure, just as tenure replaces the need to make money, it may also replace the need to achieve. In the world of business, achievement and monetary gain have a direct relationship; in the academy, they do not. Tenure is the reason why.

Tenure without Solid Achievement

Tenure makes clear that those who defend scholarship's merits can be specious and that those who emphasize teaching may be no better. Most professors who defend the system of tenure, which is linked to the past achievement of scholarship, usually practice precious little scholarship themselves. But they also do not do much in the way of teaching. As if to prove the point, faculty without tenure still favor the tenure system in surveys, but wish it were extended to those among them distinguished for their teaching. They are, in effect, seeking another doorway to paradise. They may get to that threshold, but it may be to another form of paradise. The *Chronicle for Higher Education* reported in February, 1996, that graduate students at a host of state and private schools were embracing teaching preparatory programs. Such programs, held apart from the normal sequence of specialized research required of future Ph.Ds, focus mostly on teaching skills: building a syllabus, giving a coherent lecture, constructing exams, and so on. The Chronicle cited students who enjoyed the teaching preparation so much that some were strongly considering navigating their career paths towards community colleges or small, liberal arts colleges. Scholarship and research had ceased to mean anything to these future professors. Tenure, and its protections of controversial scholarship, remained quite important. Yet without scholarship, why have tenure at all?

Academic unions, professors, and other parties to the academic bureaucracy cite tenure above all as the cornerstone of academic freedom, and by inference, excellence. Tenure is intended to provide job security to scholars whose views would destroy their careers in any other institution. American democracy, which requires the free flow of ideas, and protects that freedom through government edicts such as the First Amendment, or the Whistleblower Act, hardly gives any critic free reign. No one appreciates criticism, and numerous cases over time show that where people can be fired for holding unconventional or unpopular views, they will be. So, in the academy, where the institution's inherent value rests on the freedom to challenge any intellectual authority, the case for tenure proves compelling.

That case assumes, however, that professors with tenure have views other than about events that fill the newspapers every day. Such opinions are not only conventional, they have no bearing on the essential mission of creating knowledge. What tenure assumes, above all, is that professors need the freedom to pursue scholarship in a meaningful way. That is, their scholarship should serve the interests of an academic field and a body of knowledge. And that assumption, which lays the foundation for so much of what colleges say they stand for, has very little to do with teaching. Were teaching the goal, as some junior faculty and legislators would have it, tenure would mean something else. It would serve to protect professors who have not reached independent and defensible conclusions about the subjects they teach. Or, to put it less gently, it would protect people who have no views but lots of information. Which explains the divergence of junior faculty from legislators on this issue: some legislators would do away with tenure entirely, opting for renewable multiple-year contracts for professors who demonstrate excellence (or activity) in the classroom. Junior faculty want to keep tenure, but rid it of the presumption of scholarship.

And that raises this question: can we separate the task of teaching from the work of scholarship? The nature of the debate assumes this separation, since the two tasks appear to be focused on entirely different audiences — teaching on students and scholarship on disciplines. The advocates of teaching — by far the most powerful in this debate after tenured professors — are by nature generalists, as Green notes in his Epilogue, and so we can safely assume that they agree to this separation. Traditionalists tend to view scholars as specialists who must, above all, prove their mettle to their colleagues, not to their students. This is a correct assessment, since scholars in all fields have to specialize before they can contribute anything to their field. The traditionalists want to understand just why professors spend careers on peculiar issues, issues that may have little bearing on society or the students who inhabit it and especially on the core of subjects they have embraced. This is a valid concern, but it goes against the very character of the modern American university. The university has, since 1945, seen its role largely as a producer of information and experience for the benefit of national goals. It has done many other things, but its design leads to specialization because that is what society has rewarded.

Generalism, General Education, Generalization

That said, let us also examine the roots of generalism and general education and generalization — all three — and the movement towards better teaching. A professor who can generalize for students is not the same thing as a curriculum geared towards generalization of all things. Someone like the late Richard Feynman, the rightly acclaimed professor of physics at the California Institute of Technology, was capable of introducing beginning physics students to higher level research on the topic like quarks; among his colleagues were many who could not understand the concept, and therefore could not to teach it. Was Feynman a generalist? Perhaps, but to those who espouse teaching over scholarship, Feynman presents a challenge. He was an effective teacher because of his understanding of the deepest issues of his field. No more powerful argument for the union of research and education, scholarship and teaching, can be adduced than the name, Richard Feynman. The theoretical physicist was one of the few Nobel laureates who could actually explain his work in language understandable to anyone, yet pursue questions and issues that his peers could only hope to grasp. Similarly, Harvard biologist Edward O. Wilson hopes to synthesize entire fields of knowledge, including physics, the arts, religion and economics, with single unifying theory of a field he himself invented, called sociobiology. He has his critics, to be sure, and many of them, not surprisingly, resent his efforts to make sense of what they want to make difficult. The two men represent many others, although not so many that this union is commonplace. It is not.

By comparison, generalists summarize, teaching from a wide spectrum of knowledge, both in a field and out of it. They may have little intimate knowledge of the most developed debates in their field, but in their view, staying one chapter ahead of the class is what appears to matter most, provided they can make the material interesting. Thus is born the survey course to an entire field of study, taught by a professor who understands a piece of that field very well, and the rest, not so well. The focus is on covering a smattering of subject matter on a fairly wide band of knowledge. It requires the flexibility to teach those things one does not know intimately.

This may be a laudatory skill, but as Green notes at the end of this book, a difficult one to rely on regularly and certainly not one consistent with the traditional strengths of professors and American universities. That is because generalized education does not account for sloppy teaching any better than the system we have now, Green notes. Teaching students the same basic books, with the same intent, "can produce order, but not meaning." Order is the product of understanding and categorization. A computer database is worthless without digestion by a skilled database manager, and an academic course built around information is no different. It must be led by someone who knows how the discipline of learning works, and where the data are taking it. Only specialists have these skills.

What is driving the embrace of general education is the assumed fact that specialists make hapless teachers. That assumption enjoys popularity, especially among legislators, but like any generalizations about the quality of teaching, is hardly reliable. There are countless examples of hack teachers, including professors who have created knowledge within their subject. The problem appears to emerge from a failure of scholars to actually spend time with their students. At some of the nation's most prestigious universities, undergraduates frequently get their most intense and important instruction from graduate students. Tenured professors hold back their lectures, which may still be canned monologues, for the benefit of upperclassmen. Rare are the examples of professors who allow students to participate in advanced research in the laboratory, or on critical issues of inquiry in the humanities and social sciences. Moreover, specialists have a well-earned reputation for aloofness, having created journals, terminology, and societies all to their own.

Professors tend to view students, who seem to them mere campus interlopers, with some ambivalence if not outright scorn. In this case, with tenure as a security blanket, professors have the system on their side. There is very little to dissuade them from zoning out students as much as possible, whether they are teaching a highly specialized class or a low-level introductory one. And that explains the growth of student-activism, both from undergraduates and Ph.D. candidates, on the issue of teaching. This activism, which has made an appearance on most campuses since the early 1980s, is a consumer backlash against professors who do not speak English well, give poor lectures, do not give much or any individual attention to student performance and who force graduate students to carry the burden of teaching (grading papers, leading class discussions and most lectures, and so on). At Yale University, for example, a group of graduate students staged a grade strike in 1996 that paralyzed classrooms. The graduate students wanted more money in return for the work they produced: the evaluation of undergraduates.

But, we must ask, are those professors targeted by such protests necessarily specialists? Are the reluctant professors competent scholars? Do they conduct original research into critical issues within their field? Can they explain the importance of those issues to outsiders? Is their work well-regarded by their colleagues in other, related fields? We shall take a closer look at the definition of scholarship later in this chapter, but for now it suffices to say that scholarship does not exclude by any means many of the skills that make for great teaching.

Green remarks that the solution to the teaching debate is to be found in the context of the academic department and student majors. He describes a model of instruction that encourages both professors and students to engage in research at all times, but not because they don't know where they're going. Rather, in the Rochester model, professors share the methods of inquiry that make an academic field unique. What distinguishes this model, however, is its nonadministrative tone. It is built around the concept of the academic major, and flows from a sense that a student should not simply have exposure to a wide variety of information within a single department, but should have participated in some manner in the methodology of that department.

But such a model requires the academic world to take into account many different skills and techniques. If applied elsewhere, it would require academic departments to work together, to see a concise method of inquiry in their work. It would demand of professors an explanation for how they do their work and shape their analysis. It would, in effect, do away with the "trust me" method of instruction, which is what most lectures are all about and what many teaching-advocates are comfortable with. And it would demand a level of collegiality among professors that simply does not exist on most campuses.

So, returning to the question we first posed in this chapter — how do we build a method of teaching that can answer the question of what to teach? — we find a meaningful answer in Green's Rochester model, but by no means one that can be easily repeated. And as we shall describe in future chapters, the problems of who should teach and who should learn are no less complicated than the one we have described here. As indicators of the possibility for improvement, they are not inspiring. If universities are up to the task of reforming themselves, they have much more to face than the mere issue of how to teach. They must yet decide who should be the teachers, who should be the students, and what shall everyone learn.

Who Should Teach

This is often understood to be a political question, even now, in the waning period of affirmative action. But in the present context, the issue is not political but academic: who are the right teachers (without regard to race, creed, religion, color, previous condition of servitude, or, for that matter, "sexual preference" or lack of the same), and what distinguishes a good teacher from a bad teacher? For, as we shall now see, our principal interest focuses upon the "who" of mind, attitude, mode of thought, and intellectual ambition, not upon the "who" of gender, race, and what not.[5]

Since we regard teaching as the activity that sets universities apart from research institutes and other modes of organizing scholarship and preserving and transmitting its results that may attain greater success at research than universities do, we commence with the act of teaching. We shall argue in chapter 4 that universities, pursuing scholarship by combining teaching with research, bear the most solemn responsibilities for the preservation and transmission of the human heritage of civilization as we know it in the West. It is in the context of teaching therefore that we ask what distinguishes a good professor from a bad one.

The good professor — by "good" we mean effective, demanding, self-critical — sets high standards and persists in demanding that students try to meet them. He or she provides the right experiences. The professor who gives praise cheaply or who pretends to a relationship that does not and cannot exist teaches the wrong lessons. True, the demanding and the critical teacher does not trade in the currency students possess, which is their power to praise or reject teachers. The demanding professor knows that, like professors in research and teaching, in the work of learning students will stumble. But the ones who pick themselves up and try again — whether in politics or music or art or sports — have learned a lesson that will save them for a lifetime: A single failure is not the measure of any person, and success comes hard. A banal truth, but a truth all the same.

The only teacher who taught the senior author something beyond information, who gave something to guide intellectual life, was also the only teacher who read the work carefully and criticized it in detail. To that point everyone had given easy A's. He was happy to believe them. In time, he learned to criticize himself and not to believe the A's, unless, as on rare occasion, he bestowed them on him. The difference between a student and a professor of worth is that the student wants to grade his own work and thinks he should, and the professor wants to grade his own work but fears he cannot get away with it. Every book, or, more to the point, every major scholarly project, begins in the author's dissatisfaction with the one before and, implicitly, constitutes a massive and devastating review of the failures of the prior project. The teacher who reads a student's writing and corrects not so much the phrasing as the mode of thought and argument, the accuracy of expression, the vitality and economy of the prose, line by line, paragraph by paragraph, beginning to end, and who composed paragraphs as models for what the student should be saying — that professor may turn out the sole true teacher the student ever has. But no one needs more than one.

That is not to suggest that for each student there is a sole perfect teacher, who changes lives. We must learn from many teachers as we grow up and grow old — the one who is wise is the one who learns from everyone — and we must learn to recognize the good ones. The impressive teacher of one's youth may want to continue to dominate — as teachers do — and may not want to let go. The great teacher is the one who wants to become obsolete in the life of the student. The good teacher is the one who teaches lessons and moves on, celebrating the student's growth. And the abominable teacher is the one who entertains and curries favor — generously granted by students at the slightest effort, since they would rather laugh than learn – and treats the classroom as a place not even for adventure, but mere fun. Learning is never easy and rarely fun; it is always an adventure.

The Talmud relates the story of a disciple in an academy who won an argument over God in the academy on high. The sages found themselves compelled by the force of his argument to adopt his position as against God's. So the question is asked, "What happened in heaven that day?" The answer: "God clapped hands in joy, saying, 'My children have vanquished me, my children have vanquished me.'" That is a model for the teacher — to enjoy losing an argument to a student, to recognize his or her contribution, to let the student surpass the teacher. In the encounter with the teacher who takes you seriously, you learn to take yourself seriously. In the eyes of the one who sees what you can accomplish, you gain a vision of yourself as more than you thought you were. The ideal professor is the one who inspires to dream of what you can be, to try for more than you ever have accomplished before.

These teachers today we call mentors. Nearly everyone who succeeds in life can point to such a mentor, whether in the classroom or on the sports field; for few achieve greatness without models. It may be a parent, a coach, employer, grade school or high school or art or music teacher. It is always the one who cared enough to criticize — and stayed around to praise. But what about college professors? To define an ideal for their work, let us offer guidelines on how to treat professors the way they treat students: Grade them. Professors grade students' work. The conscientious ones spend time reading and thinking about student papers, inscribing their comments and even discussing with students the strengths and weaknesses of their work. But no professor spends as much time on grading students' work as students spend on grading their professors as teachers and as people. From the beginning of a course ("Shall I register?") through the middle ("It's boring...shall I stick it out?") to the very end ("This was a waste of time."), students should be investing time and intellectual energy in deciding what they think, both about how the subject is studied and about the person who presents it.

Since effective teaching requires capturing the students' imagination, and since sharp edges and colorful manners excite the imagination, the professor who is a "character" is apt (whether for good reasons or irrelevant ones) to be liked or disliked, to make a profound impression and perhaps also to leave a mark on the students' minds. The drab professors, not gossiped about and not remembered except for what they taught, may find that even what they taught is forgotten. People in advertising and public relations, politics and merchandising, know that. A generation raised on MTV expects to be manipulated and entertained. Yet the emphasis on edginess is irrelevant. Many students have no more sophistication in evaluating professors than they do in evaluating deodorant advertising. This should not be surprising, since they approach them both in the same consumerist manner. The one who is "new, different, improved" wins attention. In this context people have no way of determining good from bad. Let us offer some concrete criteria for knowing the difference.

Can we define the differences between a good teacher and a bad one? Students have their own definitions of good and bad, and professors generally have a notion of what students like. Let us consider how students should evaluate their teachers, examining in turn the A, B, and C professors. We will begin at the bottom of one scale and work our way up. Let us at the same time consider what kind of student seeks which grade.

Grade C Professors

The first type is the C professor. This is the professor who registers minimum expectations and adheres to the warm-body theory of grading. If a warm body fills a seat regularly and exhibits vital signs, such as breathing at regular intervals, occasionally reading, and turning in some legible writing on paper, then cosmic justice demands, and the professor must supply, the grade of B (in earlier times C) or Satisfactory. The effort needed for a student to achieve an F or No Credit is considerably greater. One must do no reading, attend few class sessions, and appear to the world to be something very like a corpse. The professor who, by the present criteria, earns a C respects the students' rights and gives them their money's worth.

At the very least the professor does the following:

1. Attends all class sessions, reaches class on time, and ends class at the scheduled hour.

2. Prepares a syllabus for the course and either follows it or revises it, so that students always know what topic is under discussion.

3. Announces and observes scheduled office hours, so that students have access to the professor without groveling or special pleading, heroic efforts at bird-dogging, or mounting week-long treasure hunts.

4. Makes certain that books assigned for a course are on reserve in the library and sees to it that the bookstore has ample time in which to order enough copies of the textbooks and ancillary reading for a course.

5. Comes to class with a clear educational plan, a well-prepared pre-

sentation, a concrete and specific intellectual agenda.

6. Reads examinations with the care invested in them (certainly no more, but also no less) and supplies intelligible grades and at least minimal comments; or keeps office hours for the discussion of the substance of the examination (but not the grade); and supplies course performance reports — all these as duty, not acts of grace. And such a professor must read papers and exams in a prompt way, while the problems are still fresh in the student's mind. These things constitute basic student rights.

No student has to thank a professor for doing what he or she is paid to do, and these six items, at a minimum, are the prerequisites of professional behavior. They are matters of form, to be sure, but the grade B is deemed by (some) students to be a matter of good form alone; the warm-body theory of this grade applies to professors and students alike. In the age of student evaluations of professors, the grade C professors thrive. Student evaluations exactly correlate with the grades students receive or expect to receive, or think they will get. As always, without variation, students give the highest grades to the professors from whom these same grades will come. Science and math professors, whose ability to inflate grades is less flexible, suffer in student evaluations as a result. So the grade C professors dominate these days, students receiving the education that, by their own word, they want and have coming. At Princeton University, 83 percent of the grades granted between 1992 and 1995 were A's or B's; two decades earlier, only (!) 69 percent were. The students weren't brighter; the professors were less exacting.[6]

Of course, when professors demand less from students they demand less from themselves. The senior author used to find surprising when he taught at Brown his junior colleagues' announcement that, unprepared, they would wing it "today." That "today" soon became every day. And the students knew, they always knew. Then imagine the lessons that Brown's professors were really teaching. Preparation for class took low priority. Just as students of mediocre quality want to know the requirements and assume that if they meet them, they have fulfilled their whole obligation to the subject, some mediocre professors do what they are supposed to do — if that. The subject is in hand; there are no problems.

The C professor need not be entirely bored with the subject, but he or she is not apt to be deeply engaged by it. Grade C professors may be entertaining, warm, and loving. Indeed, many of them must succeed on the basis of personality, because all they have to offer is the studied technology of attractive personalities. Undergraduates form the world's easiest audience. That is why the Grade C professors may achieve huge followings among the students, keep students at the edge of their seats with jokes and banter and badger students to retain their interest. But in the end what they have conveyed to the students' minds is their personalities, not their mode of thinking or analyzing. Why? Because C professors do not think much; they rely on the analysis of others.

Above all, the grade C professor has made no effort to take over and reshape the subject. He or she may have a doctorate and at one point have been a scholar but now is no scholar. For this person is satisfied with the mere repetition, accurate and competent repetition to be sure, of what others have discovered and declared to be true. If this sort of professor sparks any vitality and interest in students, then he or she will remind students of their better high school teachers, the people who, at the very least, knew what they were talking about and wanted the students to know too.

How are students to grade professors of this kind? What will tell them the difference between the ordinary and the worthwhile? At the end of a course, students should ask themselves this: Have I learned facts, or have I grasped how the subject works; its inner dynamic, its logic and structure? If at the end students know merely one fact after another, students should be grateful — at least they have learned that much — but award the professor a polite C (these days: an outstanding rating passes). For the professor has done little more than what is necessary.

Grade B Professors

An academic course constitutes a large and detailed statement on the nature of a small part of a larger subject. It is a practical judgment upon a particular field of study and how it is to be organized and interpreted. The grade of B (nowadays, with rampant grade inflation, A) is accorded to the student who has mastered the basic and fundamental modes of thought about, and facts contained within, the subject of a course.

The grade B professor is one who can present coherently the larger theory and logic of the subject, who will do more than is required to convey his or her ideas to the students, and who will sincerely hope he or she is inspiring the minds of the students. As we shall see in a moment, the same is so of the A professors. It follows that the grade B professors, as they continue to grow as scholars, are not very different from A professors; they might be described as teachers striving to become A professors. But they are very different from C professors.

Given that, let us then move on to consider grade A professors, keeping in mind that B professors will probably become A professors, if they continue to strive to grow. The grade A professors are the scholar-teachers, a university's prized treasures among a faculty. America has many faculties of excellence, groups of men and women who with exceptional intelligence take over a subject and make it their own, reshape it, and hand it on, wholly changed but essentially unimpaired in tradition, to another generation. They must, by definition, include not a few grade A professors.

The Grade A Professors

Just as an A goes to student work that yearns to reach in utmost seriousness the center and whole of the subject of the course, grade A professors are exceptional. They may have odd ideas about their subjects, but they are asking new questions, seeking fresh insight, trying to understand how the subject works, to uncover its logic and inner structure. Grade C professors may not even know such a structure can and does exist. That quest distinguishes the good college professor from the good high school teacher. It is what validates our insistence that the academy do more than transmit information. It is why universities correctly impose high standards of scholarship, not just learning, as qualification for appointment and tenure. That is why the high school or community college teacher — both who spend nearly all of their working hours in the classroom – are so different from the university professor, who spends only a small part of time in the classroom. The labor of the professor consumes him, and he can scarcely imagine kicking back after an eight-hour day, or a forty-hour week. For the grade A professor is characterized by an unending sense of unease and discomfort. "You have to permit the possibility that you do not have it exactly right," said Richard Feynman in one of his lectures on the pursuit of knowledge.[7]

What makes an effective high school teacher is confidence in one's own knowledge of a subject. What makes an effective university teacher is doubt and dismay. The former belongs in the classroom thirty hours a week. The latter belongs in the library or laboratory at least for thirty hours a week, because he or she does not. When the senior author was in Milwaukee at the University of Wisconsin-Milwaukee, he informed the dean and the Wisconsin Society for Jewish Learning (sponsors of his position) that he wanted to take a semester off (unpaid) the next year to continue his studies. He had in mind more Pahlavi and more Talmud, in equal measure. Both parties strenuously objected: "When we appointed you, it was because we thought you knew your subject. Why do you need more study?" That was taken to mark inadequacy to the task. "Don't you already know what you are supposed to know?" Yet the scholarly mind is marked by self-criticism and thirst. It is guided by an awareness of its limitations. The scholar-teacher, of any subject or discipline, teaches one thing: Knowledge is never certain, scholarship is eternal, and the truly effective teacher emphasizes the meaning and value of doubt. A wise person is one who knows what he or she does not know. And, it must follow, what is taught is what we do not know.

On whom to bestow a grade A? It is given to the professor who, stumbling and falling, seeks both knowledge and the meaning of knowledge. It is to the one who at some point in every class asks and answers the question: Why am I telling you these things? Why should you know them? It is to the professor who demands ultimate seriousness for his or her subject because the subject must be known. It is the professor who not only teaches but professes, stands for, and represents, the thing taught. The grade A professor lives for the subject, needs to tell you about it, wants to share it. The Nobel Prize scientist who so loved biology that she gave her life to it even without encouragement and recognition for a half a century of work, the literary critic who thinks getting inside the meaning and structure of a poem is entering Paradise, the historian who assumes the human issues of the thirteenth century live today, the great novelist who saw her first book in print when she reached the age of fifty years (we think of Cynthia Ozick, who exemplifies the professorial grit in her own career) — these are the inspiration and the definition of the great talents in academia. One who has made this commitment to a field of scholarship can be readily identified. He is full of concern, commits upon the facts the act of advocacy, and deems compelling what others find merely interesting. The scholar—teacher is such because he or she explains that facts bear meaning.

True, to the world this sense of ultimate engagement with what is merely interesting or useful information marks the professor as curious and odd. Anybody who cares so much about what seems so little must be a bit daft. Why should such things matter so much — why, above all, things of the mind or the soul or the heart, things of nature and mathematics, things of structure and weight and stress, things of technology and science, society and mind? Professors often remember lonely childhoods, which they enjoyed. As adults, too, great professors have to spend long hours by themselves in their offices, reading books, or in their laboratories, or at their computers, or just thinking all by themselves. That is not ordinary and commonplace behavior. This is odd. But it is also the mark of someone who loves to discover.

Let us return to our comparison of the student and the professor. A student earns an A when he or she has mastered the larger theory of the course, entered into its logic and meaning, discovered a different way of seeing. Like a professor, the student earns an A through mastering accurate facts, then seeks meaning and finally reaches the core and center of the subject. Yet matters cannot be left here. Passion is the thing. We do not mean to promote advocacy for its own sake. Students have rights too, and one of these is the right to be left alone, to grow and mature in their own distinctive ways. They have the right to seek their way, just as we professors find ours. The imperial intellect, the one that cannot allow autonomy, is a missionary, not a teacher.

Many compare the imperial teacher with the A professor, but if you look closely at their different ways of teaching, you will see that this is an error. The teacher leads, says, "Follow me," without looking backward. The missionary pushes, imposes self upon another autonomous self. This is the opposite of teaching, and bears no relevance to learning or to scholarship. The scholar-teacher persuades; the missionary preaches. The scholar-teacher argues; the missionary shouts others into silence. The teacher wants the student to discover; the missionary decides what the student must discover. The teacher often begins with fear and trembling, not knowing where he will lead. The missionary knows at the start of a course exactly what the students must cover by the end of the course. A course without surprises pleases the missionary but not the teacher.

Good professors teach, never indoctrinate. They educate, rather than train. There is a fine line between great teaching and self-aggrandizment. And this brings us back to the earlier emphasis upon scholarship as the recognition of ignorance. The true scholar, who also is the true teacher, is drawn by self-criticism, compelled by doubting, skeptical curiosity, knows the limits of knowing. He or she cannot be confused with the imperial, the arrogant, and the proselytizing. A good professor wants to answer the question, Why am I telling you these things? A good student wants to answer the question, Why am I taking these courses? What do I hope to get out of them? Why are they important to me? The imperial teacher takes offense at any such questions.

How ought students to know whether a class has accomplished an educational goal? It is by asking, what is the one thing I learned here today? At the end of every class the senior author asks his students, "So what did you learn today?" and waits for the answers. Then he sorts them out, looking for the main point, the secondary point, and on downward. Then: "What evidence did I present for the proposition I wanted you to learn? What did you find in the reading that pertained?" And, on the more daring afternoons, I will ask, "And was the hour worth what it cost you, which is...?" and he will specify the tuition divided into the hourly rate, assuming that the entirety of tuition covers only instruction and so specifying a huge sum. The honest, amazed, and ordinarily negative answers underscore the goal, which is to raise the stakes of the classroom. For the case we have to make for universities has to sustain this proposition: Of all of the things you could do with the money it takes to bring you here, of all the things you could do with the time and energy that sustain you here, what we are going to do this hour is the single most important thing you can do.[8] That extravagant claim validates the universities' lien on the country's future — if teaching scholars can make it stick.

The Enterprise of Teaching

The work of a teacher is to speak about ideas in an effective manner. To us "effective" means, to teach in such a way that students will engage ideas and find themselves intellectually challenged and even changed by what they are learning. In our view, as we have just now stressed, the entire case in favor of universities as the principal medium of higher education — not corporate schools for a particular job, not passive television instruction, not advanced high schools and community colleges or other media for tertiary education — rests on the union of research, scholarship, publication, and teaching. Anyone else but a professor, any other sort of school but a university, can offer instruction; only a professor and only a university can offer the union of scholarship and teaching, publication and personal encounter. Mass education via television or interactive computer presents information to whom it may concern. Colleges and universities nurture intellectual growth through the meeting of the "I" and the "you."

A teacher has to keep students alert and attentive. A teacher has to teach students how to listen. A teacher has to teach students how to think two or three logically connected thoughts, before teaching what problems to solve and how to solve them. A teacher has to know how to listen, what to listen to, to recognize the signs of being heard, to read the signs of being tuned out. For our work is to enter into minds and change lives. No one successful in life today, rich in achievement and heavy in responsibility, would have succeeded were it not for the kind of teachers who care about what happens in a student's mind.

The senior author writes as a teacher, because it is all he has ever been or ever wanted to be. In this regard we permanent professors really are different from presidents, provosts, deans, and those who have moved out of the classroom into other academic positions. Most of us do not want to make that move. We do not want other jobs. We depend upon deans, provosts, and presidents to guide the university, but we do not want to be deans or provosts or presidents. We who live our lives in classrooms and in our studies are doing the things we were created to do. We want no more, because we think we have it all. When we list our heroes, moreover, they turn out to be the founders and framers of our civilization. Who are the greatest teachers of all time, if not Socrates, Jesus, and Moses? What did Socrates do, if not walk the streets and argue with everybody, all the time, everywhere, about anything simple and obvious, like what is truth? What did Moses do, if not instruct his people, not always kindly, not always patiently, but always passionately, about what they should be? What teacher can fail to admire and envy the pedagogical power of Jesus, who could capture a world of meaning and present it whole and complete in a parable?

What makes a good teacher, then, is clear. A good teacher is someone who can enter into the mind of another person and bring to life the mind of that other person. A good teacher does the work by arguing, pressing, asking questions, challenging answers, asking more questions. The life of the good teacher is expressed in giving life to ideas, imparting meaning to what appears to lie entirely beyond intellect, making the obvious into a problem, turning the world of settled truths into an adventure. A good teacher is argumentative, disorderly, prepared for confrontation everywhere, all the time, with everyone, on everything — all for the sake of the vital mind, the freely inquiring spirit.

If students later in life can reason, someone somewhere has criticized them. If they can think clearly, someone has listened carefully to what they have said and has corrected them — and corrected them in such a way that you heard and grasped the meaning of their mistakes. Great teachers are the foundation of our vitality, of our capacity as a society to do our work. These teachers are all around us. In liberal arts colleges and some universities, all the classroom teaching is done by professors, people who hold doctorate degrees in the fields in which they teach. But in all large universities, private and public, much teaching is done by graduate students, people en route to their doctoral degrees, who are advanced students in the field they profess. So formal education — as distinct from the real work of learning — occurs in the classroom at the hand of two sorts of teachers; those who have completed their formal education, and those who have nearly done so. They differ in many ways.

But they are the same on one count. All professors think they teach the subjects they know. But students think professors do many things besides that. Professors come to a room filled with late adolescents and tell them things. They then measure what the students have heard and learned. They administer periodic examinations and grade the results, like eggs, with letters, even with pluses and minuses, no less. Strict logic might dictate that they should use those results to grade their own success as conveyors and purveyors of learned information, but that is a separate qudstion. It is hard to teach eighteen-year-olds, to ask them to think cogently for more than a short period, to insist they answer a specific question and not some question no one has asked, to pick out purposeful from pointless remarks, and to demand that they learn from the teacher, not only from themselves. These do not add up to a prescription for public popularity or private ease. To say the least, the professor, as much as the graduate student, risks unpopularity as a natural by-product of good teaching.

In the humanities over the years the senior author have found it difficult to get students to take seriously what he has taught in a course. To take the case at hand, Jewish students assume they know "Judaism," from a smattering of parochial education, synagogue youth group retreats and family observance, such as it is, so they care little about what the course presents. The same problem — the struggle to gain a hearing amid the static of students' prior impressions — afflicts many subjects, philosophy and political science as much as literature and the academic study of religion. On finals some insist on writing things they knew or took for granted before they took the course and ignoring the course. Students will write papers that could have been written without taking the course and doing the reading. Some write on subjects the course never took up, assuming as fact a wild range of misinformation and impression.

And then some others get the point. So we professors say what we say, and students hear what they hear, and only sometimes do the two match. For some students, the professor may become far more than a teacher in a classroom. Students endowed with confidence and curiosity, who know what they want and are determined to get it, gain the legitimate power to transform the demanding professor from enemy to opportunity. By seeking out the professor and trying out on the professor the creations of their own design, these students create for themselves a resource of considerable worth.

To other students, the professor may become a friend, for professors are people, and professors are commonly parents. Many among them value friendship wherever they find it, among young as much as among old. Students able to sustain relationships with adults, as well as professors open to friendship in age succeeding age, give to one another gifts beyond all value, an ever-renewed spring of life. For the senior author, long-term relationships can survive the end of the semester. Since the mother of the junior author was once the student of the senior author, that possibility means creations never possibly imagined.

It follows that the differences among types of professors flow from the diverse sorts of people who are drawn to this particular vocation. Some people love learning, taking ideas apart and putting them back together. If their interests center upon matters of academic learning, they aspire to become professors because they love precisely what professors do: learn and teach how interesting ideas work. These form a tiny proportion of the whole. Other people see in the life of a professor a protected refuge. Such people, unsure of themselves, seek the certainty of knowing one subject better than anyone else. Uncertain in relationships with others, they want not only to know the rules but to control them. So scholarship becomes an excuse not to relate ("too busy with my work"), and human encounter falls under rigid guidelines. To read and think and write, people have to be on their own the greater part of the day. If research institutes could absorb those who present both unusual intellectual strength and the capacity to work forever on their own and by themselves, then society as a whole would gain from their learning and not lose from the narcissism of a fair number of the great lonely learners.

Some professors are more scholar than teacher, devoting long hours to research and writing. And this too is difficult — to think up new questions and to work out their answers, to write article after article, book after book. Not many professors actually open their ideas to public scrutiny by publishing articles and books for their colleagues' criticism. But many pretend to or promise that they will, and all profess to think it important to try, while hating the few who actually do so. Tenure challenges professors, tempting them to do nothing. Some professors give up the struggle of research once they are granted tenure. Some few continue to produce. Fewer continue to learn. But the only real teacher is the one who succeeds by definition, the tenured professor who continues to labor in research and to publish the findings, for that professor never stops being a student. To be a professor is to be a student all the time — a taxing vocation indeed. So the two have much to learn from one another.

But what about the students — what do they encounter in universities? Students see teaching assistants, not professors, in most of their direct contact with university instruction. In most large universities, the professor addresses sizable numbers of students and in the nature of things cannot give proper attention to each individual student. But the professor will have assistants — normally, one for forty or fifty students. These assistants conduct discussion groups. They read exams. They maintain everyday contact with the undergraduates. In a fair number of universities, they are the only ones who will know students by name. In the education of students, teaching assistants carry far more weight than anyone else. That is because the greater part of the person-to-person encounter, of which, ideally, education consists, is with the teaching assistants. The teachers whom both authors knew, who knew them and taught them as an undergraduates, were mostly teaching assistants. When students in larger universities reach the point at which they can frame ideas and offer them for public inspection, they address not professors, who rarely hear from students, but teaching assistants, who are paid to listen. These same people normally grade students' written work. Accordingly, at the two principal points at which students do not merely receive but also express thoughts, teaching assistants stand at the turning.

Let us spell out this fact, since we believe it is at the center of the education that the greater number of large universities provide. When people learn, they do two things. First, they receive ideas and facts; second, they try ideas out for themselves. They begin by acquiring information and learning how to use it and manipulate it, whether it comes from a lecture or in reading. Normally, in higher education, it is through both media. Then, if they are to benefit from what they read and hear, students must also attempt to make it their own. This they do by stating matters as they have heard or read them and also have reckoned with their meaning or point: how they work. Teaching assistants are there to listen.

Now in an ideal world, these teaching assistants would be junior professors, assistant professors in the true sense of the word. Like residents in a hospital, they would have completed their own education and begun to practice. They would also enjoy close supervision of their actual teaching and their capacities to read an examination and guide a student paper. They also would have a proper salary for their work. They would enjoy standing and position on account of it. But in the real world, teaching assistants are graduate students, themselves in the earliest stages of their graduate education, many not even a year out of college. They are paid a pittance. They enjoy slight standing or prestige. Worse still, they are not supervised by senior professors, who rarely sit down to discuss the problems of teaching a given unit of a course, the difficulties students face in grasping a given idea, or the likely obstacles to grasping a stated proposition.

What does this mean for students and their parents? It means that when they visit a college or university, they should find out the extent to which senior professors seek an encounter in the classroom with small numbers of undergraduates. Are there seminars for undergraduates? How do you get into one? Ask students how many professors know their names, and when they last talked to, and were heard by, someone more than a year or two older than themselves. Determine the normal size of the classes in which students hear lectures, and ask also the size and schedule of the meetings of discussion sections for those large courses. Visitors to a campus will want to find out by what criteria teaching assistants are appointed — scholarly distinction or merely the need for financial support for graduate students. They should ask how the teaching assistants are supervised, the extent to which senior professors inquire into what their assistants are doing and review with them the pedagogical problems of a given topic or class. In other words, parents and their children should inquire about the possibility that they may pay for a senior surgeon but end up having an intern remove an appendix.

In the end, and realistically speaking, the particular student's own ambitions, his or her sense of self-confidence and intellectual purpose, will govern. If the critical issue is how the student feels about himself or herself, then what emerges from the interplay of teacher and student, the web of relationships spun on the loom of learning, then the small liberal arts college offers what that student must want. If the central purpose in university education is learning, and a student can work independently without sustaining relationships with professors, then come to the cold, indifferent, but intellectually vital and rigorous classroom and laboratory of the great research university. On the whole, people choose well for themselves — or transfer.

Tenure and Teaching

Now let us turn to the much-vexed matter of tenure. For tenure makes a deep impact upon the personality of the college professor, and that impact may shape the professor in many ways, depending upon the character and conscience of the person. What tenure means is that after a probationary period (usually six years) a college professor may apply for a lifelong appointment by the college or university at which he or she teaches. Unless the need for services should end, which is not common, the professor may look forward to a lifetime of employment. The professor is obligated at the most for only a few hours a week to be in a classroom. The rest of the hours of the week are his or her own, to do with as the professor sees fit. Tenure generally appeals to people who suppose that job security solves many problems. But it creates some too.

How shall we justify a system in which lifetime job security takes precedence over real achievement? We see three paramount considerations.

First, tenure serves the best interest of universities, because it preserves the careers of the accomplished professors from the machinations of unaccomplished ones. The workers taken up with their work find themselves harassed by colleagues with little more to do then disrupt the lives of the active scholars. If majorities ruled universities, and if the hard workers were not tenured, then universities would lose the little talent and commitment that they now possess, the majorities ridding themselves of the minorities that break the curve and embarrass the above-average. The scholar-teachers, always a minority, embody a critique of the rest of the faculty who are always the vast majority. Tenure is all that protects the best professors' freedom to excel.

Second, tenure protects freedom of speech, without which universities above all could not do their work. If professors must fear losing their job if they express a dissenting opinion about anything of consequence, few will dissent to whatever prevails as the norm at a given hour. Truth would die.

Third, tenure forms a key part of the compensation of professors, assuring universities that they will stay on by granting long-term career security and so discouraging the never-ending job hunt that people in the business world pursue. Tenure therefore lowers the labor costs of universities and makes the workers docile. Any one of these three reasons would suffice to explain why universities nearly always grant tenure after a probationary period (and overseas universities, in Europe for example, grant tenure upon employment or scarcely a year or two later).

Tenure was created to protect those who needed protection, and it still serves that purpose, along with the careers of others who have taken risks in scholarship or in the struggle for excellence and academic integrity in their universities. Now professors ask for courage to speak the truth — but not at the cost of the food their children eat or the roof over their family's head. Tenure protects truth tellers and intellectual whistleblowers; it allows for controversy and debate. For the first twenty years of the senior author's academic life he spent his time pointing to naked emperors pretending to be scholarly greats. That hardly endeared him to colleagues. Not only so, but had the Brown University administration been able to fire him, it would have, in May, 1981 after he wrote that the faculty didn't have much in which to take pride in the achievements of the then graduating class. Brown's then-President Howard Swearer at that time had only this to say: "Don't embarrass us any more." The only reason the Brown Corporation did not fire the controversial critic was that they could not legally get rid of him. So tenure saves careers. But tenure also, of necessity, shelters everybody else, including those who savage the university from within by acts of incompetence, stupidity, and venality.

If tenure protects teachers who give life to the university, it also prevents the departure of teachers who drain life from it. Few teachers have the courage to give up the security of a job for the freedom of having, not a job, but a choice. When the time comes to make a change, tenure forms a prison wall, albeit with lovely gardens, a nice cafeteria, and velvet-covered bars. Hanging around, the tenured teacher becomes cynical, bitter, jealous. Students no longer challenge him, they only irritate. Fellow teachers no longer help and inspire; they only commiserate. The tiredness we all feel at the end of the year, the spiritual fatigue that tells us we have given our best and can give no more. For the grouchy but immobile, these mark the beginning and middle of the year as well. And why? Because there is no choice. The present is known, the alternative frightening — especially for men and women in their forties, the point at which change is both still possible and also necessary.

Tenure locks into the job the scholar who may very well have gone on to another career at just that point that tenure has been earned. The young scholar tends to run out of ideas and energy just when he or she attains tenure. For the first five or six years after graduate school, the young professor continues to read books and think about writing books. New ideas for courses percolate. The fact that there is a tenure decision down the pike also serves as inspiration to maintain the professional ambitions as teacher and even scholar with which the work began. After tenure, inertia takes over and so does the true character of the professor. It is at this point that the one scholar who, it turns out, really loved the work and lived for it, stands apart from the many who loved and lost the love, and still others, who never loved, never lost, but received in tenure the one thing they really wanted: Status.

Some of these people find refuge in other activities, work on committees, or as department chairs, or even as assistant deans, associate provosts, and directors of this and that. They raise funds, they form institutes and associations. They attend conventions and conferences, as audience members only, never presenting their own work, because they have nothing to present. But the larger number do not. And they do little else. But they have tenure. It locks out life. It bars taking risks. It sets up the walls of the prison for those whose intellectual careers have ended.

The system of tenure, then, creates a conflict of interest between students and their need to be taught, on the one side, and teachers and their legitimate concern to keep their jobs, on the other. Students argue against tenure because they find themselves deprived of the promise of the young who care. They have a right to their complaint. It is academic malpractice to place the minds of students which are just beginning to form in the hands of professors whose own minds shut off years earlier. Administrators say their hands are tied, that tenure keeps them from tossing overboard the dead weight. Would that it were so. The record of university administrations in our time — the age of political correctness and firings for wrong opinions — proves that they should have their hands tied. Some professors will be disciplined as much as possible for making off-color remarks in a classroom; others who attack whites, men, the Catholic Church, Jews or any of the above will escape administrative wrath altogether. Some professors at State University of New York's New Paltz campus got the wise idea in 1997 to hold a conference on revolting sexual behavior, led by pornographers and sadomasochists. It was, indeed, a wise move, since it won the praise of the campus president, Roger Bowen.[9]

Professors are not the Only Teachers: Presidents, Provosts, Deans, and the Educational Enterprise

So much for the responsibilities of professors — teacher-scholars. What about deans, provosts, presidents? The qualities that make a good teacher trouble a good administrator. The pure and total freedom of encounter and expression demanded in teachers' work with students presents problems for presidents and provosts in their work. To run the great institutions of society, they must have order. They need to nurture goodwill, a good reputation, generally good opinion, so people will give the money needed to sustain the schools and colleges. A well-run school is orderly and predictable. In such a world, it is perfectly natural not only to get along, but to go along. The two tasks appear to go together.

The skills of teachers are the skills of another sort entirely. When we professors go along with our students as they are, unchanged, we do not get along in our work, we merely become well-liked. If we go along, our students cannot get along in life. To serve effectively, we must be different from presidents. To serve effectively, presidents must be different from us. What makes a good administrator is the capacity to do things regularly and routinely, to keep things in hand and under control. When deans plan budgets, they work a year in advance. They think quite properly about the ongoing life of the institution they serve. They wish to keep the peace in the community they serve. Stability, order, goodwill, good organization — these are the marks of good administration. But stability, order, goodwill, and good organization are insufficient for good teaching. A classroom should not be disorderly, though a bit of chaos helps. Ideas are disorderly. Intellectual life is full of surprises and discoveries. Courses to be sure do begin somewhere and end up somewhere else; but a first-class course is one in which the conclusions are not predictable at the outset. Teaching is an act of discovery, and adventures, while they have goals, are most exciting and fruitful when they are unpredictable.

Thus arises the conflict of interest between the good teacher and the good administrator. Beyond the campus, people do not broadly understand that presidents must lie and professors have to tell the truth, and presidents who tell the truth or professors who lie violate the moral contract of their respective callings. The long years of conflict that the senior author sustained with the Brown University administration came about because he did not understand, much as fish have to swim and birds have to fly, universities have to engage in false advertising and presidents in particular have to dissimulate, repackage, or otherwise find means to sell a faulty product – certainly a product that falls far short of its billing. And, it must be clearly understood, while professors create the product of the university, which is the classroom, presidents, provosts, and deans define the university. Professors can not make a university better than the presidents and provosts want it to be, and those who try, waste their time.

Telling the truth may not be good administration. But it will always be good teaching. When schools and colleges lose the reputation of freely teaching what is true to those capable of learning it, schools and colleges lose the public esteem and support they require. Then they turn to the community for bond issues and are turned down. It follows that the mentality of bureaucrats stands at odds with what they administer in schools and colleges. It is one thing to write the book of rules and follow them when one is a captain in the army or a director of a government bureau or the manager of a corporate office. It is quite another to bring those same values into the schools.

What makes a good teacher is not the ability to follow a book of rules, but the ability to criticize the rules and ask why they are there. That is not because criticism is what we do. It is because teaching is what we do. And to teach, we must bring to life our students' and our own capacity for response, for thought and reflection — and that means, to criticize. Bureaucracies keep things going through public relations and accepted dogma. Teachers ask embarrassing questions. Clerks and administrators pass out news releases to reporters. Teachers shrug their shoulders and tell the truth — even to reporters (Again — tenure saves!). The president of a university wants everyone to think well of the university. The professor in that university wants everyone to think. The president embraces the institution and its structure. The professor affirms life — the vitality of ideas, the good health of argument and controversy. What one builds at all costs the other seeks to question at all times, and just the same, at all costs.

Schools and colleges in the end, however, are not well served by dissimulation. They are not preserved by public relations. Schools and colleges are strong enough to bear true witness, even about education. They are not fragile, to be protected by lies. They are strong and essential, the bone of our bone, the life-blood of our society. The reputation of the schools and colleges does not rest upon the discretion of liars in public relations. It rests upon the achievement of teachers. Admit to the problems and people will believe us. Gloss them over and they will lose faith.

We teachers stand before our students to wake them up to what they can be. When we do our work, people will respect and sustain us. When we do not do our work, people will not believe in us, no matter what the public relations directors, alumni magazine editors, presidents, and board chairmen may say. And that, many presidents concede, is death to the university.

This brings us to one task of presidents in particular. In another age they represented moral authority, guiding curriculums, advising government, even moving into the White House. Today they schnorr — the Yiddish word that means, beg for money, and not always with dignity. Once upon a time, the president of a university became governor of his state, and, a few years later, president of the United States. Woodrow Wilson went from Princeton to Trenton to Washington. When the senior author was a boy in Connecticut, presidents of Yale University regularly came under discussion as possible Senate candidates. They were automatically assumed to be great leaders and persons of exceptional intelligence. Today college presidencies go to failed politicians. Once, people turned to college presidents for their opinions on a vast range of subjects, as today they turn to pundits (or controversial professors). Once more influential than politicians in the framing of cultural concerns and values of the country, college presidents made speeches about ideas, won attention for issues of the intellect, spoke out on questions of higher education. The presidency of a university was a bully pulpit, and great women and men used it. Furthermore, they imposed their views of what their universities should do, leading the faculty to make substantial changes in curriculum and in the organization of education. They were figures of controversy and they thrived on it. College presidents created universities, like Abram Sachar of Brandeis. They also transformed universities, like Henry Wriston and then Barnaby Keeney at Brown, 1937-1956, 1956-1966, respectively; or they brought professionalism and an unsentimental perspective to universities' problems, as did Donald Hornig at Brown from 1970 to 1975. And, were we to list the great presidents in public universities, the list would fill an entire chapter of this book. Not only so, but in the more distant past, the influence of presidents such as James Conant of Harvard, Robert Hutchins at Chicago, and Nicholas Murray Butler at Columbia, and the standing of the presidents of the great state universities of Michigan, California, Illinois, Wisconsin, constituted formative forces in the definition of America. They had a purpose and a program. And, by the way, college presidents raised money.

Today, as we said, all the presidents do is raise money. The picture is clear: they offer no vision, define no center, set no specific goal - just the budget. In the state systems, the counterparts accomplish political tasks of equal importance. The 1960s and 1970s promised a call to greatness in both private and public higher education, but in those years the timid administrators survived, the great educators — Clark Kerr of California is the best example — perished from the campus. In scurrying for security in the face of upheaval and chaos, boards of trustees let college presidencies fall into the hands of people who promised little more than compromise to maintain their own survival and, with it, the survival of their college. But while the colleges did survive, the presidencies did not, the average term not going much beyond five years. And in those years, the presidents did not appear to enjoy themselves. When presidents today do enter politics, like the hapless John Silber of Boston University, who lost an election for the governorship of Massachusetts by showing his true character in a televised debate, the political community learns how poorly universities are run, by what sorts of people, and the universities discover how what passes for normal on the campus offends everywhere else. When presidents do find themselves called upon to speak intelligently and express their convictions, they can not do the one and do not have the other.

The universities did survive. But survived for what? If survivors themselves cannot tell you, then what have they survived? In the aftermath of the revolution of the late 1960s and earliest 1970s a new formalism replaced the old. Those "tenured radicals," so aptly named by Roger Kimball, completed the dismantling of academic standards, finished the leveling of difference and the exclusion of distinctions based on achievement and excellence. The public imagines that the college president leads, presides, sets standards, and provides an example and a model for students and teachers alike. But these days the college president rarely leads as the educator that people rightly expect the president to be. The college president is interchangeable with other corporate presidents. Why? Good administration applies equally to government, industry, charity and the academic world. What that means is that there is no longer a career of educational leadership reaching the climax in a presidency of a college in particular. The president can be president of anything, which is another way of saying that the president of a college is not skilled in anything in particular. As a result, we do not live in the age of great university presidents, those who give leadership to education in particular. We live in the age of institutional caretakers. But for the bricks and mortar they must maintain, they would have nothing to shape their agenda.

The most recent age of great university presidencies began in 1946 and ended in 1970. We live in the age of effective and successful administrators, who keep the peace. Presidents tend to bow out of important discussions of purpose and meaning in education — like rich, absentee parents. It is probably the way things have to be. But colleges lose the opportunity of having leaders. Without a vision the people perish. Without presidents who stand for something to do with learning, research, scholarship, and teaching, universities and colleges pay their bills on time, but go nowhere, lacking all direction and purpose. Consensus decides everything, and decides poorly. Leadership depends upon opportunity, no one else on campus can do what the president alone can and should. And great leaders create their own opportunities. College freshmen give the gift of their perfect faith, believing in the college of their choice. They seek models, new beginnings for themselves, paths to a worthwhile future. Above all they look for striking leadership, for examples of what they may become, for someone to say, through example more than through word, "Follow me! After me! To life!"

But who talks to them about goals for life, and who uses the language of morality and right and wrong and a life well-lived and thoughtfully examined? What they find, in contrast to what they seek, is at best sallow competence. Presidents should impart vision and provide a view of the whole. By reason of their office, they should speak of the great and general purposes of the college: the hope it extends to its students, the high duties it demands of its professors. The president can't make things work — that is the task of the professors — but he can make things work together. In a word, the college president should define the ideals of the college, lead, and aim to attain it.

In general, that is not what college presidents do, and it is not even what they try to do. They should lead, but they administer. They should see a vision of the whole, but they worry instead about the budgets of the parts. Success for them is measured in dollars, and they yield to the excuse that real world issues are at odds with the task of the university. Like professors who claim that they would write books and conduct research if only they had more time, presidents who fail to lead or accomplish any meaningful goals claim that their administrative duties keep them from greater things. Surely, for both, the excuse is a crutch. Those with ideas do research; those with vision lead. The rest lack.

But these excuses for failing to lead can not stand. Others, in other offices of the university, could surely carry out these practical tasks quite well. For instance, no one today imagines that a college president should manage the college's investments (though in New Zealand, the vice chancellors, who correspond to presidents here, do just that — but then, they do not do much else). Here there is a specialist for that. Well and good, but then why should the president serve as primary figure in "development" (which means fund raising)? The president should do what no one else can do, what no other position in the university permits one to do, and that is, lead, inspire, call forth greatness, recognize achievement, give a model for learning in the community that the college is meant to embody. Can anyone think of a prominent college president today who would attempt to define his work that way? A handful, at best, and not where you'd expect to find them. That is, not in the Ivy League.

In consequence university presidents rarely attain eminence in education and often do not even pretend to be educators at all. As we said, industry, business, government, and now universities swap leaders. To the trustees or state boards of regents universities are interchangeable with corporations, government offices, and factories. The trustees are wrong. Colleges demand leadership particular to their tasks. Education produces something more fundamental to society than does industry, government, or business. Colleges need educators for their leaders. A great college president is great in ways different from a great industrialist, banker, or bureaucrat. Our bottom line reads differently. We pay our dividends in human lives. Our budgets are balanced in books and in great ideas and ideals. The reader now may say, "Yes, but you do have to pay the bills." True enough. But you pay the bills in order to get something worth having. More important than paying the bills is educating the students and nurturing learning.

If the president does not know what scholarship takes, he can not use the position of prominence and power that he or she holds in such a way that the college becomes more vital, more effective, then who needs a president? Why not hand over the presidency to the fund-raising office or to the business administrator, and the university to other hands entirely? Today higher education can point to few examples of true greatness in leadership — we mean, those who aspire to greatness of heart and mind and spirit. That is why we need great men and women to set an example, to lead universities and to make them places of greatness. To settle for people who can raise a lot of money hands the future over to amiable schnorrers who have no clear idea of what they wish to do with their own bags of cash. In the end, money becomes its own goal and we end up with the status quo.

Do we sound disappointed? Is this a mere diatribe? You bet. For the senior author was once interviewed for a college presidency, that of Brandeis, in the mid 1980s. Having declared himself the least qualified person the trustees could uncover, he explained why: "You people want a president to raise money. I want to be a president who walks around the campus, smiles a lot, and says wise things to people." That mysterious pronouncement closed the interview, though the conversation persisted for two hours afterward. He never heard from those people again, but since then he has thought about the matter a great deal. Why are we both so disappointed at the state of the university presidency? The senior author learned at Brown how mediocre leadership can dismantle a once-splendid university. That explains his optimistic view of matters: in those miserable failures he sees the promise and the hope of the office: If one leader can destroy things so quickly, so too can a successful one rebuild, just as quickly.

Why used failed presidencies to prove the point? We are talking about leadership that shapes coming generations of young Americans. That is why it matters so deeply that few presidents today have important views on education or offer a cogent philosophy of what a university does. Power without purpose proves as perilous in college presidents as in U.S. presidents. But more is at stake in college: the future of young women and men. For presidents without goals pass in a few years, but the effects of an aimless education for students on a lifeless campus in those same four or five years last a lifetime. Which costs more — an unbalanced budget or a wasted life? And how shall we weigh the value of a balanced budget against the cost of a generation deprived of vision and left without challenges of greatness?

The young people will follow a leader; the campus requires leaders. The college presidency should be a place for great women and men to speak out in important ways about weighty matters of heart and mind and spirit. By that criterion, that presidency today stands empty. It is like the Irish Catholic churches after Cromwell. Where God was served, the choirs stood bare and ruined, the roof open to the skies, the walls crumbling. So, too, the university may remain in gilded settings, but its core, hollowed out by two decades of bureaucratic vicissitudes, is empty of purpose.

Where Students are Learning, Everyone is Teaching

Everyone teaches in a community of learning. Universities are places in which young people go from adolescence to maturity while engaged in higher learning — in that order. The students spend only part of their time in the classroom, library, or lab. In residential universities they spend much of their time in the dining halls and dormitories, on the sports fields, all the time, socializing with one another. And in commuter universities they still spend plenty of time out of the classroom but on campus. That is why, in the educational enterprise, in relation to the things that matter to students, what professors do is useful but not critical.

Students worry about whether they are liked. We want them to be learned. Many want to know that they are attractive to the opposite sex. We care that they think clearly. They often entertain fears about their future, and we listen to the clarity of their argument and the precision of their reasoning. A gap separates the purveyors of higher education from the consumers. There is only one way to bridge the gap, and that is by transforming colleges and universities into places in which every one undertakes both to teach and to learn, not only professors to teach and students to learn. In a community of learning, exchanges of insight and even of information will take place in each transaction and encounter. In the community of learning formed by a college, the focus of education is the undergraduate; the object of education is the student's growth to maturity in mind and in heart.

Professors teach students, but students by definition educate us professors in our responsibilities. For professors in particular, the students teach teaching. This they do when they respond to what we say and do. That is why, in the classroom, our eye must be always upon the student: how does their body-language or the expression on their faces or the look in their eyes convey information on whether or not they are listening? In classroom experience professors have to learn to watch for signs that they have said something not understood or poorly phrased or merely stupid; whether they are boring the students or addressing the concerns that should occupy them that day, in response to reading done in advance. For the senior author's part he tells students to sit up straight, look at him, and not to take notes. If they take notes, he talks to the tops of their pens. If they slouch, he talks to dormant minds. If they gaze at the walls, he is not the focus of their attention, and what he is saying becomes part of a din of undifferentiated sounds — not words, not thoughts, just noise.

Students do not express thanks for being told to sit up straight and how to listen. At Bard College, where the senior author teaches in the autumn semesters, at the end of the course, students write anonymous critiques of professors, which the dean of the faculty reads. Late adolescents at elite colleges prove themselves remarkably adept at expressing their anger in personal terms, and an exact correlation matches the grade they antici-pate (and ordinarily get) with their evaluation of the professor. But later on some come around and concede, yes, indeed they learned something about learning.

Still more to the point, if students learn to listen to us professors, it must be for the goal of helping them to listen to one another. For people are used to listening to authority figures — talking heads at the front of the room. But when it comes to hearing another and responding to the thought of the other, matters are otherwise. People may regard the state-ment of the other as a breathing space, waiting to say what is on their mind; they will interrupt; they will dismiss; they will change the subject and simply ignore what the other person has said. In the senior author's classroom, he will point out, "But you have ignored what has just been said and changed the subject." In the beginning of a course, students will interrupt the professor (though not commonly more than once!), all the more so each other, and the boys will commonly disrupt what girls are saying and contradict them. By the end of the course, if the teaching has succeeded, students will not only not interrupt the professor, they also will not break in upon one another; they will carry forward and respond to what has just been said; and the women will speak in loud voices and with assurance. Here are lessons to be learned in every classroom, what-ever the subject, and even outside of the formal classroom altogether. If we succeed in turning out educated men and women, able to read percep-tively, listen carefully, and speak to the point and with effect, we know it in their powers of heart and mind. When we fail, we see it in their confu-sion and doubt and incapacity to inarticulate their thoughts. The senior author has never completed a semester without totaling up the wins and the losses, and he never wins them all. He is always glad simply to have won more than lost and in so doing, made a difference.

Given what is at stake in education — as distinct from the mere trans-mission of information — many other sorts of officials and officers par-ticipate in the work and define the character of a college or university. For example, the way in which secretaries conduct themselves may teach lessons about life more immediate and more telling than anything professors say. Why are secretaries central? Because, as soon as students come to meet professors or teaching assistants, they walk through the door of an office and confront a person in charge. That person is not a professor or a teaching assistant and may not have an academic degree. Yet the secretary guards the door and says, "Yes, go in," or, "No, the professor is too busy." The secretary answers the phone, takes the messages, transacts much of the business of professors when they deal not only with students but also with the rest of the university's management, not to mention the outside world.

The way the details of department life are carried on is all important to students. How so? If secretaries are cordial and friendly, they create a setting in which students rightly feel respected and important. If they are cold and unresponsive, they create a framework in which students find themselves abused and disregarded. Since the student is at the center of the university's mission, the way students are treated signals the prevailing atmosphere of the university, defining what it is like to be a student there. In this regard, the secretary plays a more critical part in the life of the university, so far as students' understanding is concerned, than many people who appear to outsiders to be more important. The majority of management and service staff of the university are not academicians. But in the nature of what they do, they always are teachers. They invariably teach students the most important lesson the university imparts: how much we care for you, the student. When library employees try to accommodate students' interests and help them make use of the books, when cafeteria workers, infirmary nurses, lab assistants, and custodial workers befriend the students and take an interest in their lives, then the entire university becomes a happy community.

But when the basic attitude of the staff expresses disdain, when people do not try to accommodate the students and solve their problems, then the university contradicts its purpose. The students then receive the wordless lesson that human concerns and reason take second place, and the convenience of the autocracy — and even a dean of housing may play the part of autocrat — is paramount. Universities ought to carry out the policy that education happens everywhere and all the time. Hence all procedures should operate under the policy that we are here to solve the students' problems as best we can, to make the world of learning a happy one, to accommodate their wishes so far as we can. This we do by an appeal to reason and good sense, by a consistent refusal to say no when there is any possibility of saying yes. The world at large accommodates peoples' whims and allows people in authority — however trivial — to show the world how they feel this morning. We can do very little about the grouchy bus driver who closes the door in our face. We cannot get back at the rude salesperson, the needlessly officious guard or customs inspector, the one who never smiles, the one who never says yes. But in a university we can do a great deal to cultivate a friendly spirit, an attitude of solicitous concern for students and all people. That does not mean we teach only by saying yes. It does mean that we teach courtesy by trying to be courteous, just as much as we teach clear expression by trying to say things clearly. Our example need not replicate the world beyond our gates.

For we stand for reasonable discourse and the power of argument to change minds. We demonstrate what we mean to teach not merely in the classroom but also in the use of rational discourse in every corner of the campus. Assistant deans come in many shapes and sizes. Outside of the classroom, they are the university officials students are most likely to know. Indeed, students will know them better than they know professors. The students do not choose their own rooms and roommates, but someone assigns them; students do not maintain their own records, but someone oversees them; they do not come and go without paying tuition and receiving credits and going through a considerable number of formalities. Students moreover have problems of which the professor remains ignorant. They go to deans of students, to health services, and to others as important as the professor. Universities, moreover, offer a broad range of extracurricular, but educationally vital, activities, such as student unions, bookstores, discussion facilities, clubs and organizations, and publications of all kinds. These do not happen by themselves.

Like pistols in the hands of seven-year-olds, the student newspapers, for example, make or break careers. The student paper at the University of South Florida (the *Oracle*), printed unsigned letters that libeled professors (and clearly came from other professors), and poisoned the life of a department, disrupted normal working relations in one of the University's colleges, embittered the campus, and, as a matter of fact, violated Florida law. The next generation of editors then could not understand the hostility of professors to their work. Professors remember — and, for life, so do students — what happens on campus and not in the classroom.

Deans of student life nurture students and guide them, while preserving students' freedom to make of their campus life what they will. Such people as secretaries, food service employees, library workers, physicians, nurses, librarians, deans, coaches, and guards play a vital and intimate role in the life of the student and of the college. In fact students who play sports learn more from coaches than from others, fall more under their influence and model than under the spell of even the most brilliant lecturer. The life of the residential students is lived for a dozen hours a week in the classroom, and for 156 hours a week on the campus and beyond the classroom. And the commuting students come under the influence of the campus too. That is why secretaries, the maintenance staff, library specialists, the university's police force, assistant deans, associate provosts, and all the others who run part of the university must have one ability above all others: the ability to teach, to serve as an example. Just as there must be a standard of reason in the classroom, so there should be a policy of accommodation and goodwill outside it. Let the exceptions to the norm testify that in life at large, it is normal to be nice.

How does a prospective student assess this aspect of a college? When you visit a campus, look into three specific areas. First, are students happy with the health center and related services? If they are sick, do the doctors and nurses treat them with respect? What happens in a crisis, whether psychological or medical? How effective are the responses? Second, can students see deans and professors readily and easily, or are offices tightly closed to them? Do departments make ample provision for advising students? Third, are there enough resources to deal with the many problems a student will face? Be prepared to ask students specific questions about all three areas. They will tell you how comfortable the students are with the school's facilities. Do students find it easy to get an appointment? Are there enough deans or advisers and counselors so that all students get the attention they need? Is there a broad variety of deans, covering diverse special tasks, so that a single dean can pay adequate attention to a few specific responsibilities? If there are housing problems, do people take them seriously? If a student has to change a room, does someone care? When there are problems with a tuition payment or a meal contract, does someone take charge and solve the problem? Or do students find themselves unable to conduct their business rapidly and efficiently?

These are the sorts of questions that will lead parents and prospective students into the everyday reality created by the support staff of the college or university. People who ask general questions come away with generalizations — and happy lies. If you ask students whether they are happy, they will answer that they are. But if you ask students what substantial problem they faced outside the classroom, and how they found help in solving that problem, you will learn specific and important information about the conduct of life at that college. Our impression is that colleges and universities, on the whole, do a first-rate job of tending to the extracurricular and noncurricular lives of their students. But whoever does not know in advance whether and how a college's entire system of deans and directors does its work will find out at the worst possible time.

Notes

1. We focus on the humanities, because that is what we know, the senior author as producer, the junior author as consumer. That leaves us with a high opinion of the seriousness, in both teaching and scholarship, of mathematics, technology, and the natural sciences, which seem to us to exemplify the virtues of the academy, so far as these endure. Perhaps we are too much blinded by the beam in our own eye to see the mote in that of the other. It is noteworthy that the great critics of higher education in the recent past have found little to reject in MIT, Cal Tech, Illinois Institute of Technology, and the other great centers of higher education in mathematics, technology, and the natural and physical sciences; or in medical education. Much of the intellectual and educational corruption of the universities has limited itself to the humanities and to what are called "the soft social sciences," those that do not require math and statistics. But these areas of the curriculum respond to culture and politics in ways in which the hard sciences do not; and they erect lower barriers to admission, even cancelling requirements to master foreign languages, for example, in doctoral programs. Whether the humanities will, or should, survive their present dismal condition is a question not pursued by the National Endowment for the Humanities, though at least two of the agency's chairs, William Bennet and Lynn Cheney, at least tried to raise the question.
2. "Colleges are teaching students less and charging them more" *Denver Post*, March 24, 1996.
3. "Higher Ed; The No-Longer Sacred Cow." *Governing*. July 1995
4. Ellis, John. "Poisoning the Wells of Knowledge," New York Times. March 28, 1998.
5. In what follows we recapitulate some of the writings collected in different form in *How to Grade Your Professors and Other Unexpected Advice* (Boston, 1984: Beacon; second printing: 1984). What intersects with the earlier work is extensively revised for the present purpose, and the greater part of the discussion is comprised of fresh proposals.
6. Archibold, Randal. "Give Me an 'A' or Else," *New York Times,* May 24, 1998.
7. Feynman, Richard. The Meaning of It All; Thoughts of a Citizen Scientist (Helix Books, 1998).
8. This notion is not original to us but derives from the counterpart claim in behalf of the theater that the senior author heard Lloyd Richards express at a meeting of the National Council on the Arts, governing body of the National Endowment for the Arts: "What we are going to do here in this theater for the next three hours is the most important thing you can do with those three hours, and with the money that you will spend to gain admission." Hearing that, he wondered whether we on the campus could issue such a self-confident challenge even to ourselves.
9. Kimball, Roger. "What Next, a Doctorate of Depravity?" *Wall Street Journal*, May 5, 1998.

2

What Should Universities Teach?

Scholarship, Research, and Teaching: How They Work Together

Since we have insisted that universities uniquely unite teaching with scholarship, including publication, we owe a clear statement of what defines scholarship. This is especially important because many professors (in our view correctly) view teaching as integral to scholarship and as a mode of scholarly expression. Outsiders suppose the opposite: publish (as a scholar, and therefore neglect students) or perish. But since few publish and still fewer perish, clearly reality is otherwise. So how do scholarship and research and teaching work together?

To begin with, what do we mean by scholarship? By scholarship we refer to the informed, systematic, and rigorous study of a subject aimed at solving a problem set forth by that subject. The scholar's stock in trade is criticism through which he or she creates a fresh reading of the subject, yielding a distinctive approach to a problem. What distinguishes the scholar from the teacher is that the scholar takes up in a new and interesting way a long-standing problem, or a long-familiar, yet ever-interesting text. Learning, a process of renewal, therefore goes on in teachers' minds as well as in their students' minds. Defined in this way, scholarship sets the stakes for university education. For only by studying with scholars can students grasp that fact: learning is always in the present tense. To be sure, all of us, on campus or off, solve problems and see things new. What we do in academic scholarship, in the security of the study and the laboratory, is use our minds to think strictly, clearly, and sharply. And

47

this is the quality of thought that enhances every life that rises above the mechanical. It is this process of thought that forms the primary goal of all education. That is why scholars begin so many sentences with, "But."

Scholarship forms a mode of learning based on not only accurate mastery of information but critical inquiry into the meaning of what one knows: a process of testing and retesting the established facts and truths of knowledge. Scholarship accordingly distinguishes universities from high schools, on the one hand, and from research institutes, on the other. Secondary-school teachers are expected to transmit information and lay the foundations for informed knowledge. This defines what most students at that age can acquire. The teachers are not expected to contribute to learning, and few do. Scholarship in the form of teaching defines universities and distinguishes them from research institutes. There researchers bear no responsibility systematically to share what they know with all qualified comers, or to do so in an effective way. They publish for whom it may concern, often not even engaged in discourse with colleagues.

High school teachers, like college professors who abandon critical learning, repeat the known but rarely say how we know it and why it is so. Research institute scholarship solves problems but does not then provide a model for problem-solving outside of the narrow limits of the topic under study.[1] The researcher at an institute suffices with a published article; the university research needs to share, and to do so in person. University professors ideally transcend both callings. This they do by learning critically and self-critically, sharing not only what they know, but how they know it.

A university without a faculty of hard-working and accomplished scholars does not do its job, and a university with a faculty of great scholars who disdain teaching students should close. And both deserve to suffer suits for malpractice and fraud. This country knows both kinds, but, alas, knows more colleges and universities staffed by teachers lacking all scholarly ambition than colleges with publishing scholars who cannot teach. The truth is, few publish, but, for not publishing, fewer still actually perish. Because universities form political communities, therefore sinking to the standard of the lowest common denominator, tenure rarely eludes those who go through the minimal motions. So scholarship expressed through publication and through teaching forms the heart of the university. It is its heart and the soul.

But what of the mass universities, where perhaps 80 percent of college students get their education, and where huge numbers of students search in vain for the heart and soul of learning? Can scholarship be replicated in fixed and formal lectures on television for mass audiences? These two questions form the arena for debate in the coming century, when, quite naturally, those who pay for higher education quite properly will seek ways to bring the costs down to the scale of society.[2] In some aspects, scholarship can be demonstrated before a camera. For, if works of scholarship, like works of art, cannot be mass-produced, still, the process can be portrayed.

But will "show and tell" suffice? No, for merely showing scholars at work does not shape minds. At this point William Green's epilogue to this book takes on deeper meaning, for he stresses how scholarship as a process, an attitude of mind, gains a concrete presence only when the labor is shared with the students, when, for example, professors can say to students, "I don't know the answer to that question" — and then proceed to discover it. For fresh work is work that progresses thoughtfully, in an unlimited exploration. Reducing the process to a one-way exchange, such as television teaching, or through interactive audio and video, disrupts it.[3] But, far more important, for scholarship to come to full exposure, students must participate, and that means, they must both listen *and be listened to.*

Whatever the medium, dialogue must take place: questions, answers, back and forth. Students who learn through dialogue — and that means, who are listened to and get a critical response to what they say — join in the process of discovery, transforming education into active learning. To expose processes of creative thought, moreover, there must be conversation, and people must work at it. Dialogue is certainly possible among a hundred students in a lecture room or among students located at various venues and linked by interactive television — but probably not among a thousand.[4] In very large classes — more than a hundred — as much as in small ones the senior author has managed over nearly forty years in the classroom to convey the points he wished to make through a process of question and answer, a dialectic of ongoing exchange. Those who follow enter into problem-solving; others lose their way, only to grasp the solution when it emerges. They've received only half the lesson, and not the important half.

True, authentic exchange costs money, since dialogue is always retail and never wholesale. Overwhelmed by the masses of students, the largest universities may treat as a luxury the project of teaching their students through publishing scholars. But scholar-teachers, in both vocations, represent what is essential, not what is expendable, for the mass universities. For in their teaching the scholars must always aim high, especially in the mass enrollment state colleges where the bulk of America's citizens of tomorrow are educated. The poor, after all, receive the same proportion of gifted brains as the rich, and, being many, in the aggregate will be possessed of a larger mass of sheer intelligence. And, when it comes to ambition, the rich, in their elite colleges and universities, cannot compete at all. They do not have to. That is why the largest and most local universities, faced with the most daunting numbers of students, must aim at maintaining the highest standards of scholarship and teaching. Students at Harvard, Brown, Stanford, or Duke can afford to fail; and anyhow, select and able to produce tens of thousands of dollars for tuition, they demand and get honor grades and honor degrees — whatever the state of their achievements, if any. But those at the subordinate campuses of the state universities, such as at the senior author's own University of South Florida, can not demand much of the world, except in response to their own accomplishments. That's all they have to offer. So they deserve the best. Yes, others pay more for their education, but no one takes a greater risk than the student who borrows to attend college and is a first-generation university student. Hocking the future on an unknown commodity requires the greatest commitment; and that commitment does show up in the classroom far more than in colleges where students pay cash.

Small liberal arts colleges present an ideal setting for teaching small classes. But in these colleges there may turn out to be less than meets the eye: professors who teach too broad a range of subjects and replace knowledge with impressions, critical judgment with opinions. They tend also to attract more than their share of students who seek coddling and attention but not challenge and criticism. Just as the best medical care may come from the large, teaching hospitals, where patients compete with specimens for doctors' attention, so the best education in the end may take place in the largest state universities — those with the highest standards and the most objective, impersonal rules. That is because scholars need an environment that small liberal arts colleges simply cannot provide, such as first-rate libraries and excellent laboratories and a corps of other highly specialized scholars, expert in mastering subjects and therefore worthy colleagues.

Defining an Authentic Scholar

Four traits characterize the mind of the scholar, young or old, freshman or senior, beginning or experienced, academic or nonacademic. None of them can be taught, only exemplified.

The first is the desire to rethink important propositions and to ask how they work and why by reasoned inquiry we have been compelled to accede to them.

The second is the capacity to take important intellectual initiatives, to ask questions in addition to accepting answers, to want to know not only more about what is known but also about something others have never asked.

The third is the complete engagement with the work, the entire devotion to the task to the exclusion of all else; more simply, the ability to concentrate.

The fourth is love for the work, a love that means finding the full meaning of life in what one is doing.

Any one of these traits without the others yields not the scholar but the dilettante: a politician of ideas, a dealer in manufactured and available notions, an amateur with bright ideas. Without these four traits, the intelligence never reaches its full potential of being more than a skill, a basic ability. Let us name a few scholars who thought the unthinkable — and prevailed. First, there was Charles Darwin. Second, there was Sigmund Freud. Third, there was Copernicus. In the worlds of nature, mind, and the universe, these three pioneers exemplify the power of the scholar to ask the unthinkable questions, to reexamine the basic questions everyone assumes have been answered. These men and women such as Madame Curie typify in their work the process of scholarship. Darwin allowed his careful observations to lead him to conclusions that defied long-established facts. Freud insisted on taking seriously phenomena people insisted bore no meaning at all. Copernicus explained old facts in a completely new way. The first one worked inductively, the second reasoned independently, and the third thought courageously, seeing as fresh so-called facts everybody had accepted. None, by the way, worked in a university. So the habits of mind that make great scholars belong to the scholar and not to the institution that houses him. The institution is wise to sponsor the scholar but it can never own his gift.

Teaching and Apprenticeship

Now to the heart of the matter: what has scholarship so defined have to do with education? From the opening lines of this chapter we have insisted on the centrality of our universities' unique aspiration to unite scholarship and teaching, so we owe a concrete answer to that question.

Education takes two forms, and both are necessary for scholarship. The first is the acquisition of knowledge, meaning both the facts and their understanding. The second is an apprenticeship to those who teach the work by doing it. Women and men of learning and critical capacities afford access to knowledge. Only scholars serve as intellectual mentors. Both kinds of scholarship serve, and both are necessary.

All undergraduates are well served by great professors, people who teach what is known in a responsible and conscientious way. In the century that is upon us, universities will establish their utility only by offering what people can find nowhere else, which is teaching scholars, joined to an apprenticeship to learning. If universities fail to define their unique vocation in such terms, they will lose out in the competition with far cheaper, and equally effective, media for the transmission of information, down to the humble tape recorder. In universities alone students will experience an apprenticeship as well. We can give three common examples of the master-apprentice relationship that most of us will recognize and have perhaps experienced.

First, in music school, the teacher plays, the student imitates — and tries to play better.

Second, the sports field, the coach demonstrates, the athlete copies — and does it better.

Third, students copy a parent, on the one side, and a teacher on the other, but they improve on much.

The apprenticeship offers the student an opportunity that cannot be duplicated in a lecture class, and that television and interactive computer teaching cannot convey. For there is no simple way, and no way other than the personal one, to show someone how to take intellectual initiative: how to ask questions, how to draw analogies from the known to the unknown, from the completed to the incomplete. For that, people must see one another and feel one another's presence. Perhaps, as we have already proposed, with two-way television an authentic classroom can come into being. But however and wherever we meet them — in person, on a monitor, on the web — we educate our students by example as much as by word. We cast our shadow on the wall for the disciples to see. For what students see in their teachers is related to the model of what they want to be. We may present an attractive or an unattractive model, but always a choice. The apprentice learns the craft by imitating it — or by doing the opposite. They know success when what they make surpasses what the artisan has made. That is the sole measure of a teacher's greatness.

For some students, a college education will achieve that goal, nurturing a mind that can see farther and sharper than the teacher's. The setting for this form of education is not so much the classroom as the study, the computer work-station where one thinks and writes; not the place where results of research are announced, but the laboratory and library where the discoveries are made. The setting is wherever there is a beginning. It is the place of inquiry, discovery, by doing for oneself, by finding out for oneself. But scholarship for the beginner commences in the classroom and attains concrete form through the habits of the teaching scholar, who receives student questions and exemplifies what it means to think in a fresh way. That is where the classroom meets with the life of research.

Research is what a person does when he or she undertakes to test established truths, replicate them or call them into question. Research is what a person does by proposing to find out whether what people take for granted is fact. Research is what someone does who asks, What if...? and Why...? and Why not...? Research identifies what we do not know that we must find out — and proceeds to discover it. Must professors supervise research? No, though they can help. Can freshmen undertake research? Most certainly, if they want to try and have the patience to do what is required and the humility to reckon (as all of us must) with their own limitations. But the beginners must learn also what scholarship in the setting of research is not. Research is not merely learning about an obscure subject closed to the vast majority of people. Nor is it merely collecting a lot of information about a topic. That is mere erudition, fact mongering. And beginners have also to grasp where scholarship in the form of research takes place. Research can occur anywhere; it is defined only by an attitude of mind and heart, of inquiry and stubbornness, of care and attentiveness, of clarity of thought and originality.

Many learned people can teach, but only the scholarly mind can nurture other scholars. Only the person who knows how to undertake the search can show others how to do so. Only the scholar, like the artisan, can teach by example so that others may learn by doing. The key to scholarly apprenticeship is this: scholars never cease to be students and disciples, never cease to learn, and those who are beginners in our craft never serve only as students and disciples until the day they formally become scholars.

We scholar-teachers therefore have always to be, and to be seen as, not only teacher-scholars but more especially as learner-teachers. In argument therefore we have to show the capacity to listen and even to change our minds. So, too, even beginners should take up tasks of scholarship, while still acquiring the requisite knowledge and skills we learn by doing. And while doing, we always learn. We cannot postpone the work of doing until we have learned all we think we need to know, for we will never know all we need in order to do what we want to do.

Traditional schools, with the task of training, not educating, exemplars and authorities for another age, emphasize the authority of the old, the incapacity of the young. They have no interest in educating the independent-minded, free-spirited citizens that a free society demands. Imitate the old, accept the model that has endured — that is what traditions demand. For instance, the senior author recalls how often in his student days at Jewish Theological Seminary of America years he was told, "You are worthless. You don't know enough to do anything." When he asked, "Well, when will I know enough to do something," the answer was, "When you're too old anyhow. So stop writing, shut up, and study." He heard the same message in Jerusalem. Perhaps that forms the message that a traditional and hierarchical and geriatric culture imparts. It certainly explained why the schools — the Jewish Theological Seminary of America, among many parochial institutions of its kind, and the Judaica faculties of the Hebrew University — would ultimately enter intellectual bankruptcy and lose all influence in the world of learning, as they have.[5] It is not that people disregard positions fiercely defended in these centers; it is that nothing worth an argument comes out of the humanistic part of Jewish studies in them. The archaeologists know better and take their rightful place on the world stage, and so do the social scientists working on the Jews. But for the classical subjects, the mighty have long ago fallen.

The standard critique of scholarship in sterile centers concerns mistakes one allegedly may make or has made. These mistakes turn out in many cases to stand for mere differences of opinion, misconstructions, or misunderstandings. But all of us do make mistakes, large and small, and those who venture most will make the biggest errors. The offense against learning comes not when we make mistakes, but when we fail to correct and learn from them. And the discredited scholar in the end is the one who does not learn from mistakes but defends them. Fear of publishing lest one publish what has not attained perfection masks pretense and dishonesty. The pretense is that perfection is possible. What is dishonest? It is the allegation that the nonpublisher would have plenty to say, if only he or she could say it perfectly. Professors announce that they will retire early so as to write their books. Or they will say they will apply for a year off so as to write a book. But publishing scholars gain energy through momentum and do research while teaching in semester. All excuses aside, the simple fact is, those who do not publish have nothing to say. That is why those who do not publish ought to perish — or, more fairly, give way and open space for those who do — or in their youth promise at least that they may. Tenure that protects the inactive scholar or the slothful teacher keeps the academy from doing its work. But those who do not publish rarely perish; they more often go on to chairmanships, become deans, provosts, and presidents.

Clearly, in our stress on the unique promise of the scholar-teacher, we have in mind transforming much of university education into a mode of seminar-instruction, worked out in response to possibilities afforded here and there. When students begin their studies, therefore, they ought to find themselves plunged into an ongoing seminar, a kind of laboratory for research into a common problem by individuals working together, from different angles and on different data. All can benefit to varying degrees, and those who can benefit most should receive nothing less. Then what do we mean by a seminar? It is a course in which professors do not lecture. Rather, participants — students — present their ideas to one another, always subject to the professor's guidance and criticism. They write their papers under the professor's guidance, but the papers are their own. They read their papers to their fellow students and gain the benefit of their comments and criticism.

What makes a seminar work? It is a shared inquiry, the formation of a partnership in learning. A well-constructed seminar will present a single complex problem for collective study. Individual members of the seminar will take a part of the larger problem and write papers about it. All together, the group discusses the problem as a whole, with each student contributing his or her share. A seminar on the causes of the American Revolution, for example, would present a dozen students pursuing a dozen proposed causes, advocating and analyzing the character and place of each. Taken together, the individual student contributions would produce a coherent picture. Most colleges and universities offer seminars at the upper levels of the curriculum, usually for seniors. Some offer seminars for freshmen as well. But many confuse a seminar with merely a small class. Numbers do not wholly define the matter, sharing does.[6]

A seminar offers no easy answers to a problem through the labor-saving device of professorial instruction, and the student is forced to think independently about a difficult question. It is at this point that learning takes place. The seminar requires the student to cross a crucial threshold. The most difficult thing for a scholar to learn, no less any member of today's economy, is to learn from other people, to preserve an open mind to the idea, insight, even to the questions of co-workers. In the seminar the student learns to respect the criticism and ideas of other students, and to recognize the limits on his or her own perceptions. Because scholarship requires single-mindedness and dedication, scholars face the temptation to dismiss as unimportant the questions and inquiries of others. The same is true of any vocation. This attitude of self-sufficiency, this incapacity to learn from others except what one needs for the particular task at hand, closes the path to scholarship. It closes the mind.

Professors are responsible for teaching the lesson that we do learn from others. We always carry on our work alongside that of our colleagues, and often with their help, and we must learn to listen to and consider fairly the concerns and problems of others, colleagues and noncolleagues alike. Let us give a concrete example. At Princeton University, we are reliably informed, professors routinely walk into one another's classrooms and engage in argument with the teacher of a course. That exactly realizes the promise of disciplined rationality. A more senior scholar may transform the lectures of a junior one into a dialogue and a debate — and everyone gains a clear picture of the stuff of intellectual life. For if students learn from the example of professors that what they need from others is not approval but insight, then we have opened the way to great achievement. Junior faculty giving courses in partnership with senior scholars enjoy the same stimulation — but also bestow it.

This observation leads to a difficult question: How do we as professors measure the success of our work in education? It is, alas, a measure that we are not in a position to take: the total mode of life adopted by our students. If we succeed, we open the doors of learning, the world of the mind, to the coming generations. Our young apprentices go forth, and some will carry on the work of the teacher, knowing something about teaching and much about the self-conscious and articulated requirements of learning. And if we fail, then we foist upon the coming generations a mass of closed-minded, self-important careerists, people who impose dogma and recite facts.

Here the senior author takes the floor: His own ideal is for his work to be made obsolete, of mere historic interest, by the greater achievements of his apprentices. Among his many doctoral students of years past most accomplished little with the good jobs he got them. But a few have surpassed him, especially in the areas in which they work, using things they learned from him in subjects he scarcely knows. One of them has undertaken exceptional research. Another has taken over and mastered an area of research the senior author left behind. His work now far surpasses mine. A third went on to problems of thought and theory that lay beyond the range of the senior author's ability. The epilogue of this book is by that former-student. That above all embodies what the senior author means by having students who learn from but then surpass the teacher. This is the only way he knows to transcend self and to surpass his own limitations.

The New Humanities — For Good and Ill

Now let us turn to concrete questions about what is to be taught, and concentrate on a specific field of learning, the humanities, as distinct from natural science, mathematics, engineering, medicine, and social science. Within the humanities such fields of learning as language and literature, history and philosophy, the study of religion, provide important examples of what constitutes the difference between trivia and scholarship. These form subject-areas (i.e., American history, Buddhism), but also require the framing and answering of questions. How do we study history? What do we study when we study religion? Trivia answers only one question. The humanities, studied properly, answers many others.

That is why subjects come and go, but disciplines and methods evolve slowly. New approaches that last in the academy must demonstrate the qualities of solid and rigorous intellect. Yet the topics of study, rather than the methods, attract attention, for good and for bad. These form the surface of learning — and they are what add the glitz. Take for example the new humanities of the past few decades. The revolution of the 1960s and 1970s brought to the campus a demand for relevance, to the new groups of people coming to the campus at that time. For them new subjects had to be invented, mostly concerned with groups formerly excluded from the mainstream of culture. They were principally taught by new types of teachers, people who in times past received no welcome on campus. The history and literature of women, blacks, Jews, Asian-Americans, Polish-Americans, Latinos, and others joined the established curriculum of English, American, and Western European studies. American literature had been taught from a canon that made no place for writings concerning, or by, blacks or women; the canon had to expand.

Not only so, but, during those two decades students brought about fundamental change by demanding that studies relate to everyday life. The meaning of the word relevance proved obscure — relevant *to what* was often unclear — but students insisted. They wanted to know why they were studying the subjects at hand. They asked what the curriculum had to do with them as people, with their lives and their futures. The question of relevance produced diverse answers. But one answer has won the greatest support: any interest in subjects from those who differed from typical white male students — women, blacks, Jews, Catholics, Greek Orthodox, Hispanics, Italian-, Polish-, Asian-Americans — were regarded as properly relevant. These students wanted to study books important to them as Jews, blacks, Catholics, and so on. As a result of the demand for relevance, programs, centers, and departments of Judaic, Afro-American, and women's studies (among other fields) were organized. These new subjects confront students still today, and they have vastly enlarged the college curriculum everywhere. But the new humanities have run out of energy, as the potential audience of blacks to study black studies, and Jews for Jewish studies, reaches a natural limit. The target audience has lost interest and found greater success in the curriculum that is defined by method and discipline, not by subject matter: business, science, engineering, and so forth.

But — and this was much to the good — the revolution in the 1960s and early 1970s brought about considerable expansion of the established curriculum of humanistic learning in American and Canadian universities. Departments of history that formerly concentrated solely on American and Western European history made room for regions formerly ignored, such as Asia or sub-Saharan Africa. History departments excelled, in times past, in intellectual bigotry. They gave no hearing to Jewish history, dismissed Africa as lacking history altogether, and treated Asia as an exotic episode in what was essentially a European and American story. Departments of English did the same, and classics notoriously sheltered the campus snobs, those keepers of the grail of Western culture. Where religion was studied, it was religion in the Protestant model. Even to this day, while Catholic universities appoint to their religious and theological studies departments numerous graduates of Protestant divinity schools, Protestant ("nondenominational") counterparts appoint negligible numbers of Catholics.

Much clearly has changed. Departments of literature that were formerly interested in only English, American, French, German, and Russian literature began to ask students to read Afro-American and Latin American literature. In the course catalogue today, college students find an account of whole sectors of American society that earlier generations of college students did not know, subjects that earlier generations would have regarded as private.

If the university is to serve its true purpose, which is to demonstrate the universal uses of criticism, reason, rationality, and rigorous thought, then the Roman Catholic, or Greek Orthodox, or black, or Hispanic, or woman will find a place in the curriculum, representing a subject matter the testimony that one's experience matters to the life of the college. In our view the advent of cultural and ethnic diversity in the curriculum and the mainstreaming of women are the great, enduring achievements of the student revolution of the 1960s. But, since there are no gains without pains, these form the challenge to the twenty-first century as well. Blacks have defined black studies as an exercise in exclusivity — blacks teaching racial pride (a form of racism, surely) to blacks. Professors of Jewish studies routinely assume that most of their students will come from Jewish families, whole or in part. And they orient their instruction to one notch above the quality of most extracurricular synagogue schools. They dwell on ethnic resentment and its quite reasonable provocation, the Holocaust. The ideology of the subject obscures its rationality. And that loss of academic and intellectual purity characterizes the whole of the corps of the new humanities. The premise of the new humanities then rests upon the special interest of the select few, and that contradicts the norm of the academy, which requires that we speak in a shared language of reason.

In today's humanities, special pleading replaces learning, politically correct opinions substitute for free debate, proscribed attitudes substitute for free inquiry, and a reign of intellectual terror has descended on those who dare to deviate from accepted scholarship, particularly at the most expensive and liberal universities. Indeed, the higher on the scale of the elite universities, the more restrictive and dictatorial the Afrocentric groupthink. Few at the outset perceived the profoundly antiacademic spirit in which the legitimate interests of African-Americans, for example, would come to expression in the curriculum and outside of it. These academic liberals were sympathetic to blacks' interest in including studies relevant to their experience in history and culture. They desired to learn the great literature that took to heart their suffering and pathos. They thirsted to know the history of Africa as much as the history of America and Europe. None anticipated the cruelty that black studies would usher into universities; none realized that the victims of racism had learned too well from the racists, their tormenters — and would improve upon their lessons. That is, truth belongs to the victors. And in the odd calculus of the contemporary campus, the victims are the victors, and they decide what is truth.

The Canon

And that brings us to the record of those long in control: Their canon of what is to be read or ignored, along with who is to do the reading and direct it. The homogeneity of old American universities, with their old American faculties and their old American names and genealogies, quickly disappeared in the second half of the twentieth century. Newer Americans were coming of age and demanding a place. Once universities had opened their doors to larger and more diverse social and ethnic constituencies than they had ever known, the question confronted faculties and students alike: What do we do now? The answer was simply to do more than had been done before. This meant that students could study what was familiar in their own background. Relevance became the criterion. But this was both natural and normal and just as students had always done. The old Americans had always known what was relevant to them: Classics, after all, was a gentlemen's hobby, English literature belonged to the descendants of English immigrants, and American history was the history written by the old Americans great-grandfathers. Classics, English, history — the culture-defining disciplines — unashamedly practiced anti-Semitism, dismissed women out of hand, and treated African-Americans as nonpersons. And, where they can, they still do. A certain snobbery, of course, protected these scheduled subjects. People absorbed the prejudice that, quite naturally and predictably, these were things any educated person should know. And the rest — the other, the excluded subjects stood for things no educated person would admit to knowing.

Knowing these subjects, or a list of selected books (the one hundred books for the one hundred families that count), defined an education.

Hence a core curriculum and a general education was considered possible. No one needed to ask about the missing books, those that served as classics to excluded groups, and the millions of excluded families. Before the 1960s, everybody knew what was worthwhile and what represented taste, what shaped thoughts worth thinking, what defined values worth adopting. And it should be added, people who knew these worthwhile things also could look forward to careers of worth and standing: in banks, law firms, corporations, hospitals, universities, and the other protected professions, reserved for those who came from the right castes and knew the scheduled subjects. All that had to change, and it has changed.

But, for reasons that vastly transcend the academic catastrophe brought upon black studies by black academicians, the change from the old canon to the new, realized a nightmare: The utter scandalizing of the academy. What seemed relevant to one proved remote to the next. The curriculum came to resemble the self-interested ethnic politics of large industrial cities in the 1920s and 1930s, with a slice of the pie for everyone, but no sense of a common good or a public interest. The old bigotry gave way to new bigotries: blacks against Jews, lesbian women against marriage and men in general, to name the more notorious ones. Translated into university life, this meant no one could appeal to a common rationality or shared critical criteria or universal reason. Each group had its own. This ethnicization of learning brought also particularization and only emphasized the apparent differences between the new and the old humanities. The old humanities had preserved not only privilege but also a center, a sense of purpose. Their imperial view did encompass everybody, for the old humanists imagined that they had something to say to the whole of humanity and that what they had to say demanded a universal audience. Teachers of the established humanities could indeed point to books they believed everyone should read. And they could say why.

These teachers could also define traits of intellectual excellence. A teacher of the old humanities therefore, could imagine such a thing as a general education. So, they held, people could determine why one book mattered more than another, and why one philosophical tradition deserved close and careful scrutiny while another deserved no attention. The power of the established humanities lay in the promise of educated taste and reasoned judgment. The old humanities promised to impose order upon the chaos of information. Against this intellectual order and serenity pressed the motley crowd of the new humanities. What did the new humanities offer to justify their entry into the realm of the disciplined intellect? The presence on campus of a new sort of student and teacher, both formerly excluded, hardly constituted a persuasive argument. After all, that new person, whether black, Catholic, woman, or Jew, could readily study the classics of the established curriculum and adopt its values. Generations of "minorities" had done so.

But what universally accessible human experience did the new constituencies bring to the campus, to usurp the classics of human intellect that had constituted the old humanities? So people asked, Where was the Jewish Aquinas or the Indian Plato, the black Shakespeare, the Catholic equivalent to the Protestant Reformation and its legacy of individual conscience that everyone studies with such admiration? Many were ready to answer these questions. But when the new humanities pointed to their heritage of art, music, fiction, and poetry, few but those to whom it was relevant were interested. So, people took for granted blacks would study what blacks had done. Jews would study Jewish studies. Women would study women's studies. What this meant in practice was that most students in Jewish studies courses were Jews, most students in Afro-American studies courses were blacks, and most students in women's studies were women. It took many years before the profile of students in basic courses in the study of Judaism matched a demographic sample of Brown students in general, so that non-Jewish students found it perfectly routine to take such a course. At the University of South Florida, by contrast, most Jewish students regard academic courses on Judaism as not ethnic enough, while the Judaic studies classroom is filled with a cross-section of the cultures and ethnic groups of west-central Florida. Go figure.

The Failure of the New Humanities

But then, in the revolution, the academy made one more assumption. People took for granted that everyone would still study Greek philosophy, Shakespeare, the Reformation, and other familiar subjects that everyone had always studied in the ways in which everyone had always studied them. So was formed the hollow bargain of the 1970s: ethnic insiders would teach private subjects to ethnic insiders, and everyone — the real people, the normal ones — would continue to study public subjects. Everyone accepted the compromise. The newcomers felt quite at home, as well they should, for they never left their ghetto. What this meant for students was that Jewish students took for granted they could get easy A's in Jewish studies and please their parents too. And they would do their serious work in other departments.

Even when the degree requirements imposed upon all students courses in women's or black or ethnic studies, the new humanities remained on the fringes of the real interests of students at large. That fact is shown by a simple measure: enrollments in the new, private subjects have tumbled. Not even blacks want African-American studies, or Jews, Jewish studies, for more than a course or two at the most. What the new humanities have taught — the great human experiences of the black peoples in the Americas and Africa, the remarkable record of Holy Israel — never enriched the curriculum. The old humanities remained essentially unchanged and retained their ultimate governance. Making room for newcomers only by adding intellectual ghettos staffed by ethnic cheerleaders, the old privileges endured and did not even have to be shared. What emerged, then, through the 1970s was curricular tokenism, a kind of intellectual affirmative action: The new minorities filled the classrooms, but the board of directors would come from the same folk who had supplied members for generations past. Everyone would be content. And they were.

Not surprisingly, the easy compromise of the 1970s has become a Faustian bargain by the late 1990s. The established humanities cannot explain themselves any longer and their enrollments dwindle. The newcomers have proved inadequate to the tasks and the old-timers have fallen into bankruptcy. How so? The new humanities, in their dominant form, made no important contribution to the university. They consist of Jews teaching Jewish things to Jews, and blacks to blacks, and women to women. And when it comes to the Jews, the religion departments opt for what they imagine is authenticity and — as at University of Virginia — they therefore prefer Orthodox rabbis to all less exotic comers. The new humanities undertake no reasoned response to the argument that some things matter more than others, "white" thinkers more than black, Aquinas more than Maimonides. But universities do their work only when they form places where everybody speaks to whomever is interested. Scholars speak to everybody about matters of scholarship and interpretation. No scholar talks to himself alone or speaks of experience or logic inaccessible to anyone other than those who share his biography.

Once the new humanities decided that theirs was an essentially private and particular heritage, to be promoted for parochial purposes (to give blacks self-confidence for example, or to persuade Jews to remain Jewish), they also turned themselves into mere pressure groups on the campus, extensions of political forces based outside the campus. The result for black studies has proven disastrous. James Lardner reports, in the *Washington Post,* that in the late 1960s and early 1970s, there were more than 500 formal programs in black or Afro-American studies. By late 1982 only 275 programs survived; of these, only sixty-five or seventy were full departments. Scholars of black studies concede that their field has entered "a state of near-crisis." Why? Because the black students themselves now avoid black studies. The scholars excuse themselves by explaining that the students are "more job-conscious and more interested in courses that will make them employable."[7] This is pure self-indulgence. In this same period classics has enjoyed a renaissance, although few jobs these days demand knowledge of Attic Greek or the ability to read Plato in the original. Anyone who doubts that the same story may be told of Jewish studies and other ethnic studies needs only to attend a meeting of the learned societies of those fields. Gone is the atmosphere of hope and energy. Newer subjects also give evidence of regression. The academic study of religion, which was born in the later 1940s and fully realized in the 1960s as part of the larger development under discussion here, is old and feeble.

At a recent national meeting of the study of religion, the scholars held a caucus of "endangered departments." One participant guessed, "Every religion department from Springfield, Missouri, to the tip of Maine is endangered, whether the department chairmen know it or not." People take for granted that a university can exist without black, Jewish, women's, or religious studies, but a university cannot exist without history, English, philosophy, or sociology. What went wrong? The new humanities have not yet taken the measure of universities; universities have not yet imparted their distinctive character to the new humanities. That is one fact, with two complementary effects. The new humanities have a future in universities only if they join the sort of discourse that universities nurture. The university, for its part, must build its future upon the broadest social foundations and draw upon the deepest cultural resources of human experience and culture. And that can happen only when the university demonstrates, as it has not yet done, its power to illuminate human experience across the globe through scholarly analysis, and to make interesting and public what is at present self-serving and private.

Each side, whether the new or the old, the outsider or the one at home, bears part of the responsibility for the reform of the new humanities. Professors of the new subjects will have to demonstrate how the things they know contribute to a common inquiry and a shared conversation.

They must cease to turn away from their colleagues and to assume they address a protected audience within a privileged sanctuary — as though they could not compete for attention if they tried. Professors of the established subjects will have to open their minds to areas of learning they have, to date, treated with unjustified disdain and ignorant indifference. Both sides are accomplices in the easy compromise, which has perpetuated privilege and merely expanded its range.

The only issue in the rise and fall of the old and new humanities is scholarship. Scholarship by its nature pays no heed to special claims. A proposition that one cannot understand unless qualified by gifts of genes or genealogy should gain no hearing at all. A book that speaks to people only if they believe at the outset that the book is true or important will enjoy a long, undisturbed life on the library shelf. Such books, such courses, in the end go the way of all claims at reaching judgments through other than critical and reasonable modes of thought. They enjoy the fate of every conviction that is exempt from verification and falsification. Scholarship is inductive; it aims at falsifying or verifying all claims to truth, and subjects all propositions to the same critical and reasonable modes of thought.

In the beginning, the new humanities flourished by presenting surprising information about subjects no one cared to study. Playing an endless game of show and tell, justified by self-indulgent special pleading, the professors of the new humanities gathered everything but a reason for their field. For their part, the universities proposed to accommodate what in fact most people despised and dismissed as soon as they could. For universities are not museums, and professors must add to knowledge, not only preserve and display it.

The first phase in the new humanities, now drawing to a close, has proved deeply flawed: arrival without welcome, presence without purpose. Since universities are nurtured by the societies that sponsor them and the politics that give effect to social policy, universities will hardly benefit from reverting to the earlier world of institutionalized prejudice and cultural snobbery. American society will never tolerate the reintroduction of quotas to exclude Jews, let alone the reimplementation of the bigotry that blacks cannot learn and women should not. In the same way, the new humanities will fail the universities and society if they continue to exclude the larger intellectual community. Black history must be open to the work of white scholars, and women's studies must allow men to read, write, and evaluate their work. The task of the new humanities is to gain legitimate entry into the intellectual life of the universities. The task of the universities is to draw from every group within its boundaries the same principles of reasoned discourse and public accounting of all propositions that have framed scholarship and defined worthwhile learning. Both parties must now move on from the initial uneasy accommodation.

How shall we achieve the integration of the new humanities within the university's conception of its own work? As an example, let the senior author state what he does in very simple language: *it is to teach students*. And what he teaches to students is *about* Judaism — in that order. What we teach students, through any subject, is about thinking, about using their minds for specific tasks. The curriculum then consists of two components: first, information, which students learn, and, second, an example of how we compose that information into intelligible propositions, arguments about possibilities, which students may choose to imitate and improve. Whether we teach undergraduates or graduate students, the issue is the same. Students should be concerned with modes of analysis and means of interpretation, through which they learn the particulars of information. When we impart information without articulating how we have formulated the specifics and worked out the details in one way rather than another, we do only part of our work. The other part, alas, is most rapidly forgotten or rendered obsolete.

The New Humanities versus Multiculturalism

If someone had stood on a commencement podium on a bright May afternoon in 1970 and predicted that a little-known classics professor would, one generation later, turn American academia on its head with a best-seller book, no one would have believed it. Classics was seen as a vestige of a discredited curriculum in the late 1960s, a holdover from another time. And if this prophetic speaker had suggested that the book, a full frontal attack on the excesses of a multicultural curriculum, the proclivities of anti-Western faculty and administrators and the depressed content of American culture and ideas, someone in the audience might have regarded the speech as parody. And if that speaker had predicted not just one best seller, but a series of works, all by competent and forward-thinking people, that took for granted the loss of quality in American education in general and higher education in particular, the audience might have begun to question the speaker's sanity. Imagine if this same speaker had predicted that some of those best-sellers would be written by academics themselves, people motivated not by the destruction of campuses or the resentment of youth, but by the rebuilding of academia and student life?

It would have been hard to believe, not simply because the possibility of a counterrevolution appeared so remote in 1970. Our hypothetical commencement audience would have been sitting not only in the warm glow of the afternoon sun, but at the very edge of America's golden age of liberal academia. Someone suggesting that it was one generation away from being frittered away in a morass of corrupt ideas and policy, only to serve as the future punching bag of popular cultural and academic critics — this someone might be regarded roundly as a pessimist at best, an academic Tory at worst.

By 1970, forty years of unbroken success had made American campuses the envy of American society, industry, and campuses throughout the world. American colleges had taken the lead in developing the great ideas and concepts that nourished democracy and industry. The American middle class had deemed college to be a natural step in the education of its young, more than a mere repository for the wealthy (which it once was), and more than a curricular extension of high school (which it also once was). Modern American liberalism found its roots on the campus, and for better or worse, had used that basis to form an intellectual coterie that pursued an agenda of the welfare state now regarded as sacrosanct in our nation's capitol. And at the precipice of the final quarter of the twentieth century, American colleges had begun to right the past wrongs of discrimination, in their own terms, but in keeping with the liberal philosophy that the meritorious should be rewarded, regardless of creed, color, or religion. Such was the philosophy that had integrated colleges ethnically and religiously in the postwar period, and had given American colleges the philosophical justification for government support — through the GI Bill and major research projects — that permitted skyrocketing growth.

But if that commencement speaker had the audacity, he might have said it would soon end. And he might have argued that American colleges would lose their status not with a crash and not in a flash of light, but in the shadows and whispers of mediocrity and dumbing down. And he might provide the most stunning argument, one which would have placed his speech beyond the pale of reason at that time: that American universities would be undone by their professors, and it would have to be a professor, and not a student movement, that would launch the countercultural revolution in American academia.

What would his audience have said to his arguments that professors, in the relatively unknown world of academic journals, lecture halls, and seminars, would untie the knots that linked American universities closely to scholarship, truth-seeking, and knowledge? What would they have said had he told them that definitions of excellence and truth would be decided on the basis of race, or religion, or sexual orientation? What would they have said if he predicted that the greatest thinkers of the Western world — Shakespeare, Aristotle, Chaucer — would find their works judged not on their eternal merits and truths, but on the fact that their works were written by white men?

What would the audience have said? What, indeed, other than applaud politely and thank heavens that their child's education had finished just in time. Why? Because such a scenario was as unthinkable then as a lunar landing was to Americans twenty-five years before. The structure of American higher education in 1970 had been grounded solidly in a few major concepts that helped guide it through the Cold War, a fantastic rise in enrollments and budgets, the campus revolutions of the Vietnam War and the shedding of its gilded and elitist past. But since 1970, American colleges and universities have routinely turned out self-parodies. At Stanford, requirements for American history are waived to make room for requirements in race theory and feminist studies. At Georgetown, English literature professors denigrate the works of Shakespeare as not practical enough, not open enough, to the many cultures and backgrounds of today's student body, who are almost entirely American. At Harvard Law, the faculty adopted an antirudeness ordinance — whose punishments include dismissal from the school — prompted by a parody of one faculty member's rambling attack on hate speech.

Muckraking authors don't have any trouble finding academic malfeasance at nearly any level of academia, from obscure course offerings to unread journal articles. If only, the critics argue, American colleges were as good teaching anything substantially multicultural as they are about coming up with even more exotic course offerings. Foreign language budgets are slashed, foreign campuses are closed and lecture series are transformed into harangues against established curriculum. The very mechanisms developed to widen cultural horizons are being gutted to make room for the ill-defined goal of multiculturalism.

How did this happen? The argument is not about whether American colleges should teach unusual subjects, but how and by whom. American colleges had by the end of 1970, established a precedent for accepting subjects that were unusual, scholars that did unusual work and students that had unusual interests and backgrounds. But it was not in the collection of unusual tastes that American colleges found their vitality. Rather, it was in the method to which everyone subscribed, and with which everyone agreed, that was the reason for academic success. That method, broadly understood, valued scholarship first, teaching second, and service third. Such consensus, however, only skims the surface of the tension over multiculturalism, which we view as a central debate in today's colleges and universities. And the resolution of that debate will ultimately decide who should teach, to whom, and about what.

In its most basic forms, the debate is no different from that between two schools of thought, even in the age of consensus, between World War II and 1970. It was a debate between those who argued for coherent "core" curriculum — the generalists — and those who viewed the specialization of scholarship and teaching as a strength — the particularists. Both sides left room for one another in the faculty, but both sought predominance in matters of curriculum. The pendulum swung, for practical purposes, to the side of the particularists by the 1960s, when American colleges no longer adopted core or survey courses. On the side of generalists were colleges such as Columbia and University of Chicago which viewed most knowledge as interrelated, if not in substance than in form. These generalists deduced that much could be learned from studying those ideas and thinkers that shaped the methods which led to further discoveries. Some schools still adopt this Great Books idea, which by definition is literary, and seeks unity in academic subject as well as form.

The particularists did not haggle on that point, but they had a different argument altogether. The specialization of higher education permitted a professor to move beyond mere erudition — as was the norm before the twentieth century — and develop a new understanding of science, history, and the like. The model for this revolution was medicine as it was studied at Johns Hopkins University, and the professionalization of the field yielded a new method of teaching: not by the generalist, but by the specialist. That meant placing the most knowledgeable and qualified professors in charge of curriculum and students, and allowing them to pursue subject matter as they saw fit, provided their colleagues regarded their work as serious and well-founded. We shall return to these models later to study their implications for multiculturalism.

The Old and the New in Multiculturalism

We recognize two forms of multiculturalism, one new and one old. What was the old multiculturalism? It was a scholarly outlook that valued diversity in subject matter, student body, and faculty. It was responsible, in part, for the breaking down of racial, economic, and religious barriers that once prevented anyone not white, wealthy, and Protestant from attending or teaching in most American colleges. It created the study of foreign language as a science, sociology and anthropology as tools for understanding exotic cultures and opened for study religions that had once been the province of only the yeshiva, the mosque, or the abbey. At some schools, it took on the shape of well-intentioned programs to bring promising but poor black students to prestigious campuses. It permitted the hiring of non-Catholic professors at Catholic universities, women professors onto previously all-male faculties. It was a natural extension of the history of American higher learning, which has always measured the importance of subject matter in very subjective terms. If there was, before 1945, an American canon, no one has been able to define it or describe it. What Abraham Lincoln read as a young man was far different from what Henry Adams learned at Harvard. Would anyone argue that Harvard gave the better education of the two — or that America gained more from Harvard than from Abraham Lincoln's autodidactic learning?

What is perhaps more important, and which has come to bear on the debate in profound ways, is the access brought to cultural literacy by old multiculturalism. As the debate later unfolded, the new multiculturalists attempted to portray curriculum as an issue of power; if, however, one can see curriculum as the natural extension of knowledge and wisdom, it becomes immediately clear that power isn't the issue, access is. For as soon as the class and geographic boundaries separating bright minds from academia dissolved, those elements of cultural canon were immediately accessible to all. Some academic elitists such as Harvard president, James Conant feared, for example, that American veterans going to school on the GI Bill would dumb down classrooms. The opposite occurred, with the veterans bringing a freshness and maturity hardly seen before in American universities. So the old multiculturalists provided not only a model for access, but the means with which to achieve it. That is an important contribution, and one which the new multiculturalists have struggled to emulate.

The point about power and knowledge should not leave us here. It is central to the debate over the future of the curriculum of diversity. As E.D. Hirsch argues in *Cultural Literacy*, any national culture must choose its "literacy," or the cultural boundaries by which it defines itself. But these boundaries need not be elitist, nor Eurocentric. In fact, Hirsch notes, America's preponderant use of English literate traditions doesn't just exclude Asian or African choices (and we are assuming here that the choices exist). It excludes German and Irish cultures, Spanish and French, and so on. The old multiculturalists did not debate the merits of this system of literacy. Rather, they introduced the possibility that new forms of literacy and cultures could be understood through a prism of established inquiry. Instead of revolting against the language of the dictionary, they added new entries.

The new multiculturalists challenge this method. There are, however, among the new multiculturalists a moderate wing and an extreme wing. They are united only by sheer dislike of those who argue that the traditional curriculum and canon must preserve the notions that keep democracy healthy — people such as Allan Bloom, William Bennett, Roger Kimball, and Dinesh D'Souza. Among the moderate wing, few better make the case for the diversity of knowledge than Henry Louis Gates. A literary critic and scholar, Gates has argued for the past three decades that American literary scholars have, at their own risk, ignored a whole canon of black American literature and writings. And he has gone on to show how accessible and important these writings are, and to what extent they contribute to our understanding of American history and culture. Gates could rightly be identified as an old multiculturalist in many ways: he is a self-defined believer in the humanities, which teach how to understand other groups, and how to use that understanding to shed light on how we see everyone else. But he also subscribes to the new multiculturalist view that canon is an extension of power. And in making that argument, he ultimately criticizes the very core of our definition of the sound curriculum: that it emanates from scholarship, not power.

The academics of identity politics unseat all that. Gates, for example, argues that the biological classifications of Francis Bacon represent a megalomaniacal view of the world — that it can all be organized under a single system of knowledge. "The rhetoric of liberal education remains suffused with the imagery of possession, patrimony, legacy, lineage, inheritance," wrote Gates in an essay, "Integrating the American Mind."[8] Such a system ultimately forces the inheritors of that liberal education —

America's colleges and universities — to create the illusion that education is a possession, a cultural legacy, that divides as it nurtures. It divides, he argues, between those who participate in that tradition and those who don't, and although it affords access to those who can't claim genetic links to the tradition, it never permits full ownership. The black author James Baldwin regarded himself, faced with this rhetoric, as a bastard to American culture. Gates put it differently: "I am a guest at someone else's banquet."

The use of identity then, becomes central to new multiculturalism, even in its moderate wing. It defines the Western canon as an exclusive club, precisely at the point when the old multiculturalists had proven it wasn't so. And it begins to change, by definition, the nature of all debates in the academy. If knowledge is a function of power, so too are the standards of knowledge: scholarship, teaching, writing, and truth. These arguments, raised indirectly at first, ultimately affect every facet of academic life, and have done so to this day. If the academic mind can be won over in a struggle, so too can the academic body. The use of intimidation and bureaucratic arm-twisting has permitted, for example, the resegregation of some college dorms in the name of preserving the identity of black students. It creates black study halls, deans specializing in the needs of black students, and wholesale efforts to rid the admission process of any standardized tests, since blacks tend to perform worse on those tests than whites. It has kept, Gates concedes, many fine white scholars of Afro-American studies from receiving appointments in the field, even as many departments are looking for talent (albeit with the right skin pigmentation). Gates bemoans this trend, as a moderate is wont to do. But even though these moves are the work of the extreme wing of the new multiculturalists, they are the offspring of the moderate wing's ideology.

From Intellectual Merit to Personal Identity: Higher Learning Loses its Way

By allowing for the transfer of learning and teaching from a meritocratic system to one aligned with personal identity, U.S. colleges and universities have overseen a diminution of the status of scholarship. As it was once understood, scholarship meant not only erudition, but criticism and conflict. Just as scientists must first test theories in a time-honored system of hypothesis and experimentation and statistical analysis, so too did the humanists and social scientists, in the manner befitting their fields.

That is, until the personal was raised above the eternal. For scholarship was once understood to mean that uncomfortable truths would dictate further analysis, and that the only way to set a new agenda was by eliminating prior theories through scientific and/or rational argument. Copernicus defeated a scientific falsehood with a new method of seeing existing information about planetary orbits, despite the Church's teachings. Darwin incorporated known paleontology into a view of time and species that turned then-science on its head. Neither man was made to feel good about his discoveries in his time, and nor did those defending discredited ideas feel good about themselves, but we are all richer for the discoveries.

But scholarship driven by personal and ethnic identity-considerations does not permit such revolutions. In the scholarship of personal identity, the characteristics of the scholar begin to determine not only the questions that are asked of a subject, but also the answers reached. That explains why, without fail, the study of blacks, black history, and issues relating to race are beyond the pale of normal scholarly debate: most of it is extrapolated politics, which is no better than the papal defenders of Ptolemaic astronomy in Copernicus's days. What shaped personal identity scholarship in its infancy was the notion that some subject matter needed criticism because its guardians had never taken into account latent sexism, racism, and other biases against the dispossessed and powerless. The result was, in some cases, a careful appraisal of overlooked information and resources; but sadly, most of it made the overrated case for adding more footnotes. The development of personal identity scholarship has made it impossible to study American history without studying the most exotic events, or those eliciting the most remorse, but without studying those ideas that shape the very foundations of American democracy. Take, for example, Stanford's approach to "Religions in America." The course, according to critics David Sacks and Peter Thiel, pokes into Shamanism, the Peyote cult, and the Kodiak sect, but not the Catholic Church. A class on the history of civil rights in the U.S. devoted so much effort to the protest movements of the 1960s that it left out a careful reading of the Declaration of Independence and the Constitution.[9] Here we witness not multiculturalism but distortion and disproportion — an absence of culture and canon altogether.

The result of the diminution of critical scholarship by the new multiculturalists can be measured in three distinct areas: the quality of faculty research, the quality of student learning and the standing of academics in public debate. We have in this chapter briefly described the slow decline of quality in American scholarship in the humanities and social sciences. Whereas in the four decades following the end of World War II, no nation could approach American expertise in most areas of research, the gap is closing. And we hasten to note that within the nation's borders, the qualitative distinctions between private elite universities and their public counterparts has decreased markedly, particularly in subjects where the new multiculturalists have established strongholds on private campuses. The public now perceives that the new multiculturalists, who developed their guiding principle largely as a protest vehicle, will not permit protest among their ranks. There are those who recognize this as a unique evil, something just as onerous as the quotas against Jews in pre-war private colleges, or the segregation of white and black students in Southern state colleges through the late 1960s.

But the use of identity politics exacts its costs in other ways. The lessons taught by the new multiculturalists now permeate higher education, with widely varied results. It's not fair game to say "What's in it for me?" on any campus and demand not only an answer, but satisfaction. While most legislatures set up state-run American colleges to serve a public need, like agricultural or engineering training, by the late 1960s, those functions ceased to have quite so much meaning. Now however, colleges are being asked to pursue the subject matter reflected in the community around them. This particular form of identity politics means that on a coastal campus, oceanography might receive huge state subsidies while in an area surrounded by poor neighborhoods, social service and medical aid might be a crucial institutional function. These are not, by themselves, worthless goals by any means. But the trend towards geographic pandering has more than one dimension: in Florida, the decision over a new state-run law school was fought over its geographic placement — should it be affiliated with a historically black institution or be located in the Miami area, where Hispanics would be mostly likely to attend? The fact that the school would have perceived benefits for one minority group at the expense of another never appeared to bother anyone in the debate.

But this crossover has deeper implications for more than the location or ethnic identity of a school. When identity issues enter the curriculum, they yield onesided courses that tend to merely mimic the structure of a college class while pursuing the agenda of something very different. The University of Maine has a Lobster Institute which recently published a study saying lobsters don't suffer when boiled alive. Whether that finding has any scholarly meaning is up to someone else; but it certainly helped the state's seafood industry, which just so happens to subsidize the institute. Universities now rent out respectability, their surest commodity, to institutes sponsored by companies, industries and others willing to foot the bill. Georgetown University's Credit Research Center, which publishes studies friendly to the credit card industry, gets most of its funding from that same industry. University of Wisconsin's Milwaukee campus has an institute for the study of environmental air quality, paid for by Johnson Controls Inc., a company which happens to build air systems for big buildings.[10] The list goes on and on, and the message is simple: Universities are for rent to the highest bidder. And that means truth is also up for rent. Identity-led instruction yields an educational philosophy that critics find abhorrent: an unsubtle blurring of the boundaries between a right answer and a wrong one when the answerer happens to be of a certain background. That made it possible in the 1960s for the City University of New York to experiment with changing the status of remedial courses to accommodate the poor educational background of many of its affirmative action applicants — many of whom were black or Latino.

The teaching of writing, for example, now takes place in many cases in an atmosphere without criticism of structure and with a great deal of grammatical equivocation. "Many teachers now consider the traditional idea of teaching to be intellectually suspect and morally offensive because it is tainted by the authoritarian idea that there are defensible standards and by the inegalitarian idea that some people do things better than others," wrote George Will.[11] In fields such as linguistics, sociology, historiography, anthropology, and other soft sciences, truth and fact now have nonmeanings — the upshot is, we shall later see, ironic. Even the writings of a historical figure are analyzed for meanings that were never intended. Such deconstruction of literature goes on not by accident, but on purpose, so the argument goes, because literature is more interesting when the author doesn't matter anymore.

That has prompted the critics of the new multiculturalism to complain, but the debate is carried on only in theory. In reality, the new multiculturalists have taken control over certain subject matter. It is an empty victory; the subjects they control lose their students. English and history, for instance, now have half the majors they did twenty years ago. But when English professors will not define literature and cannot explain why one poem is better than another, they announce they have nothing to teach. And when history professors conduct mere tirades of ethnic resentment (such as black history and Holocaust history deliver), even the insiders grow tired, even bored.

But the line is being drawn elsewhere, and on grounds that the new multiculturalists are finding hard to conquer. In an extraordinary conference called "The Flight from Science and Reason," 200 high-level scientists, physicists and other scholars decried the movement away from respect for science to simple apathy and aggressive nonbelief. Popular manifestations of scientific irrationalism — psychic and herbal healing, poltergeists, firewalking — had become so commonplace that the group had to study just what had happened to the institution of American science. After all, this was an enterprise that had helped win one world war, deterred another, developed vaccines that had saved millions of lives and medicines that extended millions of others. These were the minds that birthed space exploration, agricultural efficiencies, and intimate knowledge of the human gene.

The conference participants, and still other critics, now recognize that the hostility to critical science comes from the new multiculturalists, who distrust science as a Western, male-dominated vocation. That view imparts to scientists antienvironmentalism (looking at nature as a tameable beast) and an excessive belief in logic. There are now "scientists" from the new multi-cultural school creating out of ideology and unproven theory that a women's Golden Age existed before "violent, male-god worshipping Indo-European invaders on horseback," writes Christina Hoff Sommers, a professor at Clark University.[12] Thus the new multiculturalists have attempted to replace real science with soft science, research with optimistic guesswork. In those cases of success - and there are many — the scientific method is replaced by identity politics, which yields precious little scientific knowledge. Scientific illiteracy is now rampant among American college graduates, not only because they are required to take so little hard science, but because their heads are filled with invented facts. It is no wonder, the critics concede, Americans are superstitious, believe in ghosts, and resort to healing techniques that have little provable value.

But deeds do not go unrewarded. The movement to remove boundaries between those who are right and those who are wrong has not just eliminated truth-telling, it has undermined public confidence in the college diploma. Malfeasance on a grand scale is difficult to coordinate, but it hasn't been hard to identify. The American educational establishment is now openly hostile to success and public displays of student intellect and public repudiations of student failure. The result, as we shall see later, has been a widespread view that American academics are destroying the very methods that helped make the nation what it is. It has, on the elementary school level, fed a movement among parents to teach children at home, or send them to rigorous private schools usually led by religious organizations. On the college level, it has exacted a different cost. Graduates of four-year programs emerge unprepared to face the reality of the workplace, where success is rewarded and failure punished. In this regard the elite students, smart when they got to their elite college, no smarter when they leave, face a disadvantage: they cannot draw on experiences of failure and achievement. They bring to the workplace only a rich sense of their own importance, a deep commitment to that to which, they think, they are entitled by their smarts. Few parents are surprised to find that four years of college leave their children just as clueless about their futures as they were when they graduated from high school. The result is a healthy demand for graduate school spots.

The irony of new multiculturalism — in this sense, there are too many to mention — is the destruction of standards in general. The one thing that the old multiculturalists sought to defend and take full advantage of, were the very definitions of excellence built into a curriculum. Such definitions insured those with talent against those without, and gave credence to the views of anyone who had the ability to make a cogent and critical point. Now, making a cogent and critical point is viewed not just with skepticism, but with hostility. In the new multiculturalism, both faculty and students must tread carefully when negotiating an argument, less they damage the self-esteem of protected groups, their views, and their histories. The examples here are too many to mention. But the upshot, besides routine public dismissal of the vocation of academics, is a view of academia as a hovel of hypocrisy. Institutions pledged to the pursuit of truth and knowledge, goes the view, have turned into protectorates of patently silly views. Roger Kimball, in *Tenured Radicals*, notes the fixation of academics on destroying, for example, the ability of a reader to read a great novel without considering subtle sexual messages. "Champions of the new rationale like to pretend that they are merely thinking more critically than the tradition had allowed. In fact, though, they have often degenerated from the rigors of criticism to a rootless and sharply politicized nihilism," he wrote.[13]

What characterized a prior generation of scholars was its capacity to question. Now, the new multiculturalists deem questioning too dangerous to accepted practices of scholarship. Why? Take the example of Yale's fascist anti-Semite from Belgium, Paul de Man. The legendary deconstructionist was found, in 1987, to have written anti-Semitic, Nazi collaborationist invective for a Belgian newspaper in the early 1940s, at the height of Nazi power. Normally, such a discovery would destroy a career, and certainly one in literary theory, once one of the premier subjects in the humanities. But in the world of de Man, one populated by theorists who deny to authors the right to impart clear meaning, such conclusions of character do not come easily. And, as Kimball notes in his bare bones analysis of the de Man affair, the defenders of de Man demonstrate — many of them Jews — not merely the sophistry of their chosen field, but of academia in general. In de Man's theoretical world, text never means what it appears to mean, so just as easily as he had penned his anti-Semitic diatribes, his Jewish defenders — some of them active in Holocaust remembrance projects — could say he never meant it. So truth, even fact, has no meaning anymore, and Kimball notes, de Man's defenders could argue breathlessly until "the distinction between guilt and innocence beings to blur, and begins, in good deconstructionist fashion, to seem merely linguistic." Needless to say, those who condemned de Man were ignored by his allies. Some even said they were guilty of the same sins as the Nazis. No glory, then, is owing to de Man's strongest advocates who were Jews on the Yale faculty, using cleverness to invent excuses in defense of their hero. But, a few decades earlier, de Man would have gladly joined in murdering them.

So what is happening on the other side, where those ideologues who seek to preserve the way of the old multiculturalists? We referred vaguely at the beginning of this chapter to a little known professor of classics as a major figure in the comeuppance of American academia. It is crucial to note here that Allan Bloom's 1987 *The Closing of the American Mind* is not a mere diatribe, and while it is usually grouped together with the muckraking works of Kimball, Charles Sykes, and Dinesh D'Souza, Bloom vests great power and weight in America's elite universities, and observes that as they go, so does the rest of the country, for better or worse. Which explains Bloom's interest not only in Great Books, but in moral education. So Bloom believes in the power of the system. The problem, and Bloom's negativity bordering on nihilism, stems from his estimate that not much can be done to stem the slow decline of American morality and integrity. The rest of the argument, as they say, is commentary. Bloom dissects the philosophical roots of apathy to morality in academia, observes its modern symptoms, and issues the standard clarion call for change.

That said, Bloom's work took on much greater importance than he could have ever imagined. He was attacked from both the right and the left, by some for elitism, by others for populism. Some feminists pilloried the work, other feminists cheered him. Some critics regarded him as a wistful Europhile; others compared him to an agrarian's intellectual, like Thomas Jefferson. In essays published in the years after the book's publication, Bloom became the lightning rod for all cultural and political views of academia, although he was usually championed by the right.

What is striking, in retrospect, is that this was the first successful challenge from the right to the pervasive liberal culture of American academia. It was successful in its popularity, its ability to set the agenda of debate for the next ten years and its raising of a position that had little academic clout before it was voiced as a best-seller. Bloom's debate was not simply about getting "back to basics," as was often the philosophical banner carried by the right during the 1960s and even today, but to make sense of modern problems with the tools antiquity bestowed on us. Bloom's legacy, forcing academics to acknowledge the value of teaching works that are great and not just old, set forward a definition for cogent curriculum that has, as yet, not been matched.

The new multiculturalism has defined curriculum as a servant to the identity of either teacher or student. Bloom argues that curriculum leads, that it imparts the values that set forward everything else in a classroom and a college. When he sees relativism about truth in the classroom, Bloom sees the seed of relativism in every other endeavor in the academy, which trickles into the professional and private lives of every American. Again, Bloom is optimistic about the power of the classroom, but pessimistic about its effects. It should not surprise anyone to see now that Bloom's harshest critics were those that called him elitist, sentimental, and close-minded. Bloom argued that moral judgments were part of the vocation of academics; most academics do not agree, or do not agree with his moral judgments.

Bloom formed his judgments following his personal experience with the student riots of 1969 at Cornell University, so it follows that his critics tended to view those disturbances as intellectually liberating events. The new multiculturalists were willing to accept Bloom's gift of the power of the academy, but not his prescription for its use. They preferred to view the power flowing from the classroom as a force emanating from the presence of a genetically or sexually or ethnically or geographically diverse faculty and student body. The curriculum, as a result, followed that self-adoring identity theory, and reflected solely the "native" concerns of those faculty and students. The question, ultimately, is whether Bloom and the new multiculturalists share the same failures in logic. For Bloom must ultimately define what is best in Western thought, and he must make decisions that exclude other subject matter. And the new multiculturalists must do the same thing, weighing the relative value of certain identities over others. Why gay romantic literature of the nineteenth century instead of something just as exotic? Who is to say?

Needless to say, the new multiculturalism has routinely foundered when asked to account for its choices. So, too, did Bloom. His arguments about the moral, and immoral, behavior of students struck more than one reviewer as grumpiness. "Bloom the teacher is a jilted suitor who has watched his beloved sneak giggling away with the strumpet relativism," wrote critic Robert Pattison.[14] And Bloom's definition of great works in the Western tradition — mostly Greek, Latin, and English classics — raises yet another issue: is this just another plank in the fence of new multiculturalism? For when Bloom wrote this work, the debate over curriculum often settled into two camps: the "Hey hey, ho ho, Western culture has got to go" group and the "West is best" group. Neither side, we maintain, made a compelling argument that their curriculum held some deep truths that the other could never offer. And both smacked of the ideological fadism that has wracked American higher education since the early 1960s, when the general education model was finally defeated.

Casualties in the Culture Wars

At what cost? What was lost, in the culture wars, was the love of teaching and love for subject. When identity replaced scholarship as the arbiter of truth, and when ethnic breast-beating made a mockery of 50 years of advancing multiculturalism, the two major achievements of the prior three generations of academia were sullied, and perhaps lost. The central property of learning and academia was always that it could be transitive: you need not have been French to study French literature, nor Jewish to study Judaic studies. But in the age of identity politics, love of learning appears only measured in terms of the ethnicity, sex, sexual habits, race, or other political identifying characteristic. We have seen America's universities move beyond affirmative action admission and hiring policies to realm of affirmative action learning. In that world, literacy is oppressive to the illiterate. Science is misogynistic and antinatural. History is meaningless.

Those who have embraced the new multiculturalism do so while risking the very future of their subject matter and their institutions. They too can find their beloved subject matter out of favor, and therefore, out of sight. And so, too, do those who argue for the supremacy of the Western tradition solely because that is what our grandparents studied. The question a curriculum must ask, and then answer, isn't what is most important, but what leads us to understand virtually everything else. That question, and the answer that comes with it, marks the beginning of cohesive learning and a plan for both professors and students to follow.

"Teaching means to teach students how to do something, how to know something, how to understand something"

And this brings us back to what matters, which is, teaching by highly accomplished researchers; active through both scholarship and teaching.

In the words of William Scott Green, "Teaching means to teach students how to do something, how to know something, how to understand something." By this criterion, one subject serves teaching as well as any other, the history of the Jews as much as the history of medieval France, the literature of the American blacks as much as the literature of the English, the religious world of Islam as much as that of Christianity, the Roman Catholic experience of Christianity as much as the Protestant. For whatever we teach stands or falls by the same criterion: Does the subject at hand present the possibility of analyzing generally intelligible propositions? Does the area of learning generate theses worth sustained testing, ideas capable of providing insight beyond themselves and transcending the context that gave them first light?

That is why the white male experience is no more the norm than the black or female experience is abnormal. For human experience properly described, analyzed, and interpreted speaks to us all. But without analysis and argument, no experience safely establishes the norm (or diverges from it). Accordingly, universities engaged in scholarship would do more than simply accommodate the new humanities. Colleges can no longer imagine scholarship in ignorance of the corpus of human experience and achievement taken up in those new humanities. Rigorous thought about what matters must by definition focus on black as much as white, just as biology inquires into the blood of anyone. The very nature of the disciplines and of the discourse of university scholarship requires the full recognition of the new humanities alongside the established ones. Why? Because we cannot do our work without them all.

How shall we who represent the new groups — women, blacks, Jews, Hispanics, Catholics, and many others — proceed? In our view the task now falls upon the shoulders of the professors of the new humanities. If we claim right of entry, ours is the burden of presenting a valid ticket of admission. We professors have to teach everyone equally. And we must first teach students to broaden their sympathies. The books people wrote in the submerged and ignored sectors of humanity, those of the "other" religions, races, sex, parts of the world, have won our place for us. Ours — professors and students alike — is the task to ask what do we know about our experience that will speak to the heart and mind of others. The answer to that question will emerge in our answers to other questions. How do we all exemplify a common experience of humanity? What can we share with outsiders? When we see the ways in which we are like others, and the way in which we are not like others, then we may speak intelligibly and claim a full and solemn hearing for ourselves.

Because of the failures of the new humanities, their self-ghettoization, special pleading, ethnic cheerleading, and racism, many find sound reason to repudiate the revolution of the 1960s and early 1970s, and therefore repudiate the new humanities. But like all revolutions, it not only destroyed good and bad together, but also brought needed change that mixed good with bad. Today by reason of the policy of inclusion that has taken hold everywhere, we stand nearer the true goals of education than we did before the events of the 1960s and 1970s. A lasting change of those revolutionary years is a change in attitude, a change in the heart and mind of scholars. This is the change that will affect students most profoundly since it dictates what and by whom and how they are taught. New subjects, new classes of persons, and new modes of education, take their place alongside the familiar ones. Attitudes toward education have changed too. And they never will go away, which is a blessing.

Who Teaches What: Defining the Humanities after an Age of Revolution and Reaction

The significant change in attitude concerns the humanities and their new definition. The revolution of the 1960s brought new studies to the university. The appearance of these subjects has forced many — teachers and students alike — to grapple with the concept of "the humanities." People know what sciences teach, and in general they also can make sense of economics or sociology or political science or the other social sciences. But the humanities, one of the principal components of education in colleges and universities, remains elusive. What do people do when they study literature, philosophy, languages, music, art, and religion? Or, as any college student's parent has asked, what can you do with it?

The question demands an answer, simply because every college student faces requirements not only in practical subjects such as natural sciences, social sciences, computers, and mathematics but also the subjects such as history, literature, philosophy, music, art, and theater. These, all together, sail under the flag of humanistic learning. At the outset let us say what the humanities are not. First, they are not "humanitarian," meaning, about being nice to people. Second, they are not "humanistic," or secular and therefore not about religion.

Can the humanities be defined by a specific intellectual goal? No. Clear thinking, lucid and simple expression, cogent and connected argument, characterize intellectual power wherever it is found. Just as sociologists write jargon and anthropologists talk like barbarians, other sociologists give us classics of insight and other anthropologists create literature of enduring human interest. Medicine, engineering, physics, mathematics, all with their languages and technical vocabulary, can conduct their business through clear thought and cogent argument. And they can fail at it too. So subjects don't dictate the quality of content.

Each discipline and field has its own standards of elegance and good argument. A biology student who does not learn how to analyze clearly and to think critically through a laboratory experiment will do no better in English or philosophy (except that the thing studied may more firmly seize his or her imagination).

Is there a standard body of knowledge we can look for within the humanities? Some have argued that there is, but experience strongly suggests the contrary. Since we cannot settle debates concerning what belongs and what does not, we have now to concede that there is no common core of facts that everyone, everywhere, must know, and that we in the humanities in particular must teach. The age of academic imperialism ended when people came to perceive that there is nothing more "classic" than something else. No book, painting, symphony, philosophy, language, or religion can say otherwise. All things are subject to taste and critical judgment. All the peoples of humanity now are the subjects of the humanities.

Yet by common consensus, outside of a few idiosyncratic or aloof colleges — the Stanfords and the Yales and the Oberlins and the Antiochs, we still teach Shakespeare in preference to rap lyrics, look at Rembrandt, not graffiti, pay more attention to Christianity, Judaism, or Buddhism than to the ephemera of tarot cards, and think about mind, metaphysics, and ethics, rather than the transient philosophy of newspaper cartoons. Within those distinctions lies a new classicism — the application of taste and judgment. This definition of a new classicism raises some obvious questions. What are the criteria of taste and critical judgment? Why these criteria and not some others? Asked in this way, the question yields yet another: What is the value of the books one chooses to read? What can be classic at this moment?

In the humanities, the intellect common to us all focuses upon a specific aspect of our being. It is our imagination and sensibility, our capacity to appreciate and respond to the being of humanity, which gave the humanities its existential context. Let us say this in another way. What we teach, that thing which sets us apart is imagination. Such imagination gives us access to the unmeasured capacities of humanity: to laugh and cry, to feel pain and joy, to hope and endure, to surpass what we are. The intellect and imagination are common to us all. The use of intellect for the discovery of what we may become is the work of humanistic study. For what humanists study is the potential of imagination, in history, philosophy, and literature. For these disciplines explore the great works of imagination and passion (not only of intellect) and allow us to experience, in the deeds and visions of other men and women, those hitherto unimagined thoughts, unseen visions, unheard sounds, and unplumbed depths of mature emotion, by which we may measure and shape our own humanity. In this way we may transcend our small and limited selves.

The senior author did not always see things this way. Coming from that old and rich tradition of the Talmud, he thought all things devolved solely upon the rational intellect, and what mattered most in humanity was mind. But a colleague at Brown persisted in asking, Where in your scheme of education is there room for imagination? To feel with Othello, to weep with Achilles, to admire the heroism and be awed at the nobility of Socrates in the Phaedo? As he grew older and endured bitter, difficult times at Brown, with no happy ending in sight, the senior author experienced genuine suffering, disloyalty, ingratitude. There he suffered contempt and rejection from students who learned deeply from him and betrayal of trust from colleagues whose careers he had supported. So he learned to appreciate the experiences of the heart and began to reflect upon what there is to be learned about feeling and emotion, as much as reason. Out of bitter times came a sweet conclusion.

So out of the resources of the humanists, he had to think long about what he truly believed to be the stuff of life, the value of education, the truth of scholarship. He has come to understand that not all the world is mathematics — that (to him) highest achievement of the intellect — nor is reality contained solely by the perception, beneath the accidents of the world, of the enduring patterns of relationship and relation. The Book of Job is not an essay on the problem of evil, but a work of surpassing art, because therein is the problem of evil made human and accessible to the heart. Behind the dense abstraction of the great German philosopher Immanuel Kant is the urgent problem of the limits of knowledge and the reach of faith and feeling. This one person, at this one place, thought more deeply than had any before him about mind and belief and sentiment and, in a compelling way, also about their complexities. So too are the eye and the ear to be shown what there is to see and hear. In music and in art we discover how blind and deaf we have been, how much there is to be learned about seeing and hearing — and about the structure to be sought through sight and sound — from the better eyes and ears of others.

But in enhancing our capacities to imagine, the beginning lies in the imagination of potential emotion and sentiment. For not all will ever see or hear or think about reason, but everyone has sentiment and heart. All love and are loved, bury and are buried. None ever passed through life without that, the experience of love and death. But since the educational revolution of the 1960s, there has been no common core of facts that everyone everywhere must know and that we in particular teach, and surely nothing so compelling as the raw experiences shared by all humanity. Nor is there a distinctive grace of intellect that is ours alone. All we have to offer is a particular access: to those moments in history of significant humanness; to those powerful minds in philosophy; to those observers in literature; and to those anguished, searching hearts in religions in which we may perceive not what we are, but what we too can be.

This attitude expresses another kind of classicism, which is the conviction we in the humanities espouse and profess. By the exercise of catholic taste and critical judgment we may make choices among works of human greatness of mind and emotion. Through the selection of what transcends ourselves and surpasses our former expectations, we too may know and therefore be more than what we know we are. When students come to college, they tend to limit the range of feelings and emotions they are willing to express. They care deeply what others, particularly of their own age group, think about them. So they do not develop their imagination, and suppress it.

The last thing late adolescents want is to be different. For them, striking out on one's own is dangerous. It means to be different. Imagination is for fools. Anguish, failure, self-doubt are to be dulled. Tears and laughter — these are permitted only in careful measure, about some few things. It is precisely for this trait we pledge to teach some subjects more than others. For them we tell the story of the Cross and all it stands for; and the suffering and enduring Israel, the Jewish people; the blacks and their painful record of toughness and inner power; and of all the families of humankind, with their hatreds and resentments, their hopes and unmet aspirations, their fantastic sense of worth, their equally unreal fear of inconsequence. It is closed ears that we want to open, dull eyes we want to brighten, confused minds we want to clarify and expand. And this we do in the only way open to us: by showing what humanity has been and has made and has thought. This is how people have become more than what they are, and what students can feel and do and be and think. Some men and women have known how passionately to care and dream. And what we teach in the humanities is the creations of their caring and their passion.

The Scholar's Apprentice: An Afterword on Graduate Education

All that has been said here pertains to undergraduate teaching alone. But universities define the future not only for the country at large, but also for themselves. They educate the future faculties, and that brings us to the special tasks of graduate education, both for the master's degree and for the doctorate. In forty years on campus and thirty years of graduate education at Brown University and at the University of South Florida, what has the senior author learned? It is that the same rules for good teaching apply, without distinction, to whoever is taught, and for whatever academic degree.

Works of scholarship, like works of art, cannot be mass-produced, and neither can the scholars or the artists of the next generation. For the scholar is not someone who merely knows more than other people. The scholar is someone who lays claim to know something in fresh and interesting ways. Scholars are distinguished from merely learned people, just as poets are not merely those who appreciate and memorize poetry or even those who make poetry, but who know the good from the ordinary in poetry.

It follows that the education of scholars is not only different, but discontinuous, from the education of informed people. Not all bright and interested undergraduates are suited to the discipline of graduate education, just as not all people who dabble in water colors aspire to be artists. Not all who want to call themselves professors should enter the calling. Mere profession of enthusiasm and interest in a subject or discipline does not suffice.

What is called for is something else, and how to define and pass on this distinct attribute of mind is the continuing task of those engaged in the making of scholars: the nation's graduate educators.

Four traits of mind characterize the scholar, young or old, and none of them can be taught. The first is holy simplicity, the desire to rethink important propositions and to ask how they work and why we have been compelled to accede to them. The second is the capacity to take important intellectual initiatives, to ask questions in addition to accepting answers, to want to know not only more about what is known, but also something others have never asked. The third is the complete engagement with the work, the entire devotion to the task, to the exclusion of all else, at the moment of the doing of the work — a skill which we may reduce to one word: concentration. The fourth is love for the work, therefore the finding in learning the full and whole meaning of life.

Any one of these traits of mind without the others yields not the scholar but the intellectual; or a politician of ideas, a dealer in manufactured and available notions, an amateur with bright ideas, and a dabbler in many things. To put it differently, without these traits of mind, intelligence yields a reviewer of books, a teacher, a good guesser, and a Sunday painter. All of these have their place in the economy of the mind. But none of them aspires to greatness, and none will ever know failure.

There is simply no way in which someone can be shown techniques of taking intellectual initiatives: how to ask questions, how to draw hypotheses from the known to the unknown, from the done to the unattempted. It follows that in graduate education we aspire only to exemplify — or, more honestly, adumbrate — the things we try to be. We educate our doctoral students by example as much as by word. For what they see in us naturally becomes the model of what they want to be. If, then, we read or hear their work with a simplicity which leads us to ask questions — i.e., What does this mean? —we show no shame in asking simple things. If we respond to their ideas by asking questions they have not thought to ask, we exemplify how to take intellectual initiatives. If they perceive in our labor dedication to the task at hand, then we do not have to tell them the meaning of hard labor. And if they find in us not merely dedication to the work but the example of fulfillment in the labor, then there is no need to talk with them about finding happiness in the obscure and mostly never-acknowledged and unrecognized life of the mind which is all we have to give them as a future.

Graduate education takes place in two dimensions. The first is the acquisition of the knowledge needed to do the work. The second is the apprenticeship to those who teach the work by doing it. Undergraduates are well served by great professors, people who teach what is known in a responsible and conscientious way. Graduate students, needing this same form of excellent instructions, require another quality as well. For them, the model of the scholar at work is required. The right relationship is one of apprentice to the craftsman, not merely student or disciple to the teacher and master. These diverse relationships begin and end together, but they work differently.

The disciple learns from the teacher by doing. The apprentice does what the craftsman does. Disciples succeed when they know what the master knows. Apprentices gain success when what they make surpasses what the craftsman has ever made. The teacher reproduces learning through the minds of students. The craftsman wants above all for the apprentice to become the master, to transcend the limits of the craft as practiced by the craftsman. It follows that graduate education is best left in the hands of scholar craftsmen. The comfortable setting for graduate education is not so much the classroom as the study, not the auditorium where results are announced but the laboratory and library, where they are attained. While many kinds of learned people are fit to teach, only scholars are suited to create more scholars. For only the person who works in the laboratory or library and shows others how to work by practicing the craft in public, in the presence of apprentices, can do what needs to be done: teach by example, so others may learn by doing.

Here the senior author takes over. With a measure of hesitation, the senior author may report how he has chosen to do this, because in the humanities it is uncommon.

His conviction is that just as we in the university never cease to be students and disciples, even while we labor as scholars, so those who come to join us in our craft never serve only as students and disciples, while they await the day when they too will become scholars. We always are learners as well as teachers. So too even beginners should take up the task of scholarship, while still acquiring the requisite knowledge and skills to do their work. We learn by doing. And while doing, we always learn. So there is no postponing the work of doing until we have learned all we need to know, what to do. When, therefore, students join a well-crafted graduate program, they find themselves plunged into an ongoing seminar, which meets twelve months a year, and which is devoted to an immense labor, in which all participate. It is a kind of laboratory, therefore, for the conduct of researchers into a common problem by individuals, working together, from different angles, and on different data.

In the natural sciences this kind of collective research project is commonplace. In the humanities it is not. We in the humanities have taken for ourselves a problem of the most fundamental character and importance. We labor at it over a great many years (in this writer's own case, four decades now). The facts required for the solution of the problem are so numerous and difficult that there is sufficient work for all to do. The documents on which we work, while immense, also exhibit the requisite cogency, so that, when we have results, we are able to talk with one another about them. Since the seminar ideally brings together students who have worked for four or five years with those just beginning, a continuing tradition takes shape. Much of the work of teaching is now in the hands of the older students, while the younger ones, in time, take their place at the lead.

The practical plan, therefore, is to give a student a long-term project on the day on which his or her studies commence, and to keep the student at work for a period of four or five years. The practical result is a piece of work that is produced for the public, for the student will write and read the research reports, which ultimately constitute a dissertation, over a long period of time. The other students will both criticize and learn from the results. When, at the end, a dissertation emerges, it is one that has come from a long process of public criticism. Line by line and paragraph by paragraph, the work unfolds, subjected to many eyes and many minds. It is, of necessity, a work of consuming detail. The task of holding the whole together and seeing its larger traits, of remembering why, in the end, we are working on these things, is not always accomplished.

We then have to point to one disadvantage of this mode of graduate education through apprenticeship, and one advantage.

The disadvantage is that the student must make a commitment to a long-term project before he or she is ready to exercise independent taste and judgment. And this means more than the problem of a malleable mind entering into a rigid way of thinking. It also raises the specter of the formation of a rather tight, impenetrable circle of people who talk only with each other and agree to disagree only about trivial matters; that is, a scholarly cult or an academic sect. In my own experience, in order to overcome the tendency toward sectarianism bred by this peculiar system, every summer was called a "conversation," in which other scholars in our field as well as their graduate students were invited to join in shared, public analysis of common issues. That is how we seek in deed to teach the lesson that others have important things to say, and that ours is not the only, or the most important, approach to the common tasks of learning. Second, our students are encouraged to pursue studies elsewhere, in the course of their graduate education, and so to learn important things, essential to our own work, which we do not teach but need to know. Third, the students faithfully attend the meetings of learned societies in our field and related fields. There they confront for themselves other academic agendas and diverse methodologies.

This brings us, finally, to the advantage to which we have alluded. We think the most difficult thing for scholars to learn is to learn from other people, to preserve an open mind to the ideas and insight even to the questions and scholarly programs, set forth by co-workers. It is in the nature of our work, requiring, as it does, single-mindedness and dedication, that we face the temptation to dismiss as unimportant the questions and inquiries of others. It is not because they threaten the results we seek or the methods to which we are committed, but because those questions are distracting. The real sectarianism is that expressed by the one alone, the individual scholar who forms a clique unto himself or herself. This attitude of self-sufficiency, this incapacity to learn from others except what one needs for the particular task at hand, closes the path to scholarly greatness.

We have defined the problem of narcissism because we perceive it to be a common failure of scholars, particularly of publishing scholars. We have, rather, to learn how to learn from other workers in the same field. Indeed, we always carry on our work alongside and with the help of colleagues, and we must learn to listen, to concentrate our minds upon the concerns and problems of others. If our students learn that what they want from others is not approval but insight and even criticism, then we have opened the way to great achievement. When the senior author worked for a year at the Institute for Advanced Study, he saw a single instance of scholarly greatness among an entire community of self-important preeners and over-the-hill primpers. A senior scholar, working in the mathematics of biology, from the Rockefeller University (not a permanent IAS professor), approached a young mathematician and in this writer's hearing laid out a problem on which he needed help. Though the inquiry clearly was routine, in his career he had never seen an older scholar ask for anything of a younger one but a glass of water. It showed him, in a brief glimpse, what an authentic community of learning — mathematics in particular — could be.

This observation leads to the final question: How do we measure the success of our work in graduate education? It is, alas, a measure we are not apt to take, not immediately anyway. If we succeed, we open the doors of learning to the coming generations. Our young apprentices go forth to do the work, knowing something about teaching and much about the self-conscious and articulated requirements of learning. And if we fail, then we foist upon the coming generations still another clique of closed-minded, self-important careerists, rather than craftsmen who, having turned the potter's wheel ten thousand times, still wonder at the wheel, the clay, the pot, and the capabilities of their own hands, hoping their own apprentices can help them find the answers.

The senior author's ideal, already partially fulfilled, is for his work to be made obsolete, of mere historic interest by the much better achievements of his sometime apprentice. That is the only way anyone can know to surpass his or her own limitations. The stakes in graduate education are high. The obstacles are formidable. Those outside the academy divert our attention. It seems that there is a cycle which regularly requires that we defend our work and to persuade the university of its worth. Perhaps that is healthy, but it also is distracting. For more formidable obstacles confront us: tough and intractable clay, infirm and unskilled hands, a wheel on a wobbly pivot, and the vase that has never before been imagined, or dreamed of, but not beyond our ability to make.

Notes

1. We have in mind research institutes in the humanities and social sciences, where on-going teaching does not take place. The contrast between the world-class excellence of mathematics and astrophysics and particle physics at the Institute for Advanced Study and the rather ordinary work in social and historical studies that goes on there underscores the stress in these remarks on the aridity of humanities research conducted outside of the university and its corps of students and colleagues.

2. Our counsel if asked would be, limit the number of students to those who can benefit from the opportunity — and can make the case, beyond the mere desire to go to college. Cut back on the tasks of universities and eliminate all those offices — and they are very many — that have no bearing upon the work of scholarship, research, and teaching. Assign to community colleges all work in the categories of "lifelong learning," "classes for senior citizens," and other outreach programs. Reduce the size and mission of universities to those dimensions and tasks that pertain to the only thing they do better than any other institution; these are matters discussed in the next chapter.

3. It is very easy to criticize as fraudulent all university efforts at distance and technology-mediated learning. But the senior author has made a long-term commitment to this form of instruction, as part of his interest in learning about the strengths and weaknesses of that medium of teaching. The early returns suggest both advantages and disadvantages. The latter — not forming ongoing assessments of students' learning — may be overcome by two-way video as well as two-way audio such as we now have. In addition, weekly writing assignments provide ample data for assessing the progress of students. One clear advantage is the depersonalization of the classroom; students tend to censor themselves when on camera and late adolescent psychological events and personal transactions, commonplace events in some classrooms, do not take place. In the costly environment of a school like Brown, students quite brazenly would announce how much in tuition they were paying and how, therefore, they were owed A-grades so as to gain admission to law school. In front of television cameras, aware of the possibility of eternal embarrassment via videotape, they lean towards reticence.

4. But the technology must work. The senior writer once was asked to "teach" via long-distance telephone a seminar-session at a theological seminary in Toronto and found the questions barely audible. But then, the first question the students asked was, "How good can you be if you've never held a job at a first-rate university?" And that did encourage turning down the volume. These Protestant divinity students did not seem to have much more on their minds than common gossip. Distance learning has its drawbacks: you never know what you're getting into.

5. That is not to suggest only the institutional culture of Judaism works against independence of mind and opposes initiative and innovation as it does when cultivated outside of the secular academy. The same is so of the cultures of other religions, as is self-evident. In the now-declining age of political correctness, moreover, a rigid thought-control, extending also to supervision of correct and incorrect word-choices, governed. So these references merely exemplify the antischolarship attitudes that compete with those characteristic of the scholarly academy that the Enlightenment left as its heritage to us.

6. Nor is a "seminar" the same thing as a student bull session. Some of the elite colleges give course credit for student-initiated, student-managed, student-taught,

and student-graded seminars, Brown University and New College of the University of South Florida being cases in point. Predictably, students give their seminars the highest grades. But how do they know whether they have learned something of worth, and by what standard of comparison and contrast do they assess their self-declared success? More to the point, what can a college degree represent, if no value is added by qualified scholarly instruction? No wonder colleges that bestow such dubious degrees cannot claim to add a great deal of educational value to the elite—students they admit and graduate, smart when they come, smart when they go, but not much changed by learning.

7. Lardner, James. "Black Studies Program Suffering." *Washington Post.* Dec. 3, 1982.
8. Gates, Henry Louis. *Loose Cannons: Notes on the Culture Wars* (Oxford University Press, 1992), p. 109-110.
9. Sacks, David and Peter Thiel. "Happy Indigenous Peoples' Day." *Wall Street Journal.*
10. "Ivory Tower Inc. When Research and Lobbying Mesh." *Wall Street Journal,*June 9, 1998.
11. Will, George. "Lessons in Academic Malpractice." Reprinted in the *Tampa Tribune,* July 2, 1995.
12. Sommers, Christina Hoff. "The Flight from Science and Reason," *Wall Street Journal*, July 10, 1995.
13. Kimball, Roger. *Tenured Radicals: How Politics Has Corrupted Our Higher Education (*Harper & Row. 1990), p. 75-103.
14. Pattison, Robert. *Nation*, May 30, 1987.

3

Who Should Go to College?

Selling "Reputation" — Let the Buyer Beware

Willing sellers and informed buyers make a true market. The academic marketplace competes with the used-car lot for not merely uninformed but really stupid customers. For those choosing a university, reputation is glitz, and they go for not the steak but the sizzle. But people should buy a college education at least as thoughtfully as they buy a car, and certainly a house, not only because the cost may prove the same, but because the results of education last longer.

College-bound students and their parents, alas, smell the sizzle more than they try to sample the steak. That is why the Ivy League prospers long after many of its academic departments have lost all standing among insiders on the campus. Like every other college and university, those that form the football league called "Ivy" do good work where they do good work, and whatever else they do is mediocre — except selling themselves. There they excel. Ivy League colleges sell tradition, and sometimes solid, more often self-invented, reputation, but mainly the chance to send kids to college with the children of some famous or notorious families. Everywhere the smell of money pervades. None of this bears upon what colleges are supposed to do, which is to teach things to people.

If investors chose to buy $150,000 worth of stock the same way they decided where to send their children to college, Wall Street would compete with Disney World. Companies would sponsor athletic teams to drum up publicity in the sports pages, they would host huge parties for investors to enjoy the finest cuisine and beverages, and they certainly would tout other investors who have bought shares in the company. But investors — conscious that money can be wasted on poor management, poor products, bad industries, and bearish markets — don't care much for reputation. Just as astute consumers go to the car lots with lists of credible information about gas mileage and safety features, investors make their best decisions on solid research of a company's fundamental value. Indeed, analysts spend much of their time trying to find companies no one else has discovered, in the hope they will make a killing when others see the same opportunity. Picking established stocks, the financial journals tell us, is decidedly dull, offering little risk and, alas, modest reward. Even conventional thinkers do not observe lemming-like loyalty, and blue-chip stocks easily fall out of favor if they do not reward investors.

To see the counterpart on the campus, let us return to our original metaphor: the college as a company. On a basic level, the college does not sell shares, so an investor of much more than $120,000 in tuition (the going rate for the most prestigious private liberal arts universities) plus thousands of dollars for other costs (room, board, books, incidentals, travel, to name a few) will not see the money, plus dividends and share value improvements, at the end of a four-year period. But, and this is where the metaphor shifts away from our interests, the human capital gained in college is supposed to be worth infinitely more. So college is an investment, not just of money, but of time and effort. The rewards, colleges tell parents, can hardly be estimated. Risks are not mentioned.

Yet they abound everywhere. And we shall address them here. For the annual debate over where to go to college, goaded by national "rankings" of colleges, usually avoids two more central questions: First, Should one go immediately after high school, second, Should one go at all?

The myth that all high school graduates must immediately set their sights on a college education has destroyed more than a few adolescents who could have saved themselves effort and their parents money by putting off college. It is a myth fed partially by the federal government, which subsidizes American colleges with billions of tuition loan guarantees, interest payments, and scholarships every year. So incentives to take the money and run to college outweigh the negatives: Why?

Because many suppose a college education opens the doors to a good job and career. And so it should, if colleges add value in the form of improved intellectual capacities, for example, the ability to think clearly and analyze a problem imaginatively. The vision of an American meritocracy is still alive and well: that vision specifically includes attending a college. That need not mean, however, right out of high school, and it should not mean only right out of high school. Professors at mass-enrollment, urban, commuter-universities, teaching students from age seventeen to age eighty-five, find the best students out of the ranks of adults, who provide a model for youngsters in the classroom. But the prestige colleges and universities take for granted that most of their students will come at age eighteen and leave at age twenty-two. And few advertise the failure rate, meaning, the percentage of a class of entering students that actually completes the degree four or five years later. At New College of the University of South Florida, no less than 40 percent of the entering freshmen leave before graduation, perhaps studying somewhere else; that would raise warning signals to parents and prospective students alike if they asked the right questions.

That meritocracy, which counts virtually everyone born to the middle class as its adherents, developed the college ideal quite by accident, and without serious debate over its consequences. After World War II scarcely ten percent of the population was college-educated. Today 60 percent of American high schoolers go on to enroll in some form of college. Starting with insufficient motivation and purpose, only half of those who actually attend full-time, four-year colleges earn degrees. The human cost is unimaginable. Before they have succeeded at anything, the young people have failed at everything. Students lacking the skills to attend college fail both themselves and the institutions, and walk away with a legacy of disappointment in themselves. Diploma mills — trade schools, unaccredited colleges — use students for their government-paid and supported tuitions, a tidy transaction for a third-rate administrator searching for a quick buck (unless the government gets involved, especially when these trade schools invent student rolls or borrow student identities). But the institutions roar on. Why? Supported by the meritocratic goals of the American middle class, they wave their successful students before prospects, and make accessible a range of scholarships, grants, and loans that dramatically drive down the near-term cost of attending. In fact they cut their rates in the face of a competitive, dubious market. Even the most prestigious universities find they must do so at the undergraduate level — or lose students they, for their own reasons, covet. To be sure, anyone in industry recognizes this habit of setting artificially high prices as a sign of inner rot: All you're buying is the brand image, and there's no intrinsic value to the product.

So four more years of schooling beyond high school define status and success in the adolescent years, and the purpose of further education scarcely finds clear definition. Consequently, the fall of the freshman year finds one generation after another of aimless young people setting their feet on the moving stairway, the escalator (in an exact sense) that leads, they hope, upwards. But for many it turns out to be a moving sidewalk, going from nowhere to nowhere else in particular. The mesmerizing presence of college in a high schooler's life transforms logic into mush, careful planning into decisions based on peer review and momentum. That is because college hangs over the perception of the American dream of prosperity in an ethereal, and often foggy, cloud. No one — so people persuade themselves — can conceive of ordinary success without passing through college, the rare exceptions getting rarer. The implicit message colleges send students on their frequent recruiting trips to the high schools: pass through our halls, and you will be proud and thankful you did. The explicit message is quite different, and we shall touch on that, too.

Whether on Saturdays in the fall, or on March weekends, or on a sun-splashed May day, colleges orchestrate well-planned ways to promote an image of themselves. They may not always do it well, but it is surely a sign of the cheerleader status of most college presidents that they tout their football team's prowess with great cheers, and quietly ignore the failure of their athlete-students in classroom. Publicity and perception matters to colleges, which explains why, on graduation day, professors and administrators dress up in funny robes and act out traditions that few understand and fewer appreciate but that most agree inspires awe. They follow this spectacle with hosannas of praise for themselves and great promises for the future of their students. And of course, heaps of thanks on the parents. With song and celebration, colleges sell themselves to students and their parents. Rare is the university that boasts of the achievements of its professors — either in the classroom or in print. Rarer still are the prospective students, or alumni, who care. Learning takes place in colleges and universities, but it does not define why they matter, what is at stake when they succeed or fail, at least not in its ceremonies.

With the dream so firmly planted in so many young minds, colleges merely have to sit back and wait for legions of applicants. American ambition, a powerful force, will find its outlet somewhere. In nearly all cases, parents and children plug their ambitions into colleges, not travel, not language-study, not apprenticeship. It is, without a doubt, a great fit. American colleges feign exclusivity, yet are open-armed. They pretend they are as traditional as Cambridge's and Oxford's dons and Bologna's masters, yet derive most of their habits from a college in Baltimore (Johns Hopkins University, the first truly modern university in the U.S.). They appear to offer a rational way for youth to choose a career, yet now graduate legions of noncareerists, students so vague about their abilities that they must attend a graduate school to sort it all out. So for those who rely on perceptions of what college can do, colleges transform themselves, like a chameleon, to fit the need.

The Adolescent Stranglehold on Higher Education

But the myths are none too clear to the ambitious. Guided by the self-imposed ideology of opportunity, high schoolers view their future almost entirely through the prism of higher education. So how do these future big spenders choose where to apply? If we remove from the mix the thousands of students who go to local community colleges (a huge number), most act as consumers. They evaluate their own ability to pay, look closely at price tags, and then whittle down the list. As consumerism takes over, the inevitable occurs. Familial and local loyalties take precedence, so do issues of reputation and hype. A university which joins a top-twenty list in some magazine inevitably sees more applicants than those that fall off the list; the next year, if the places are reversed, so do the trends in applicants.

Consumerism is so rampant in the college selection process that guides offering consumer-oriented advice flood the market, and not with the same perspectives. Some are fairly buttoned-down, offering mostly perfunctory descriptions of major universities, with statistics filling out the picture. Others are unique, telling potential students about a college's social life, its easiest majors and professors (who teach "guts") and whether good marijuana is available on or near the campus. Amenities like athletic facilities are important; so is the beauty of the campus and its environs. Students looking for urban universities can get a full sense of whether Ithaca is a city in its own right, or whether it only revolves around its two colleges. Glaringly absent from these guides, however, are some of the points of advice that we hope to provide — and feel are part of the recipe for a fruitful college education and experience.

Like what? Like choosing a major according to the quality of a university's professors and according to the interests of the student, and not necessarily according to the potential preprofessional benefits implicit in its selection. What does this college or university teach particularly well, and how have its alumni in various fields of study progressed beyond college years? But, as many students discovered after relying on those guides available during the 1970s and 1980s, college didn't seem so complicated and so important. The more irreverent guides, which gained popularity in the 1970s, are sometimes published by students, with the explicit argument that only students truly understand what matters in the college experience. But students are notoriously easy to please, and they respond to stimuli that are cheap to administer. A few good jokes, generous grades, modest requirements — these form the ingredients of the popular professor's reputation. Study after study has shown an exact correlation between high grades and professorial popularity. So much for student guides to colleges — would they were the blind leading the blind! They are know-it-alls leading know-nothings.

Armed with this kind of dubious information, plus the dubious, episodic impressions gleaned from campus visits and conversations with recent alumni or current students, a high schooler and her parent can design a list of candidates. One example of how unprepared high school students find themselves in visiting colleges suffices. When the senior author taught at Brown, a young woman from Chicago came to his office to discuss her coming to Brown. She was choosing, she told him, among Brown, Harvard, and Yale. He asked whether she had been admitted to all three, and she said, not yet. She was just deciding whether to apply. He wished her luck and told her, once she knows her actual choices, he'd be glad to help sell Brown. She then insisted on asking her questions now. These turned out to concern his opinions of his counterparts at Yale and at Harvard, whom she named: what does he think of professor so-and-so, and is professor such-and-such really a good scholar — and a nice person? He (somewhat self-righteously) told her he does not gossip about his colleagues (not with total strangers) but if she wanted his opinion of a particular book or article that fell within his range of competence, he would gladly give it. What have you read by professor such-and-such? She had not read anything by any of the named professors. It struck him at the time that she had not got the slightest idea of how she might use the forty-five minutes she asked of him. Still, to solicit common gossip (it became clear that that is what she wanted, complete with names) struck him as falling beyond the bounds even of normal adolescent self-importance.

Again — and we stress this only to set up the argument below — very rarely do parents and children consider whether going to college is the right decision at all. To return to our metaphor, an investor would never plop $150,000 on an investment he was not sure he wanted. He surely would not even consider it for a moment if he was not sure he needed it, either. But in the college application industry, the assumption of need rarely gets discussed. Why? Higher education is a by-product of American middle-class values, transformed during a 45-year Cold War into an iron-clad truism: leadership and success depend heavily on education and learning. Since that is manifestly not true — some of the giants of industry skipped, left, or flunked out of college (Ted Turner was expelled from Brown, Bill Gates left Harvard early) — we must wonder who sold so dubious a notion to so many people.

How did this happen? American prosperity in the immediate two decades after World War II rested on a confluence of factors, both economic and political. More importantly, in the context of this chapter, the growth of American wealth among the middle class led to a number of trends for young Americans and their parents: no longer did most young Americans have to go to work immediately after the completion of their compulsory education, American parents had excess income to spend on their children and their children's futures and American families grew accustomed to greater wealth with every generation. The government pitched in, too, sending U.S. veterans, many of whom came from families with no college graduates, to college on the GI Bill, a government guarantee of paid college tuition. Combining those commitments with the prestige American colleges held in the nation's formal and informal lines of defense in the Cold War (working for the government, yes, but also preparing students for a global struggle of the mind — these topics we cover in greater detail in *The Price of Excellence*),[1] those with the time, aspirations and the money had a place to invest all three commodities. The ensuing "golden age" of academia saw the number of American college graduates spiral up, as a growing professional economy — one made up of highly trained specialists who emerged from a documented regimen of graduate education — sucked in many of these first-generation American college graduates.

The American economy, moving rapidly from agrarian to industrial to commercial foci, had created a new kind of student for the American university. In the business world, which a generation earlier had been run by entrepreneurs, seat-of-your-pants management no longer sufficed. For a revolution had created a market for professionals capable of managing and understanding the institutionalized growth common to American business and organizations between World War I and the Depression. In an earlier generation, future free-marketeers sought college for connections and perhaps the erudition and honing it offered. But by the middle of the century, students needed an education - even a liberal arts education — focused on practical matters like management and principles of understanding mass society. Moreover, American entrepreneurship, a fabled nursery for American businesses during the turn of the century, suffered a blow in the Depression, driving many bright prospects to seek credentials and safety. American universities were quick to realize this, offering a curriculum that bestowed credentials. So the credentials made the difference, not the learning they attested, not the intellectual skills they promised.

Taken together with economic studies showing a correlation between incomes of college-educated students, as opposed to high school-educated only, the sociological trend of education as a commodity starts to make financial sense, at least to most parents. That explains why college education, and its price tag, is sold as an investment. After all, a male with a college education will make 1.6 times the salary of a male with only a high school education. [2] So the investment looks like a good one — although some are beginning to question this. We will visit with one critic later. Meanwhile, almost everyone else's middle-class children are going to college, so the same logic that sent a tiny sliver of very upper-class boys to Ivy League colleges before World War I is sending many American children to college today.

That is, the search not only for credentials, but acceptance, social polish, and connections. That explains why, in certain states, bright students shrug at going to private colleges, since the main campus of their state school is where they plan to start their career path. There they join fraternities and sororities, secret social clubs, academic societies, and other groups informally designed to bring together future politicians and business leaders. So they get what they want. But do they get what they need?

It was precisely this trait — bestowing credentials and the chance to make connections — that has taken us to where we are today. In the hyped glamour world of college applications, no one doubts that some colleges bestow better credentials than others. So, an outgrowth of the effort of many future college students to wear the fashionable college sweater is a huge industry of aptitude test coaches, tutorial agencies, summer schools, college counselors, and even publishers of invented honorifics, like resume-padding lists of notable high schoolers. High schools get in on the act, and have altered their curriculum to prepare students for the kinds of tests their students will take to qualify for college applications. This preparatory industry, complemented and fed by scores of college recruiters, rests on the premise that higher aptitude test scores in particular, and essay inventiveness and sociability in general, make a student qualified to attend certain colleges. Naturally, high school grades count a great deal, but few have asked whether the equation should be reversed.

For example, should a student look at a college because her aptitude tests match the mean aptitude test of incoming freshmen? We argue that such a student ought to disregard that correlation altogether, choosing a college for other reasons. The mere fact that two students come out of four years of the same college with a full spectrum of experiences, good and bad, should render the logic of the college application industry meaningless. And in the ultimate irony, colleges feed potential students the argument that individuality is celebrated on their campuses, but most everyone recognizes that as a falsehood, from a social and academic view. But the myths steam forward, riding on the backs of parents who believe that their children's careers and income will be guaranteed by a diploma from a respected college, or doomed by a diploma from an unknown.

Consumerism and the Campus

So how well are the consumers staying on top of this expensive industry? How accurate are the rankings that determine who's good and who's not? Do all students make the right decision — and do they know it? And, considering the cost of a college education, are consumers as well-informed as investors, or even toaster-buyers? Who is paying for this industry besides parents, and what are they saying about it? Sadly, the evidence is not encouraging, especially for the parents.

On April 5, 1995, the *Wall Street Journal* published a startling article by Steve Stecklow showing that dozens of institutions regularly doctor the information they send to national magazines that rank colleges. The investigation included interviews with current or former employees in admissions departments, all of whom said that the process of giving false aptitude test averages, admission percentages, graduation rates and other key academic indicators was done to make students believe universities are more selective and harder than they actually are. Elite schools turned out nearer the ordinary than they wished people to suppose. In addition, these officials said that rankings were a huge pressure for them, since a positive one connoted excellence to not only potential students, but to alumni. Conversely, poor rankings implied a loss of prestige, even when the university hardly changed. The story's investigative light swept into the administrative halls of the Ivy Leagues, as well as schools perennially listed as "great buys," including New College, a component of the University of South Florida, which selected for calculation of its "average" aptitude scores only the most suitable candidates and left out the embarrassing ones. Elite colleges looked much like General Motors when people learned they were putting Chevy engines into Cadillacs. It took GM a whole generation to overcome the scandal.

The *Journal* discovered the real academic information by comparing the data printed in the college-ranking magazines and those sent by colleges to investors who buy debt so that the colleges could borrow money. Our original metaphor — that of the college student as an investor — now offers a striking utility. Whereas financial investors — those who post only their money — can find out the health of the institution, those who post not only their money, but their effort and time, cannot. Compound that shock — if you are a parent who just spent thousands on a reputation earned from falsehood — with this growing trend: college admissions officers readily admit that in order to keep their application standards seemingly high, they encourage students who stand a slim chance of admission to apply anyway. Why? Because high rejection rates connote respectability, even excellence, to many parents. Campus consumerism makes choice easy — but stupid. And there is no Pure Food and Drug Act, no Food and Drug Administration, to protect the innocent.

The Groucho Marx syndrome — "I would never join a club that would let me in" — so perverts the college-consumer process that students and their parents will gladly take on debt to attend a prestigious private university with high rejection rates than a more affordable public university system that admits nearly anyone from a certain state with a high school degree and respectable aptitude scores. Even this is changing, with public universities regularly jockeying to include themselves on the "Public Ivies" lists that circulate annually. Some of these schools, like University of Michigan, the University of Virginia, and the University of North Carolina at Chapel Hill, milk those reputations for hefty out-of-state tuition. Nor are even prestigious public institutions the only ones reaching for the gravy. Small, little-known colleges such as Bethany College in Scotts Valley, California employ telemarketing and sales shops that artificially raise enrollments by as much as 20 percent in three years by hawking college in the same manner as encyclopedias or vacuum cleaners. They visit students at home, call them up to gauge their interest and hard sell them on one institution over others. ``How can a salesperson who is quota-driven be thinking about the best interest of the kids as opposed to themselves?'' asked William McClintick, vice president of admission practices at the National Association of Admission Counselors.[3] Truth is, everything about the college admissions process is quota-driven, and prospective students are no more than financial inputs for a huge system that, to save itself, creates the false aura of selectivity and excellence.

But parents are not the only ones who are misled. So is the government, state and federal, which pours billions into the college industry. But they are not quite so interested in the pomp, and that makes even bureaucrats keen-eyed about waste. When trade schools and yeshivas were enrolling students (real and fake) and then signing them up for government-paid educations, the federal government perked up. Such scams were perpetrated by the outer ring of colleges, not generally considered part of the middle-class fast track, but nevertheless full participants in the industry of ambition. Some state legislatures have enacted "slacker laws" and other measures meant to prevent students from taking more credits than they need to graduate. Why? Some states still view their public campuses as places of state-supported opportunity, and refuse to permit students to outstay their welcome.

But some governmental authorities are not so perceptive. Federal education bureaucrats insist that removing government loan guarantee programs would doom many needy and deserving students to a life without a college degree. *Boston Globe* columnist Jeff Jacoby calls this logic a "wing of the welfare state," arguing that loan default rates at trade schools and historically black colleges, adding up to 30 percent, amounted to organized fraud on the government. For every dollar guaranteed by the taxpayers in education loans, the taxpayers end up paying about 27 cents — no wonder commercial banks decline to underwrite so many of these students' ambitions! We dredge up the analogy of the investor once again: no one with any financial acumen is buying into the myths colleges would have all of us believe, no one except parents, students, and the educational bureaucrats who dominate federal policy on higher education.

Reduced to its base level, the admissions and applications process is a huge industry within the macro-economic scale of higher education, but without the traditional free-market safeguards for consumers. Its presence in the consciousness of middle class America transforms normally frugal people into spend-happy consumers in search of high-priced brand names. But the myths and irrelevancies that prop up this vast system are starting to erode. The first of these myths is that everyone can afford to go. Even in the middle class, that is no longer the case; as a result, most entering college freshmen require at least one of the following: a loan, a scholarship, financial aid, or some kind of job. So many students now require financial assistance to pay their way that colleges now say that financial-aid need, or lack or it, can play a role in the admissions process. Prevented from colluding to fix these packages by federal edict (once a habit among the elite privates), colleges now find that some students play one college off the other, seeking the best possible deal. Those students with particular traits — a special skill, a special racial or ethnic group, a unique form of study — can bargain for free trips to visit campuses, financial aid, work-study programs, and other freebies. So consumerism has taken its toll on everyone, and what was once a blessed event — going to college — has been reduced to the art of the deal.

The by-product of the first myth is a spurt in students choosing to attend community colleges for two years before transferring to public universities. Among the poorest communities — rural whites, blacks, Hispanics, and immigrant groups — community college remains a favorite. But the sociological and academic implications of this trend are unmistakable: community colleges are hardly universities, and their students are not getting the equivalent experience of a four-year university, despite what their credit hours tally says. Two years after the end of World War II, President Harry Truman convened a group of the nation's best minds on higher education to lay out a strategy for training the next generation of the country's elite. At that time, community colleges were mere shadows of their four-year cousins, but the Truman Commission saw a better future for them. Now, five decades later, community colleges are occasionally effective, usually larger and more prosperous, but some critics wonder whether they are providing a service that should be provided in high school, or could be provided elsewhere. Meanwhile, hundreds of thousands of students spend time there, usually under the misguided impression that it will serve their interests to do so, whether they want to or not. The upshot is that the poor miss out on the first two years of university education, receiving instead another two years of high school-level studies, and these of a dubious order at that.

And what are their interests? In one radio advertisement for a second-rate college in Tampa Bay, the word diploma is accompanied by the "cha-ching" sound of a cash register, and dollar signs fill the print advertisement for another. Money, that old motivating stand-by, remains the big draw for many of the college-bound, especially those adults who return to college after beginning their careers. But college educations don't always mean bigger paychecks. The myth of earning power exploded in the early 1990s when millions of college-educated managers and professionals lost their jobs in a national recession. The results of that recession were not temporary. Earning power of college-educated professionals fell during that recession; many have not returned to their previous levels. One out of nine adults ages twenty-five to thirty-four are living with their parents. No statistics are available on whether these "boomerang" children have college diplomas, but most have probably attended college at one point in their effort to move up the career ladder.

Is College Dispensable?

In a stinging indictment of the entire education system — public, private, higher, elementary, and so on — Lewis Perelman's 1992 *School's Out* cited exactly these factors as signs of the coming demise of the college diploma's significance. His prime interest was in promoting the concept of learning as a continuous process that takes place at all times, in all situations, and now, with the aid of technology. This interest gives him a unique perspective on the investments most make in a college education. In particular, he notes with scorn that most colleges bestow diplomas, with subsequent years of bragging rights, for attendance, not performance. Since, as we have already argued, grades are a meaningless arbiter of performance, Perelman's arguments need to be addressed. Are they true?

Few can say otherwise. A college diploma sums up the credit hours and successful completion of the requirements for a major, or concentration of study. Whether a student takes full advantage of a library — or even knows where it is and how to use it — is not measured. Nor are other areas of initiative, like the capacity to conduct independent research (which, however, can be noted on a resume), or exceptional work in an ungraded task. Nor do diplomas attest to such matters as reliability, attentiveness, prompt completion of assignments, punctuality, let alone intelligence. The diploma says, this person took these courses and got the following grades — opaque information, much of it misleading. For the real issue must come out of the future: what can you do with what you have learned? And have you learned how to learn? Perelman's concept of the new learning — hyper-learning, he calls it — models itself after the ways most people take on new tasks. That is, they learn when they have to. The automobile companies call it "just in time" manufacturing. We conceive of learning in different ways, and will lay out exactly how that works.

But for the moment, consider Perelman's arguments as a worthy challenge. His expression of disgust for formal education, taking place within four walls, and only in the presence of a trained and tenured professor, is more than a reaction to other factors, like politics. He has described an alternative way to teach, and even cited an example: the television documentary. By his estimate, Ken Burns's documentary on the American Civil War, which cost $3 million to make, would have cost $6 billion to present to students in a traditional, lecture-style, format to as many students who saw the television version. That is, a format just as interesting, with as many "live" allusions to the music, literature, and politics of the Civil War era, as it was presented in the series. So Perelman has set the boundaries, which is instruction of information in an interesting way whenever and wherever it is needed, as the paradigm of learning. And using that definition as a guide, he finds plenty to criticize within the $143 billion spent annually in the college industry. A host of other critics have followed, pointing up deficiencies in professors, teaching aides, refried lectures and a host of other examples of academic incompetence or malfeasance.

We have arrived at yet another myth: that a diploma connotes learning. Agree with Perelman or not, he argues that the distillation of facts and theories in today's college education hardly suffices to comprise an education. That, he argues, is carried out, from a vocational perspective, by companies and, in some cases, computers. So what can students, wearing heavy graduation robes on a hot May morning, point to, besides a diploma, as their main achievement in four years? What, other than social polish and credentials, can they walk away with?

Values and Other Ineffable Nonsense

The answer, coming from those who now run the colleges, is "values." We put the word in quotation-marks, because we're not sure what people mean by it. Nor do those who validate the piece of paper they hand out by claiming to be inculcating values try to say what they mean. The rhetoric gets heavy, the substance, lighter and lighter, as graduation day wears on. But that is wise, for immersion into the peculiar values of most universities would lead most students to believe quite unique things about the world around them. And that explains why such ample material exists to show not only what colleges teach in the way of values, but the effects of those lessons. A by-product of the surety of this point of view, we see, is that the debate over fraud has shifted away from moral issues to financial ones. The institutions of higher learning, having lost the confidence that everything they do is important, now face a rash of critics, many of whom simply investigate or challenge accepted truths of how colleges operate, on questions of institutional diligence.

A law school in Andover now questions why the American Bar Association will not grant them equal standing with other law schools. Is it, Massachusetts School of Law Dean Lawrence Velvel asks, because the ABA, by way of accreditation, fixes law school professor salaries to a so-called "Harvard standard"?[4] The ABA had no answer — it settled to avoid an antitrust investigation of the federal government. Why, the federal government wondered in 1992, were so many prestigious universities using federal grant money for lavish parties, flowers, and other nonresearch costs? They soon found a nest of academic reverse Robin Hoods, taking from the public till to feather-line their already comfortable habits. And, as we have alluded to before, federal regulators have clamped down on trade schools, yeshivas, and other colleges which regularly pad their government scholarship rolls with names of people who, knowingly or not, do not attend the schools. State legislatures are beginning to wonder about the salaries not only of their professors and presidents, but their once-untouchable athletic coaches.

And people are starting to pay attention. State legislatures, who only took umbrage with their state college systems during the Vietnam War demonstrations, now routinely wonder whether there is much economic benefit derived from those systems. In Ohio, where a governor in the 1960s won public approval by promising to put a state college campus within commuting distance of every state resident, the state legislature is dismantling the system and stripping away its many inefficiencies. In Minnesota, legislators want to submit tenured professors to performance review and possible layoffs. The academic community could comfort itself if these challenges were solely related to the ludicrous orthodoxies of political correctness. But they are not. The debate has moved from ideology to issues of fiscal integrity and utility. If, as some university advocates argue, they were only being judged for their political views, the tenor of the criticism would be much different. But this is not Governor Ronald Reagan gleefully twisting arms at Berkeley. In most cases, state-supported education faces questions relating to the same commodity that the campuses promise to create more of: money.

Why, for example, do university tuitions rise at an annual rate of about 7 or 8 percent, far outpacing the nation's current rate of 3 percent? Everywhere in the U.S. economy, inflation is practically dead, and yet American colleges cannot sustain programs without large new infusions of cash. Why must state legislatures now dictate to colleges ways to transmit a college education in no more than four years — a directive that, to an outsider from an earlier generation accustomed to that schedule as normal, would be like enforcing gravity by papal bull — to save the state money?

And the questions are coming not only from outside the ranks of academia. Many in the admissions process wonder why colleges spend so much time recruiting students who do not stand much of a chance of admission. In the 1960s, universities like Brandeis and Tufts universities abandoned rigorous admission standards, largely to keep enrollments at a healthy level. In *Vanity Fair* President Gregorian of Brown gleefully admitted "reserving" for the president "a few" places in the freshman class for the children of super rich families, and he even pointed with pride to the endowed professorships he garnered by selling out the admissions process. That trend is now epidemic, with most every college manipulating the admission process not so as to craft a geographically, academically or racially diverse student body, but to make sure enough students can pay the full bill. Now banned from the practice of colluding to fix financial aid packages to needy students, the Ivy League schools and their elite colleagues find themselves in the quandary of competing for the truly bright (but also truly incapable of paying $25,000 a year). As colleges slash programs to make ends meet, increase the size of many classrooms, and embark on five-year, fund-raising drives simply to keep buildings from crumbling, they look to the only sure way to keep their machinery humming: student tuition.

So it is with a wary eye that most should view the glitz and glamour sold by colleges. We have offered a basic metaphor of the student as a consumer whose sole stake in the selection of a university is financial — how much will it cost me, and how much will I make when I get out? That question asks that we calculate the value-added, even though the calculation takes up intangibles such as the capacity to think clearly, express ideas accurately, and argue rationally. Students should demand a great deal more when they choose a college, and should base their decision on more than cost. Moreover, the evaluation in financial terms should not be one-way. Students should view their dollars as precious, because universities are competing for them. It is an equation worth keeping in mind while perusing the many rankings of colleges that now exist. Some students have wised up to the chase, and now play colleges off each other. For institutions who sell their wares as the equivalent of entry into model middle-class life and prosperity, the formulas do not work anymore. Relying on hard-won academic prestige, except for a very small percentage of students, ceases to count for much anymore.

What now takes its place is something akin to the cola wars. Instead of selling their product, colleges now sell a way of life. And they infuse that marketing message with an debatable economic justification that college is good for everybody, then combine it with a false mystique. But using reputation to sell an institution can be a dangerous game, as many colleges have discovered in the last decade. For as soon as colleges build their pitch around the mystique of their institution, those within the college are likely to do the kinds of things that destroy credibility. Professors justify racists if the skin-tone matches their prejudices. Students invite anti-Semites to the campus and print their Jew-baiting advertising in the name of free speech. But the same students would hesitate — out of naked fear — to bring David Duke or print his advertisements.

Academic departments sponsor charlatans who make things up and call it truth — their truth. Speech codes make mockery of academic truths. Nowadays students show up at graduation wearing nothing underneath their baccalaureate robes, which they drop upon receiving their degrees (as happened at New College of the University of South Florida in 1995). Football programs run roughshod over campuses, their players raping and assaulting other students. Hitching a ride to the middle class on the backs of institutions that permit such behavior has clear risks, as graduates of speech-code havens can no doubt attest. Colleges that build credibility on the number of the children of rich and famous who attend, or the number of people they reject, or the rankings they achieve every year, invariably pay more attention to their reputation than any other detail. When that reputation fails, the college passes along the legacy of that quest to its students. In college, as in the supermarket, you pay mostly for packaging. And in that sense, you get what you pay for, and little else.

Who Should Go to College

We therefore insist that college is not for everyone, and certainly not for everyone who has just turned eighteen. We point to mature men and women in their higher twenties, thirties, forties, fifties, and beyond, who bring a thirst for knowledge and contribute life to the classroom. Demanding from the professors more than light entertainment and good grades, they settle for nothing less than an education. But eighteen-year-olds do not always bring that kind of mature purpose to the enterprise of learning, and that is why not everyone can or should go to college directly out of high school — or at all. We now have learned this contrarian view in the age of the democratization of higher learning. We opened the doors not only to the stupid along with the smart, but to the utterly disinterested — indeed, to the completely disoriented — as well as to the focused and engaged. That is why this banality requires articulation: Students should go to college only if there is something they want to learn there. Who should go to college? Anyone, at any age, who is ready for college; this means someone who can and wants to learn what students learn in college. Who should not go to college? Everybody else.

Why stress such banalities? The reason is that in the present climate, higher education finds itself treated like an entitlement program, colleges and universities like public utilities. And like any monopoly, the academy bears full responsibility for its own failures, and in this case, the dumbing-down of higher education. In our own day, professors have compromised the three principal freedoms that make learning possible: (1) freedom to choose whom one finds qualified; (2) freedom to teach what one wants; (3) freedom to teach whoever is competent to learn. But the freedom most severely abridged concerns the competence of students. We have claimed the power to teach anything to anybody, and that claim seriously damages our reputation for probity and honesty — because we can't. No one can. Not everyone can think abstractly, read responsively, or write intelligibly and correctly. And the fact is, many cannot. The few who can will benefit from higher education, the many who cannot will do better in other kinds of post-high school programs than the ones we offer on campus. As Professor Green argues in the epilogue, the major forms the cutting edge of higher education. And, forced to choose a major, students more often settle than select: none of the things we actually offer interests them. Open admission confers the right only to fail at studying what students may not be able to master or want to.

But why should it, since in the end we are not everything to everybody. Medieval history, cultural anthropology, and biochemistry — representing the things we actually teach in the liberal arts — are not equal-opportunity subjects, nor, for that matter, are engineering, educational psychology, computer science, modern dance, or African-American studies, or marketing. Dumbing down the universities and conferring fake degrees fool no one, certainly not those who in that way get themselves credentialed. If among proportions of eligible high school graduates who go on to college, 10 percent of the high school graduates represent too low a figure, then what shall we guess is too high? Surely 100 percent, perhaps 50 percent — experience suggests a third is about right. But because we have taken for ourselves the right to bestow credentials upon the workforce and to designate those who, by reason of knowledge of medieval history, cultural anthropology, or biochemistry, have attained the qualifications required to sell life insurance, we also have assumed responsibility for educating a work force for a vast variety of skills to which our curriculum and traditions are simply irrelevant.

The damage done to the good name of universities in abridging those three freedoms accounts more than anything else for the present disesteem from which we all suffer. And we professors gave up those freedoms ourselves. We in universities stopped telling the truth about matters of solid achievement and demonstrated competence. No one gained, and everybody lost, when we academicians — professors and presidents — lied. About what did we lie? About the very substance of our work, for we pretended that anyone could learn what we have to teach, and that is simply not so. Some people simply do not have the intellectual capacity to master the various disciplines of higher education, but we took in everybody and granted degrees to whomever could produce work at an abysmal standard.

Criteria for Readiness for College: Purpose above All

Then who should go to college? The first consideration is simply the purpose in going. Do students know why they want to go to college — meaning, specifically, can they define what they want to learn there? And explain where and how, in college, they will learn it? Do students have a clear notion of at least some of the subjects they want to study there? College is not the only option after high school. Not only so, but in college students learn a very particular set of subjects. They study literature, history, language, philosophy, mathematics, biology chemistry, physics, geology, psychology, economics, engineering, education, and nursing. The curriculum has no bearing on the processes of maturity or on the development of good character, nor does it nurture conscience. That is, the academy gives no courses in patience, honesty, courage, loyalty, goodness. The curriculum rarely promises preparation for a specific job, which explains why there is no major in street-sweeping or stock-brokering. Even those who come to improve their athletic skills for professional sports careers still have to take courses in other things.

Looking for practical skills? Look elsewhere. We professors teach mainly through talking about, rather than acting out, mostly through reading and writing and studying. Throughout the curriculum we talk about theory and abstraction, aiming at useful generalization; we talk about things much more than we do them. In the study of religion, for example, students may analyze the ideas of a prayer book, but they do not pray in class. They may study the purpose, meaning, conduct, and symbolism of sacrifice. But, they do not kill a sheep and burn up its kidneys, as they learn, in studying ancient Israel's Scripture, God prefers. In politics students may participate in an election campaign, but mainly as a laboratory exercise. For doers college may present a trial of patience and restraint. We think about things and ask questions more than we try things out.

Learning takes place in many ways, but a college education in only a few. Students must have sufficient reason to study the particular subjects taught in college. Those who really are not interested are not going to learn much, even though they may pass courses. The saddest students, and there are many, really do not know what they are doing in college, even while they earn their degrees.

False advertising is everywhere. Only rarely do universities warn people not to come. The entire higher education industry serves an artificially inflated market — a market the industry itself has created and now plunders; what it sells is either failure or deceit — but in the end, never self-deceit. People know. Promising that those who graduate from college will earn more money than those who do not, the academy has invoked crude logic: since college graduates earn more, therefore college education explains why. Nowadays the gap between the incomes of college graduates and high school graduates narrows, because college diplomas in such high numbers cease to stratify incomes any longer. So that argument loses compelling force.

But even if that were not so, we should still wonder why knowing what universities teach relates to what alumni will do for a living in later life. The critical question — what is the correlation between learning and practical result? — scarcely comes to the fore. Precisely what the liberal arts degree has to do with the world of jobs and careers, why knowing history makes for a better bank executive or studying philosophy insures a future in home construction — few address these questions.

The world outside the campus has formed its own judgment of our achievements. Since industry itself now educates workers for their jobs, with vast programs conducting remedial courses for the real world of work, even the colleges of business administration no longer may claim the self-evident practical worth of their work. And when it comes to colleges of education, the success of their alumni in conducting the schools of this country has thus far received only modest recognition — and most of it negative. So whether we speak of colleges of liberal arts or of education or of business administration or of social work or of the many other baccalaureate schools that universities run, the self-evidence of the practical worth of higher education awaits articulation. We leave out schools of medicine and law, for whom relevance is assured by monopoly. That fact does not prevent professors from taking for granted that students, for the most part driven by hope of making a better living, have a clear idea that they want to study and concerning what they want to study. They take as their task to open minds to new ideas. Yet people who send us their children and the young men and women who come to us often expect us to do something quite different. Education is pushed into the background, and the purpose of college may be lost.

Society's Purpose and the Academy's

And that carries us to this difficult matter of the superfluous and non-academic tasks we claim to carry out, such as conferring not education but credentials, serving as public policy research institutes, and otherwise wandering away from our vocation as centers of research and teaching. Let us list some of the things people expect from us who staff the universities.

First, having been made keepers of the gate, we serve as a means of determining who will undertake what kind of work: who will be doctors and lawyers and who will work in factories. As more and more areas of work require degrees, more and more people find their futures determined by a college admissions officer. Should that kind of selection process be made the responsibility of the schools? Lawyers used to master their craft by a strict apprenticeship rather than in course of study. Successful businessmen need to know things schools cannot teach — how to gamble, how to evaluate people on the spot. There is no reason why these skills should not be learned after college through practical experience and with the guidance of a mentor. So why are we granted the claim to teach these things? No reason, really.

Second, we serve as a means of bringing about social change and are expected to change students, in part through what we teach. You can't read — take remedial reading. You can't write? There's remedial English. Add two and two? Here's remedial mathematics. We pretend to sweep up the detritus of the ruined middle and high schools. What charlatans we are in the cause of ever-larger admission rolls! These courses, requiring only basic teaching skills and no background in scholarship, are fabulously profitable for colleges, and explain why City College of New York's administration fought unsuccessfully to retain them in the spring of 1998. Half the freshmen entering the California State University System require remedial work; Florida succeeded in ending that trend in 1985 by saying to students requiring remedial work: "Go to a community college and get ready. Then call us."[5] Whether students are expected to change their manners or their morals, schools are entrusted with the task and responsibility to serve as guardians, critics, models. What the home cannot do with three fourths of the day, the public schools are supposed to do in the other fourth. What the first eighteen years have not witnessed, the four years of college are supposed to bring about. And we promise that we will bring it about! Again, a lie.

Then there is, third, the matter of educating good citizens. We teach math. Society expects us to produce conscience. We teach the correct usage of the English language. Society demands that we educate tomorrow's leaders, tomorrow's workers. Above all, we teach skills of mind meant to serve a lifetime. Students want us to give them skills to sell in the marketplace tomorrow. We teach habits of work and habits of thought. People expect us to find them jobs. The expectations laid at our feet bear little relationship to what we know how to do. We are asked to signify who is smart and who is not; to serve as instruments of social change; to bring about moral regeneration; and to impart the salable skills of the moment. In the current dumbing down of the universities, we are supposed also to produce a uniform result to level differences of ability, motivation, and wit. But by its nature learning highlights inequities: one is simply smarter than the other. The discipline learning requires underscores the diversity of character and personality: one is simply lazier than the next. Opportunity and outcome part company, and when universities pretend otherwise, they do not change the facts of life. So again, we are lying when we say we can produce uniformity in results. In truth, we endanger it, at least if we're doing our job right.

Learning in the Public Interest

That is not to suggest that we make no contribution to the common good. What do we offer that the marketplace values? A liberal education teaches students how to work, but it ordinarily does not give them long-lasting skills in a particular job. It teaches the disciplines of logical thinking, clear and accurate expression, sustained analysis, but it does not give an easy formula for solving a specific problem. Whether students study chemistry, geology, sociology, or philosophy, whether they master a foreign language or mathematics, history or the study of religions, they learn little or nothing they can sell to an employer tomorrow. But they gain a great many things they can draw upon through a long career of useful work. Just as counseling may nurture the power to love but not discover the ideal mate for the patient, so teaching fosters the power to work purposefully and intelligently, but will not thereby define, let alone find, the ideal job for the student.

True, whenever there is a change in the economy, students become conscious of the financial realities of life, but this awareness cannot change what goes on in a college. Professors ought not teach students how to write software in a certain language. These are salable skills today, but they may well be obsolete tomorrow, just as a course in typing or shorthand or other saleable skills twenty years ago would prove useless today. There are other places prepared to teach these things. And they do them better than we do, and more cheaply. A good rule of thumb to guide universities seeking to define what they ought not do is this: adopt the Catholic Church's principle of subsidiarity — make all decisions at the lowest possible level — and turn it into the governing law. It yields this humble rule: universities should not teach any subject or skill that elsewhere can be taught more cheaply — or more effectively.[6]

We promise to teach how to compose students' thoughts into a paragraph someone else will want to read, how to express themselves in a language other than their own, how to analyze properties of the natural world and qualities of society, how to frame and answer questions. These intellectual powers will always be with the graduates, and on them they can build. Whatever technical skill students gain for a specific career will be vacant, simply hollow without the depth of students' mind. A logical mind, strengthened through philosophy courses or mathematics, will approach the technical skill of the computer programmer with far less doubt and far greater confidence than the mind of one who has only sought skills marketable at that moment. Education for that first job leads to a dead end. To state the obvious: those who value what universities offer belong in universities, and those who do not should not impose upon themselves four years of boredom and inner torment.

When the senior author taught at Brown, he would systematically ask beginning or failing and disconsolate students what they had wanted to learn here and why they had come. A few beginners presented persuasive replies. Most did not. To the many he then asked, Why not leave, and come back when you have an answer? You cost your family a mountain of money, and you take the place of someone who would gain from the chance. The many who did not leave — he observed as the years went by — also did not find answers to their questions. All they contributed to Brown was another aimless, unhappy adolescent, of which in those days, eschewing all required courses and ignoring failure, Brown attracted more than its share. So all they got out of Brown was a Brown degree, the (dubious) value of which, to the purposeless students themselves, could not have proved commensurate to the years of frustration they had endured. Seeing the faces at graduation only sometimes brought pleasure, but, finally, provoked the reflection that produced an essay that ran in the student paper a week before graduation in 1981: "The commencement speech you'll never hear." There he announced that the faculty could not take pride in their achievements, as educators, with such students as received their degrees that day. We at Brown had educated our students for life in a career society does not offer and cannot afford — in both senses of the word "afford." It was not well received by the students who read the essay in their student paper or by the professors for that matter. But many understood that the problem of the aimless undergraduate had overspread much of baccalaureate education, not just a particularly troubled East Coast college.[7]

In the senior author's nearly quarter-century at Brown the one answer the students — aimless, lazy, rich, and, consequently, entitled as they thought themselves — never attempted to give was, to get a better job or get into a better professional school, Brown made life tough for impoverished students, many of whom found they had to pretend to be rich. Students at the University of South Florida, by contrast, bear a heavy burden of honesty: which is why they tell professors, in precise terms that college will improve their lot in life. And, elite and mass university alike, that paramount motivation governs. And it is not the students' crass incomprehension that explains why. Students do not invent on their own this quest for a marketable skill. Parents do; college costs time taken away from earning and money for tuition and much else. So why is it worthwhile? For a few it represents social status, for most others it stands for a better living, but for a scarcely palpable minority does it stand for learning important things and growing in intellectual ways.

The choice of a major explains the incongruity between what people learn in college and the reason they want to get the degree that certifies the learning. In many instances, the parents present obstacles to their children's choice of study. They want to know what the student can do with the major. Can the student make a living with it? And parents do not like a professor's proudly negative answer to their question. Most of the fields of the liberal arts cannot supply knowledge that is immediately saleable. For how much is learning worth, and what do we have to pay for entry into a poem? True, chemistry or applied math or engineering majors can get jobs in their fields of concentration, while classicists, historians, and students of religions cannot. True, but trivial compared to what all students attain if they choose the right major for themselves, whether electrical engineering or philosophy. The real issues for students at the conventional time for higher education — ages eighteen to twenty-two — are learning how to think and growing toward maturity. The tangential question of what the student will do afterward answers itself in due course. Rarely does the answer derive from what has been learned in the classroom, but it always depends upon what has happened on the campus. Parents who themselves went to college should ask how much on an everyday basis they use what they learned many years ago, and to what extent their earning capacity rests upon what they chose as a major. Then they will allow their sons and daughters the freedom to choose.

In the exercise of students' powers to learn to criticize an idea or a picture, how to take apart and put together an event of history or a piece of literature, students learn that there are things worth knowing and saying beyond the weak "Well, that's my opinion." The difference between an educated and an uneducated person is that the educated person can also say why that is his or her opinion. Further, people of learning can attempt to persuade another person that an opinion is sound and should be adopted. And in this the educated person demonstrates an important lesson that discourse between intelligent people has rules, rules of relevance, cogency, and coherence, and, more important, rules that acknowledge the mutuality of reason and reasoned respect. Students will listen, respond to questions, disagree, probe, consider. Liberal education aims at giving students the power to use their mind. It is meant to give students the experience of thought, of critical learning and careful expression of students' ideas, of listening to others and responding to the point.

Now, we recognize these skills are not highly prized — until they are missing from common discourse. When people discover they can not grasp what others are saying or they can not make comprehensible what they want to say, they realize what they have not learned in college. When in business or the professions recent graduates find out that mere technology does not suffice to do the work, that they have to think through problems freely and solve dilemmas imaginatively, students find out what intellectual powers they have learned to use in a liberal education. Yet even if these things we teach were of little social value, instead of serving, as they do, as the bridge from mind to mind, they would still count. For we are not made out of flesh and bones alone. We are by our nature thinking people, reflective and questioning. The substance of life is not merely to eat and sleep. It also is to attain consciousness about ourselves and our lives. All of us sometimes are philosophers, in the old sense of the word: We are people who love to know things, who love wisdom. By our nature we question, learn, respond to the world we perceive — not merely experience. That is why a liberal education is essential, not merely for making a living, but for living a worthwhile and fulfilling life.

How Should Students Choose their Courses

In this context let us turn from the ends to the means. Exactly how should students choose students' courses — when they have a choice? We identify four reasons for choosing a course.

1. Students should choose what is new, a challenge, something they have not encountered before. Entering students naturally assume that at college they will do things they already have done, but at a higher level. That is why freshmen commonly select subjects they have studied in high school: history, English, a foreign language, chemistry, math. It takes a

year to persuade freshmen to take subjects they have never studied, such as art, classics, music, economics, or psychology, or to pursue courses in fields that they did not even know existed, such as philosophy, Judaic or women's studies, sociology, urban studies, Afro-American studies, and semiotics. There is nothing wrong with history, chemistry, English, math, and a foreign language. But one thing students should do right from the start is explore new areas. That is why we offer them.

2. If students come to college expecting to study the same subjects as in high school, they come expecting very different relationships with their teachers. Students expect to know, and be known by, their professors. Yet if students take four courses, each with more than fifty students, they probably will never know a professor as a person. If students are typical, they may take two or even three years to reach those courses of modest size in which professors know students, and students know professors. If students want professors to know them, they must find at the outset at least one course in which a senior professor can identify students as individuals — and does. Professors cannot reach out to students if students are one of two hundred students in a semester. Students must make the effort.

3. Students should select a course for the professor who gives it , not the subject matter, no matter how small or out-of-the-way the class. Although education requires learning facts, it is also about learning how first-rate minds work. Ideally, the subjects students want and need to study will be taught by first-class intellects who show how they think while they teach. But often what students need to study and the person with whom they ought to study do not coincide. Students should select at least a few courses that will enable them to study with truly distinguished scholars, especially those who want to teach as well as contribute to their own fields.

4. Finally, some courses impart information and other courses undertake sustained inquiry, analysis of problems, testing of possibilities. Students therefore should try to take those courses that exercise their minds in preference to courses that merely teach students things they want to know. The courses that demand analytical effort may tax students' abilities and test their confidence — math and philosophy, for instance. Students may have to listen more carefully, think more slowly, and speak more thoughtfully than students are used to doing. That is all good. That is why students ought to try to take at least one course a semester in which they acquire not only information but also powers of analysis.

More specifically, students should select courses that will teach them to write. In the social sciences and humanities, that means taking a course in which students present papers for close criticism. The most important step they take is learning to use their mind to unpack an idea lucidly, on the one side, and accurately express it, on the other. Students will come to understand that good writing is not a gift or an accident: It is knowing the right word and using it correctly, and clarifying an idea in all its implications — writing for a "you" on the other side of the dialogue on paper that writing should sustain.

If students have clear-cut career goals, they obviously will know that these will require them to take one set of courses rather than another. Students in engineering, premedical programs, business, nursing, prelaw courses, and the like find their free choices limited. But if among students' courses in a given year there are at least some that meet the criteria we have outlined, then students should enjoy a stimulating and interesting year of study. If, on the other hand, students sit in large classes and take notes, repeat them on exams, and leave unknown to the teachers; if they spend years learning more about essentially the same subjects they studied in high school; if they miss the more challenging and controversial teachers at college; and if for the most part they just learn facts rather than think through ideas and problems, the fault is entirely their own.

In choosing courses students bear responsibility for their own mistakes — and also for their successes. That is the only way they will grow up. We who teach in books and classrooms and laboratories and academic activities beyond the classroom hope for students to grow up in mind and soul and spirit and heart. Who should go to college? Anyone, at any age, who can benefit from what the academy offers. Who should not? Those who cannot accept the responsibility to choose wisely, to seek challenges, and to accept criticism. In other words, those who do not seek discovery.

What is the Best Time for College?

Clearly, many enter but few belong. Would that we could appoint a keeper of the gate, to ask each student who knocks to enter: Give three reasons to explain why you should go to college and I'll let you in. The gatekeeper would admit the few who respond credibly and advise the many who do not to find some other way to spend the next four years, or as long as it takes before forming a competent response. For as everybody realizes, the academy takes in many who possess neither motivation nor qualification for learning. They may offer money or some other meaningless trait, such as gender, race, or famous last name. And in doing so, as we said, we take money under false pretenses, promising to teach many who cannot discover — at least at that time. We end up running society's most expensive babysitting operation.

Since the proportion of college graduates who go on for tertiary education has vastly increased through the Cold War, the fault lies not only with the academy but with those who selected the university as the medium of mass education, with slight regard for what actually is taught and how the learning takes place and what consequences are likely to come about from the pairing of scholars with unprepared minds. At the end of World War II, universities offered something to the masses. We meant to afford access to learning, but we ended up teaching other lessons altogether.

Motivation, Ability, and Timing

Learning is dictated by three factors: motivation and responsibility, ability, and timing.

Motivation and Responsibility

The important difference between high school and college education is the degree of responsibility vested in the student. The high school teacher takes responsibility for students' learning and monitors progress from week to week, even day to day. The process of quizzes and regular exams spills over into the domain of motivation; students learn to prepare because they have to. Everyday supervision not only motivates but also infantilizes. Students learn to do what they have to do, learn what will be on the exam. On the campus we receive the results of this system and try to reverse them.

The college professor does not and should not take the students' learning temperatures every day or even once a week. The college course usually involves an hour test in the middle of the semester and a final examination at the end. Students have to learn to plan and to pursue the subject on its own terms, not in response to quizzes and exams. Further, the college course always requires the student to take full responsibility. No one asks whether the student has done the reading. No one carefully investigates whether or not the student has understood the lectures. Like a game of poker, the truth is revealed only at the end, when the stakes are highest.

Students who miss class, for instance, ask professors to provide copies of papers other students distributed or notes that the senior author gave out (to make it unnecessary to write during class). The right answer is, ask someone in the course and take care of yourself. (Or, more humanely, "here is what you missed, but next time...") It is an important signal: you are now responsible for what you do or do not do. This aloof position toward students' everyday activities, though cold and cruel, is the first way for colleges to do their work. Those colleges that coddle students corrupt them, creating false expectations both on campus and afterward, triggering demands that later on no one can meet, prolonging dependence. For what the college education should do through the work of teaching is take a half-formed adolescent and send forth an independent citizen. Students arrive as dependents and should leave independent, ready to shape their own lives and define their own careers. What better way to promote independence than by holding students fully responsible for their own mistakes?

But at some point in life, people must have the right to fail without long-term consequences. And how better to do it than in the classroom? In the college classroom, mistakes do not have to indelibly mark the student as a failure. If a student is irresponsible, the result merely is a poor grade. If a doctor errs, the patient may die. If a lawyer misjudges the value of certain evidence, the client may go to jail. If a salesman cheats a customer, the company loses its reputation. In college, mistakes are not permanent; the consequences are limited. After college things change. Knowing this, colleges provide a trial run in the realities of everyday life by making students responsible for themselves and their work. That explains why colleges should not continue the controlled education of high schools. Nature decrees that students grow up in college, not afterward. The modes and attitudes of the academy should conform.

Let us spell out what students' responsibility for themselves means in the concrete situation of writing a paper. When students prepare papers, the first step is to choose a topic. Exercising choice must confront the student as a principal task: not what the professor wants, but what does the student think makes sense? And that leads us to the critical nexus of a university course in the humanities, the course essay or term paper, and how the paper serves as a medium of teaching that course, perhaps as the principal one.

The first point is, the term paper requires long-term planning: a proposal, an outline, a first draft, a final draft — and these demand professorial time and attention. In fact the senior author never considers an oral proposal, but only one in writing, one to which the student has made a commitment. Otherwise the student will catch some signal, a frown or a smile, and that reinforces dependence on the teacher. Then the professor wants to see an outline, so the student works out not only the proposition, but the argument, the facts, and the logic to sustain the proposition. Then he wants to see a first draft, to make sure it all works. Then he wants the students to go to a writing center — all colleges and universities that take education seriously have such centers — since there they teach skills he does not know how to teach. Then he wants to see a second draft. Then the paper is ready to be read and discussed in class.

The governing educational theory is framed for the student in this language: Do it once this way, and you'll be able to do it many times again — and never any other way. It is labor-intensive. It is also the best use any professor can possibly make of his or her, and the student's, time. Those students who benefit want to take the time, not just go through motions for a grade. And at a commuter university on the urban frontier, with students who work half- to full-time, these kinds of demands may well exceed what the students can devote to their education. So they may not get it, and that's why an education demands attention. It is not a method of teaching that will succeed in the setting of distance-learning, in huge classes, or for thin-skinned students. But the reasons are not the same. Distance-learning (two-way audio, one-way video) does not provide the opportunity; huge classes do not accommodate relationships between the professor and his students; and thin-skinned students in small classrooms do not sit still for the criticism of their ideas.

Ability

Most colleges and universities today admit nearly everyone who applies and promises to pay; only a small minority pick and choose. Accordingly, students, not the college admissions officer, must decide whether they can succeed in college, and if so, in what kind of study and at what sort of college or university. More than half of all Americans of college age now find their way to some kind of school of higher education. Before World War II, the figure was scarcely 10 percent. We were wrong then, or we are wrong now, about the abilities of our population. But if some students end up sitting in a classroom and watching others make sense of what to them is gibberish, if they find themselves bored while others are interested, the fault may not lie in the subject or the teacher.

How then ought students decide whether they should go to college? Here are some criteria.

1. If they can listen carefully to what another person says and reply to the point that the other has made, then they can listen to a lecture and concentrate on it.

2. If they can write in a cogent way, from beginning to end, they belong in an examination room. If they can express ideas carefully and accurately, then they will succeed in whatever they do.

3. If they have the patience to follow an argument or an experiment through three or more successive stages, they will do well in the pursuit of learning.

4. If they can read thoughtfully and remember what they have read, they will succeed.

These constitute not gifts of heavenly grace but intellectual skills. They are found not only in the gifted but also in people who have been well-taught to use the gifts they have. Listening carefully, thinking to the point, responding thoughtfully — these acts of intellect take place in kindergarten as well as in the senior year of high school. Parents who listen to what their children say teach them how to listen. Parents who read to their children teach them how to read. Parents who ask pointed questions of their children teach them how to reason. Parents do the probing, and children do the learning.

The senior author once spoke to the students of a Jewish day school in Winnipeg that called itself a "collegiate school," meaning, that it claimed to prepare students for university education. He found few of the students equipped to listen to a simple argument and conduct an analysis of the problem and propose an answer to the question. Most just could not manage. One sat with his back to the speaker, reading a novel. At the end, he advised the students and their teachers (who were visibly embarrassed by the students' failure of intellect and manners) that this may be a collegiate school, but at this time, few of them were ready for university education, lacking the skills, either intellectual or social. That won little gratitude, except from the fellow-teachers.

Timing

Students should go to college when they think it is the right time for them. Tradition brings students to college after high school, usually not before seventeen or eighteen usually not later than twenty-two or twenty-three. That is the conventional, if not standard or routine pattern. The average age on a given state university campus, including all degree-seeking students, may well reach thirty. Still, people take it for granted that the right path leads right from high school to college. That is bad counsel. In college the best students, those with visibly the highest motivation, not uncommonly, have spent a year or two working between high school and college. Or they served in the military. Or they traveled.

What they accomplish is maturity; they season themselves and develop a range of interests and questions. When they finally turn to college, they understand and appreciate the opportunities. They may even value the concern and commitment of their teachers. They also have clear goals for themselves. The senior author revels in teaching at his mass-enrollment, full-service public university on the urban frontier, which attracts students of every age, from seventeen to way past seventy, and his classroom includes both last June's high school graduates and retired accountants, veterans of twenty years of military service and middle-aged matrons. His happiest encounters in the classroom take place with adults, in their twenties or even in their thirties and forties. They listen with intense interest to what younger students think are commonplace facts. The reason is that they have reached that point in life at which higher education answers important questions, not just displays mere information. And they have attained that level of maturity at which they concede, the world owes them nothing, and they are entitled only to the results of their own achievement.

Here then the character of universities also defines the quality of the students, and by character, we mean just that: the wisdom, conscience, and maturity that the universities themselves exhibit. If the senior author finds one decisive difference between teaching at Brown University and at the University of South Florida, it is the overwhelming sense of entitlement he has found among students at the rich kids' school, and the humility and capacity, even, for gratitude common here at the open-admission, commuter college. The one advertises itself as elite, the other claims no special traits.

That is as it should be: there are name — and then also no-name —

universities. Just as no metropolitan area leaves itself without hospitals, so none can survive without universities (Catholic, private, public, as the population requires). So USF stands for dozens of universities bearing the same responsibility for the mass education of a huge, local population. We should all call ourselves "no-name-university," and then just add a number, as in the New York City system, Public School Number 92, so we should be No-Name University Number 84. For from us, wherever we are, whomever we teach, comes the country's future citizens and workers. And America is fortunate that they do. We estimate this country has, in addition to community colleges and junior colleges, at least 500 "no-name-universities." We who take pride in our anonymous character — just the folk who do the work — are the hewers of wood and the drawers of water of higher education: professors who earn their salaries, administrators who manage with professionalism and panache, and students who place their hopes and trust in their teachers and are not disappointed and never betrayed. That is where the senior author of these pages takes pride in casting his lot.

If therefore, we could offer one fixed rule to every high school student contemplating college, and every college student wondering what he or she is doing there right now, it would be this: Consider the alternatives and try some of them. If students in high school are not sure they belong in college just now, let them defy fate and peer pressure and go to work for a year or two. If they are in college and cannot say with clarity and purpose what they are doing there, let them take a leave of absence. Work or travel, if they can afford it, or consider other forms of advanced education, for example, technical school or an apprenticeship. College is not only not for everyone, it surely is not for everyone at the age of eighteen or twenty. If we could persuade people of this proposition, we should contribute materially to human happiness. For if the saddest sort of student is the one who has no reason to study, only slightly less sad are people who, in their thirties, realize what they missed before, when they wasted their college years. It is a waste, a tragedy, an invitation to needless failure, to send young people to an experience they cannot yet grasp.

The main cause that students fail in college — whether a student gets a degree or not — lies in bad timing matched by low motivation. Not everyone can or wants to learn the specific subjects we teach at the very moment in life traditionally scheduled for them. Why at the age of seventeen or eighteen, but rarely at twenty-eight or twenty-nine do college bells toll — "Come and learn! Ask questions"? It is not because of the natural rhythm of a person's movement toward maturity. It is because of the need for everyone to do pretty much the same thing at the same time for the convenience of the larger society.

The fault lies not only with social patterns but academic policy. College tradition does not consider that all people do not mature at the same time. They do not enter at the same moment into that realm of questioning that opens its doors to some through speculation and reflection. To most, this dawning comes through tough experience outside the classroom first. What then might a student learn from working or traveling? Among the most interested students are those who have worked for a year or two in a foreign country, for they have learned to ask themselves precisely those questions that, in theoretical form, academic learning often raises: how to master a foreign culture, how to explain difference, how to describe, analyze, and interpret another world. We teach best when we can appeal to concrete experience in our students' lives. Students learn best when they can relate what they hear in class to what they know outside. The wider the experience, the greater the learning.

Moreover, the learning is not only of an academic nature. Students with experience in a larger world appreciate things that other students do not even notice, for example, a moment of personal concern, a routine courtesy, a casual act of kindness. They know that concern, courtesy, kindness, come as gifts of grace and are not to be taken for granted. So once more: who should go to college? Young and not-so-young people who want to learn the particular subjects taught there, in the specific ways in which they are taught. And who should not go to college? Those who are not really interested, who cannot explain to themselves why they are in the college classroom and do what they do there.

Learning and Growing Up

But in the nature of higher education in this country, most college students are late adolescents. Those who teach must adapt to this reality. How does what the late adolescent students study relate to the process of maturing? This is a crucial question for professors. If we cannot relate the encounter with learning in college to the student's experiment in defining an identity, we ignore the essential. If we can show that what we do — that is, learning a subject in a particular way — is critical to what the students want to become, mature and independent women and men, then we will realize the ideal of the college experience. Students arrive in college thinking they know the answers to certain basic questions — What am I doing here? Why now? Why me? Then they find out they do not know the answers. They have the difficult task of shaping an adult identity. But where should they do this? Why college in particular? If students are in college, students are involved in higher reeducation. But if these subjects do not relate to that other important task — growing up — then there will be tension between what the student is learning and what the student hopes to accomplish in personal growth.

The scholar and the adolescent have in common the capacity to look with fresh eyes on a stale world. The student is full of idealism, can see the future ahead, is not tired or jaded, and has high hopes for himself and the world. Professors also take a fresh look at old perceptions, an idealism in its own way. We take on the task of rethinking what everyone takes for granted, just as the student does. We ask ourselves the most fundamental questions about the part of the world or of human experience that forms our work, just as the student asks basic questions about world, experience, and self. We, the scholar and the student, both have high hopes, for learning and for the people who learn from us.

For the scholar is loyal to a vision, and youth is the time of new vision and dreaming. And the scholar is, in the nature of things, granted the blessing of a continuing encounter with youth. No profession enjoys a greater privilege than ours, for our work is with and for students, who are our future. The themes of our curriculum must pertain to the issues of the student's unfolding consciousness. But even more, the very method and substance of our scholarship, the persistent, tenacious asking of basic questions, correspond in a close and direct way to the very substance and method of the student's task. The scholar's mode of thought is congruent with the adolescent's personal search. The search for relevance to one's own concerns, pursued self-consciously with a measure of restraint, must lead to the scholar's mode of study. We are both inquisitive children, capable of great wonder and discovery.

But these points of congruence should not obscure the conflict between scholar and students, particularly in the adolescent years. The primary goal of the student is to achieve an adult identity. What the student actually does rarely points toward that goal. A student's everyday life consists of attending lectures and participating in discussions, reading books, writing papers, working in laboratories — of devoting most of the day to the disciplines of the mind. One may do these things in form, and many students do. One can go through the motions of learning; indeed one may well learn a great many things doing so. Yet if learning is irrelevant to one's personal situation, then the forms are formalities; the center; the spirit, will be lacking. And nothing that is learned will matter. Many students find exceedingly difficult the discovery of what within the academic curriculum relates to their personal problems and concerns — the problems of growth and the discovery of identity.

So from ideal, we turn to the reality. Most liberal arts students come to the campus from high school or a very few years beyond high school (for instance, after two years in a community college). As we said, those professors fortunate enough to teach at the large, urban state universities face a far more diverse classroom, where the average age exceeds twenty years, and where resumed education, second-career education (military retirees in their early forties, for example), and senior citizens bring to study serious commitment to learning for its own sake that young people engaged in career preparation may not muster. But the prevalent pattern is otherwise. The conventional pattern brings young people without a material break from secondary to higher or tertiary education, and universities deem themselves successful when students complete their degrees in four or at most five years. Since that is the case, we have to reflect upon the implication of that reality. The academy serves in particular the young and touches their lives at late adolescence in particular.

What that means is that the generality of students come to college not only to learn but also to grow up. That defines one legitimate task that universities can help students carry out. But therein we find our fault. For universities that do not then collaborate in the work of maturing — relating what students learn to their quest for a worthwhile life and career — fail in what they assume as a fundamental responsibility. Teaching trivia to faceless rows of lecture hall desks not only leaves a mere residue of episodic facts of no particular use but also impedes students' progress toward their personal goals. Only by shaping the stuff of learning in so purposeful a manner that students relate learning to maturing, can universities realize one critical goal of pursuing curiosity and sharing the results. For scholars take for granted that curiosity forms an urgent and necessary task, and this task is more than of intellectual character.

College for young people is time standing still, an enchanted moment, forming a benchmark in their lives. Students leave their homes, or if they continue to live there, assert their independence in other ways. At the same time they do not take up the tasks of the workaday world. In the elite schools they rarely support themselves but depend in some measure upon others, whether parents or universities. In our mass enrollment schools most students work part time, and not a few, full time. Students come to us, in the main, at the last stage of childhood, toward the end of adolescence, and they leave us, in the main, as mature men and women.

During the four swift years between, they have to solve the last problem of their earlier life and the first of the life beyond: Who am I? During this time, they declare a moratorium on making firm decisions and begin a period of subdued inner searching. They play many roles in this period, experimenting with each of them in search of a place in society, a niche, as Erik Erikson says in *Identity: Youth and Crisis,* "which is firmly defined and yet seems to be uniquely made" for them. The time of college education marks a waystation between the complete dependence of a child and the total independence of an adult. What do people do during this interim period? They study.

Since much is asked of each student, much expected by those who send young people to college, the inability to find answers to questions of purpose of study leads to a sense of betrayal and shame. The students will feel they have betrayed those who helped them go to college — parents and high school teachers. They will feel ashamed of themselves. Rather than endure either of these feelings, they may retreat within, to the protected world of their peer group, avoiding a confrontation with the disturbing and distressing issues of a larger world. They will move insensately from classroom to dormitory, from dining hall to the movies in the company of others like themselves. We do not exaggerate the consequences of the inability to find a bridge between learning and maturing. If anything, we understate them. It is easy to pretend the issue is an illusion. Many students are able to give a clear-cut answer to the following questions: Why are students at college? What do students seek in this classroom? Those students who have (for the moment) declared themselves premedical, prelegal, or preprofessional solve the problem without ever facing it during the college years. But the solution will not serve. The problem is only postponed to a less propitious time.

And identity is not the same thing as knowing how one plans to make a living five, ten, or twenty years from now. A preprofessional commitment in the liberal arts setting is an evasion, not an answer, to these questions: Why here? Why now? Why me? These questions add up to a single one: Who am I? Questions are addressed to their teachers as well. Why are students telling us these things? What is important for us? What is relevant to us in students' lessons? If few students know the answers, still fewer professors are able to help. Rarely do professors wonder: Why am I telling you these things? What purpose is served, apart from the sheer pleasure of knowing, in your learning them? To professors knowledge is self-evidently illuminating; to gain and share knowledge they devote their lives; and that is, after all, also how they make their living. But for students it is equally rare to correlate knowing and understanding with the subjective issues of ordinary life. That explains why between professors and students there is a conflict not only of interest but also of orientation.

The conflict between professor and student actually revolves around very specific issues. Secure in an identity formed through the years, the professor strives to solve an external problem, alert to his or her and to others' ignorance. Further, the work is conducted as part of a life that includes a distinguished personal history, including relationships of love and of responsibility to a larger world. A teacher's work is to criticize, to rethink established knowledge. The goal is to come to a finer and more critical perception of learning and, inevitably, to a carefully circumscribed segment of knowledge. In part, the faculty member has to communicate what he or she is learning; that communication is central to the teacher's work within the university. But a university is what it is because men and women work through what others accept as truth; they make their own, through the power of the intellect, what others may take at face value.

To this, students offer only a contrast. Their problems are subjective and are resolved as their identity becomes clear. As they struggle with their problems they are barely aware of their ignorance. Students enjoy little past and almost no personal history; most are not married and do not make a living for themselves. What brings men and women whose problems are those of maturity together with adolescents who are not yet certain about what problems they are going to confront? Why do professors with answers seek students who are unsure of the questions? For the student, confronting and taking seriously a person well along the path of life can stimulate a greater maturity. Or it can intimidate.

Certainly, meeting men and women who sincerely hold that what is important in life need bear no relationship to material comfort, who earn less than they might in other callings, who work much harder than they would in other professions and yet do not think they "work" at all — to meet such people is apt to have salutary benefits, to offer a vivid example of how life may be lived. But the teacher needs the student as much as the student depends upon the teacher. For the teacher, the student's fundamental question about the worth and use of knowledge is necessary. Such questions lead back to the basics of a subject; and it is there that true insight is found. The student, if open to the answers to his or her questions, will vivify the life of the teacher.

Let us then spell out what we conceive to form the relationship between learning and maturing, between study and the formation of a strong and autonomous personality? Learning affords access to the experience of others. That explains why through learning — mastery of that part of human experience accessible in books and laboratories — we both prepare for life and engage in living. There can be no purpose in the discovery of the self without the exploration of the context in which the self takes shape. Liberal learning brings the person out of the self and leads to an encounter with other people, their yearnings and complexities. We are not alone; others have walked this path — these are the lessons not only of the humanities, well presented, but also of the social sciences. Through the record of civilization — that is, through the part of human life preserved in books and enshrined in permanent sources of knowledge — we confront the collective and accumulated experience of vast numbers of people and can make it our own. Repeatedly in these materials, whether in their legal documents or in the tales for pleasure, we find a record of earlier men and women grappling with the same problems.

Learning frees, not merely by relieving us of ignorance, but by supplying us with understanding and insight, with knowledge of the reality in which, and against which, we form our sense of self. Joseph Stone and Joseph Church, in *Childhood and Adolescence: A Psychology of the Growing Person,* write, "It is, after all, in literature, with its power of enlisting strong identifications, that we learn the profoundest lessons about human relationships and the nature of social institutions. The scientist and the philosopher have been grappling for years with exactly the cosmic problems that intrigue and frighten the adolescent." In that profound observation we identify the link between learning and growing up. In college, the student finds new avenues to explore in the search for answers and new minds struggling with the same issues.

These observations remain abstract. Let us now ask concretely, what of the formal curriculum? Behind all that we do as students and scholars are the three great components of reality: humanity, society, and nature. These are the center of our curriculum in the humanities, social sciences, and natural sciences. For all our impersonal devotion to our several subjects, good teachers do not forget the central issue of study: the understanding of humankind, of the complex structures formed by men and women, and of the natural setting of our brief life together on earth. We cannot think of a more promising opportunity than that presented by this curious conflict between the subjectivity of the student and the objectivity of the teacher, between the excessive self-obsession of the young and the equally excessive submergence of self by the mature person. Neither is wholly true; each must correct the other. The teacher must draw the student out of his or her personal preoccupation in part by demonstrating the shared nature of that experience among many men and women, alive and dead; but in greater part by introducing concerns and questions, interests and commitments currently lacking, yet important and relevant to self-identification. Let us look specifically at what this relationship between teacher and student can mean.

Consider as an example the unfamiliar subject that the senior author teaches, which is the study of religion, with specialization in the history of Judaism, an old and influential religious tradition. The relevance to students derives not from their origin, for, by his own design, he teaches atheists, Muslims, Christians, and ethnic Jews, as well as religious ones, whites, blacks, Latinos, both genders, and, so far as he can tell, every sexual proclivity. Reasons for taking his courses vary. For instance, the Christian students want to know about that "old" religion, some because of their correct belief that Christianity emerged from Judaism, others simply because Judaism is interesting. The Jewish students have a different motive. They are part of a minority, and they wonder why they should not join the majority. Their religious tradition makes demands on them, makes them different, limits their choice of a marriage partner and restricts their diet (in theory anyway on both counts). The Jewish students want to know why they should be Jewish. When they come to us, they perceive that we teach not about Judaism, but Judaism itself, and conflict arises. They want to be told why they should be Jewish. We don't teach that. Rabbis do. This is a conflict of interests, a conflict between the professor's academic interests and the religious or cultural or ethnic aspirations of his students, ordinarily the ethnic.

For the senior author wants to teach the students, whatever their origin or motivation for taking his course, what makes Judaism a complex and interesting religion, within the context of a larger study of religion. True, students for diverse reasons may have a deeply personal problem to work out, and he, for his part, has a profoundly objective inquiry to carry on. The students introduce issues of self-identification. What students contribute is to remind him that this "interesting and exemplary thing" is a religion that real people live by and die for. Still, if students want to know only what is relevant to themselves, it is hard to see what rote learning and teaching can play in their growth. We intellectuals insist upon analysis and interpretation, not solely upon feeling and commitment. In this conflict of interests is located the resolution as well. The student draws the teacher back from the pretense of objectivity and the claim to indifference to the human meaning of learning. The student serves the teacher well by asking, What does this mean to us? or What ought this to mean? And in attempting to answer, despite the frailty and impermanence of the answer, the teacher will serve the student too.

The Social Contract of the College Classroom

So what is at stake in the end? Given all of the many things students can do with their time and money, why should they turn their back on everything else in the world and in any given academic year spend the next nine months here, in classrooms and laboratories and library, and with professors? Only if the answer is, because there is nothing more important, should students stay here. And why should that be so? Because they are going to learn things here that matter, and that they cannot learn in any other place or circumstance. What that means has nothing to do with acquiring information; students can learn more facts from an encyclopaedia than they can from professors. What it means is that students are going to learn in a way in which they can only learn here and nowhere else: that is the social contract of the college classroom, it is what we professors promise students, and what students must demand of us.

Since everybody can learn all the time and everywhere, that is a considerable claim on behalf of college. Why do we think students have made the right decision to come to college? Why is this the most important thing students can do with their lives — not in general, but this year, this month, this minute? The answer is, because here, if teachers teach and if students learn, students will learn a new way of learning, one that will guide them for all time. That is why students should demand of their teachers and themselves not merely information but a way of learning that students can use every day and for the rest of their lives. It is what we professors promise, and sometimes even deliver: the secret of how to learn by discovering things on their own, not by asking but by finding out on their own.

It is the particularly American way of learning, which is by discovering things for ourselves. We American professors at our best aim at teaching by helping students learn on their own. Our theory of teaching is to tell students: Don't ask, discover! The more we tell students, the less students learn. The more students learn, the more we teach. And learning takes place, in a country as practical and as rich in innovation as this country, when students find out for themselves. Professors are there to guide, to help, to goad, to irritate, to stimulate. Students are there to explore, to inquire, to ask questions, to experiment, to navigate.

That attitude toward teaching and learning, not entirely common in this country and Canada, makes the North American colleges and universities unique in the world. In other countries where the senior author has taught or lectured and observed the procedures of higher education, in Latin America, South Africa, Sweden and Finland, New Zealand and Australia, and especially in Germany and Britain, Israel, and Italy, students come to class to write down what professors say. The British system, dominant also in New Zealand, discourages assignments to be done for particular lectures, so students have to be told a mass of elementary information before the professor can start the serious work.

Overseas, students do not prepare by reading in advance, so they bring nothing to class. They do not ask questions or propose propositions or much participate in classes. Indeed, he found in New Zealand bitter resentment that he expected otherwise. There students wish to be examined on an on-going basis through the year and take no responsibility for their own education. Then he made headlines throughout the country when he asked in public whether New Zealand could build its future on the strength of a population able to do only what it is told. Intellectual independence begins with informing oneself, and conformity takes over when all students learn is what a professor tells them. The violence of the answers told him he had touched on a raw nerve; people were asking themselves the same question. Later in the same year New Zealand showed up at the top of the international lists for teen-age suicide, the reason being given that being forced to conform to someone else's model in the end produced despair and self-destruction. The Kiwi saying had it that the tall poppy lost its head to the scythe. Folk wisdom was never more appropriate.

To show the difference between American higher education at its most distinctive and overseas modes of instruction, let us record what happened when the senior author taught in Germany. It was a catastrophe, for there is no one less well-equipped to teach there than he was. He teaches — as do many American professors — by asking questions — but also listening to the answers, then asking more questions. Not alone among American professors, he then builds toward the more complex analytical problems, and his theory in responding to first-rate student questions — and they are many — is, if you have asked a great question, it is because you have already intuited the answer, so you tell me. Now he doesn't know any other way than that dictated by his philosophy of education, which consists of three words in two clauses: *Don't ask, discover.* He realized how different is that theory of teaching from that of Europeans when for a semester he served as a visiting professor at the University of Frankfurt, in Germany. For the professor's part, he had a very good time; but for their's, the students didn't. That is because, as they put it, "All you do is ask us questions. When are you going to tell us what you want us to think?" When he said, "I hope, never," the students all dropped the course, and none of the professors of theology ever talked with him again, except one who soon thereafter left for Switzerland.

The senior author has spent a quarter of a century teaching through asking questions and listening to the answers and then asking questions, teaching through a process of negotiation and dialogue. He is really not equipped to walk into a classroom and tell people things. That strikes him as boring, unproductive; it preserves the authority of the professor, reinforcing the passivity and inferiority of the student. To him, the good teacher is the one who draws students in and guides them forward, not so much like a cowboy driving a herd of cattle from behind as a sergeant weaving up the hill and hoping the troops are following — all the time braving a hail of doubts. So when he got to Germany and walked into the classroom and laid out a problem for the students to solve, a text meant to serve as a guinea pig for analysis, two cultures met — and neither understood the other. Those particular Germans (Frankfurt need not represent all the universities; the theology students do not necessarily stand for all German students)[8] make good students: they take notes and learn lessons. American students at their best make great students: they take risks and draw conclusions. And that explains the reason that the best American students demand real teachers, while at least these particular German students don't want teachers, only lecturers.

Out of years of experience generalization emerges. Overseas, the senior author has found, students rarely ask questions in class, rarely argue or propose ideas, rarely participate in the shaping of a proposition. At an American college or university it happens all the time. In the University of Frankfurt, Germany, as much as in the University of Canterbury, Christchurch, New Zealand, where the senior author taught for some months, professors talk, students write things down. But he has found overseas exceptional classes, where American professors feel right at home, in Åbo Akademi in Finland and Tel Aviv University in Israel, for instance. But the norm is otherwise. In our colleges some students engage with some professors in a shared inquiry. If going to class is not an adventure for students here, it is the student's fault. No college in the country is a better place for a partnership of learning than this one: that's what small liberal arts colleges sell. It is a student's job to walk into a professor's office; once he's there, it's the professor's job to make the student glad he came. American students in general, when asked, do ask questions, do know how to argue, do reading, do work on papers, do review after one class and prepare before the next one.

Only rarely has the senior author found an overseas academic audience able to take up the challenge of helping solve a problem, asking searching questions, joining in the work. In an entire semester at Frankfurt and another in Christchurch, in a week of lectures at Uppsala University, in a series of seminars and lectures at Göttingen University — everywhere the senior author has taught or lectured outside of the U.S.A., from Sydney, Australia, to Bergen, Norway and Rejkjavik, Iceland — not one student asked him to suggest a single reading for the course, not one student prepared in advance of a course meeting, for instance, by glancing at the text the senior author had said he would work on, not one student reviewed after a course meeting, not one student wrote a paper or asked to, not one student came to his office to ask a question on anything, though he worked with his door open and took German seminar students out for supper to get to know them and let them get to know him. It made no difference. Colleagues at Göttingen tell that on standard IQ tests in Germany, theology students consistently score lowest as a group. So he may have taught at the wrong places or presented the wrong subject.

These impressions contradict the headlines about the inferiority of American students on standard, international exams. Don't foreign students know more than Americans? Without doubt, they know more about more things. They know languages; we can scarcely write our own. In Germany, all students have studied English for nine years, French for five, and Latin and Greek. German students certainly have been taught more history and literature. Dutch students speak four languages fluently. New Zealand students such as the senior author saw at Canterbury are fluent in this and that as well. But what they know about the things they have been taught is inert: mere facts. When it comes to learning, it is as though they learned the vocabulary and grammar of a language but could not use the language — much like the Japanese when it comes to speaking English. If students ask them a question that requires using in a strange way some set of familiar facts, they fall silent. It is hard to teach through questions in a German or in a New Zealand classroom. The one really bad day he had in the classroom came when his students really did know the facts, but then could not do anything with what they knew. He asked them to add one and one. They could not make connections and therefore draw conclusions. And then, for his part, he understood the costs of that educational philosophy he had long ago discarded. A German colleague, who had taught for many years in the U.S.A., understood the situation and recognized the sad truth.

Great teachers don't teach. They help students learn. Students teach themselves. The ideal teachers therefore are people like Socrates, Jesus, and Hillel. What students have to ask of their professors is that they measure themselves by the model of Socrates, Jesus, and Hillel. They shared a dislike of heavyweight speeches. They spoke briefly, painting pictures and telling tales (parables), and always raised more questions than they settled.

Socrates was the greatest philosopher of all time, and all he did was walk around the streets and ask people irritating questions. Jesus was certainly the most influential teacher in history, and his longest "lecture" — for instance the Sermon on the Mount — cannot have filled up an hour of classroom time or a page in a notebook. And Hillel's greatest lesson, in answer to someone who told him to teach the entire Torah while standing on one foot — "What is hateful to you, don't do to someone else. That's the whole Torah, all the rest is commentary, now go study." — directed people to go off and learn on their own. The great teacher makes a few simple points. The powerful teacher relates one or two fundamental truths. And the memorable teacher makes the point not by telling, but by helping the students discover on their own. Learning takes place through discovery, not when you're told something, but when students figure it out for themselves. All a really fine teacher does is make suggestions, point out problems, above all, ask questions, and more questions, and more questions.

Good teaching in our system encourages not only discovery but initiative. Good teaching in our schools leads to risk-taking, good teaching overseas leads to note-taking. Successful professors in our system present learning as answers to important questions, successful professors in their system go over familiar facts and pass their opinion on this and that. They tell people things. We want people to make their own discoveries. So we don't think Socrates would have found a very warm welcome in a German or a New Zealand classroom, with all those relentless questions of his. All he did was ask questions, he never really gave any answers, nothing students could memorize and say back on an exam. Jesus did not dictate long lectures, so the students could carry home thick notebooks. And Hillel would have lasted about a minute and a half — "now, go study" — indeed! American kids would have given Socrates a good time, and we think they would have patience for a teacher who just told them stories, like Jesus, or who advised them while they stood on one foot, like Hillel.

In this country, with its tradition of pragmatism and experiment, we aim at helping students teach themselves, asking them questions to stimulate their own inquiry. At our best, we do not indoctrinate, we stimulate. We do not just tell people things, we try to make knowledge important because knowing helps answer urgent questions. The best classes state the problem for students to find the answer. We have an educational tradition that serves the needs of a society in process, a nation never fully finished, a country in quest, a people of peoples in perpetual search. That is why entire fields of learning are founded here — social science and modern medicine as we know it for instance. That explains why new ideas, new sciences find in this country a ready hearing, a warm welcome.

True, we pay a price for this intellectual restlessness of ours: our kids are better at process than at proposition. They seem to know less; when they need to know, they go and learn. So they spend more time in the laboratory, work harder at writing their own thoughts, do research on their own. But then they spend less time learning what we know, work less hard at fully understanding other peoples' thoughts; sometimes do research aimed at reinventing the wheel. We've made our choices. For an open society, an always-changing economy, a responsible politics of participation and endless negotiation, we need an alert, inventive citizen. The cost sometimes is the independent pursuit of irrelevance. The rewards can hardly be measured.

If students were to write their half of the social contract of the college classroom, what should students ask of their professors?

1. Don't tell us things, let us find out for ourselves
2. But when we need help, give it to us;
3. And when our work is poor, don't tell us it's good.

Many professors would rather be liked than be understood; not a few find it easier to indulge the students than teach them. So one clause of the contract must read: Don't accept from professors compliments when they owe students criticism. And love them when they're tough. Proverbs says, "Rebuke a wise person, and you'll be loved, rebuke a fool and you'll be hated." To translate into this context: Show yourselves wise, and you'll get professors who care about what you know and how you are learning.

What should their professors ask of students?

1. Don't ask us to sell students our subject, let us explain it to students. Once we're in the classroom, relevance is a settled question: this is what students want to know, now let us teach it.

2. Don't stop work in the middle of the semester. It's easy to start with enthusiasm, and it's easy to end with commitment. But in the middle of a course, it's hard for students to sustain the work; the beginning is out of sight, the end not yet on the horizon. In the northern climates, the contract should add: Do your best when the weather looks bleak. And, it goes without saying, the contract must include the critical, elastic clause:

3. Don't sit back and wait to be told things, stay with us and allow the logic of the course to guide us both; join us, think with us.

One of the most remarkable students the senior author ever taught was a late middle-aged woman who audited a course of mine at University of South Florida in Sarasota; after five minutes in each class session of three hours, she would say, "Oh, is this what you mean?" And she would proceed to lay out for us the entire argument that was beginning to be developed, one that the senior author imagined would take an hour and a half fully to expose. Yes, a remarkable student but not typical. The senior author never has walked into class without fearing that he would run out of things to tell people in the first ten minutes. Students owe their teachers that moment of trepidation: make them afraid they'll run out of things to tell students. They won't, of course, but the students will make them work and give them life. The challenge is not in disagreeing or agreeing, but in uncovering a professor's logic and accepting its principles. That is what students owe their teachers.

Notes

1. *The Price of Excellence. Universities in Conflict during the Cold War Era,* (Continuum, 1995).
2. Perelman, Lewis. *School's Out: Hyperlearning, the New Technology, and the End of Education* (Avon,1993), p. 92.
3. Stecklow, Steve. "Some Small Colleges Hire Recruiters to Get Bigger Freshman Class." *Wall Street Journal.* Sept. 5, 1997.
4. "ABA Settles Charges a Panel Fixes Law-School Salaries," *Wall Street Journal,* June 28, 1995.
5. Arenson, Karen. "Classes Are Full at Catch-Up U." *New York Times,* May 31, 1998.
6. But, then, community and junior colleges also should not pretend to do our work. Too often, calling themselves colleges, they amount to little more than pretentious high schools, and not very good ones at that.
7. And even there, students fell into more than a single category, disconsolate and aimless. Some of Brown's departments and programs proved competitive and attracted students of high seriousness, mathematics, engineering, biological sciences, computer sciences, for example. They earned degrees of substance, because their professors offered demanding courses. Nor should we ignore entire classes of higher education, the excellence of which is missed by the critics. Once again, we hasten to point to MIT and Cal Tech and Illinois Institute of Technology, to the schools of music and of art, to medical schools and graduate schools in engineering, mathematics, the natural and physical sciences, as conforming to a different rule. In colleges and universities and schools of those and kindred classifications, students, whether for the bachelor of arts or for a higher degrees, show themselves purposeful and professional. One of the errors of the contemporary critics of higher education has been to ignore the diversity of education all called "college" or "university."
8. But when as a research professor he actually gave a lecture at Göttingen University a few years later, the students told him he simply was talking too much, so, perhaps, in Germany there is a happy medium that he has not yet found (and is unlikely to). But if some German theology students show themselves to be louts, others, in other subjects, display angelic dispositions.

4

What is at Stake on Campus?

Can Colleges Compete?

The three major issues in the debate over the future of the academy cover who teaches, who learns, and what is taught. But the ultimate question, the one that begs for an answer more than those three practical questions, is why? What is at stake for America in the colleges and universities that provide postsecondary education for more than half the nation's high school graduates?

American higher education is both expensive and time-consuming. It is inefficient and politicized. It is heralded for its traditions yet often bound to them needlessly. And most of all, it is only now coming to recognize its competition. As American society begins to use the technologies afforded by time- and space-saving computers and computer networks, as commercial enterprises demonstrate the efficiency of the profit-motive, as unconventional postsecondary, degree-granting operations reach maturity, the university loses out. So we return to our starting point: universities must begin to ask themselves what they provide, if not information, then learning that cannot be found elsewhere.

If not disembedded information, then what? Defenders of the college experience report that their graduates develop skills and career ambitions that make them valuable members of society. It depends. In the hard and natural sciences, mathematics, engineering, and related fields, the rigor of college is a mere precursor to a lifetime of learning, whether in computer science or medicine. As for other fields, career skills appear to be very low on the list of intended effects. Businesses now report that they seek American college graduates because they are likely to have achieved a passable state of literacy, not because they have some unique skills. They want students who can think critically, analyze perspicaciously, write lucidly — about whatever comes to hand. Are these the standards to which universities now aspire?

For forty years and more, American universities could not only point to greater achievements, but a distinct mission. The creation of knowledge was for that period a primary purpose, when knowledge and information were armaments in the global struggle for democracy. To achieve that purpose, universities adopted and supported a system that rewarded scholarship and gave access to students who would need certain skills to man a growing and vibrant economy. Those who supported universities with money — legislatures, foundations, parents — saw the immediate value of that vocation. Universities were part of the firmament of democracy, but were not simple flag-wavers. Scholarship demanded independenceand money, and universities got it. They still do. Universities receive about $16 billion in federal spending.

Now, universities talk about the value of diversity, of exposing students and professors to exotic ideas and cultures, of protecting certain ideologies from extinction. And those who pay to support such institutions are paying attention to this new goal. It is perhaps most telling that the biggest problem (as determined by those who lead the institutions) facing American universities today is not the rampant disrespect for independent scholarship, but the legal case against all forms of affirmative action. That legal case, which is now formidable, could upset fifteen years of administrative and ideological hegemony on the campus. The California state system of higher education now prohibits admissions policies which set ethnic, racial, or any other kind of benchmarks associated with affirmative action. Several other schools are following suit. And while universities spent their vast energies into upholding an ideological construct that was to be toppled, universities relied on little else to validate their presence in a society more dominated by information than ever.

Two things have happened. Affirmative action declines, either by force or by habit. Most Americans, and now, many federal judges, simply do not support the ideology of race- or sex-based, other-than-merit systems. This poses a major problem to universities, who tend to argue that they assist in creating a more equitable American society by favoring some groups over others. The inherent logic of such an ideology is reprehensible in a meritocracy, and goes against what universities stood for from the 1930s to the 1960s. Abandoning that meritocracy, which applied to professors and students alike, has cost universities dearly.

The second development: the application of technology to the disbursing and management of information. Knowledge is available everywhere and through technology accessible to nearly anyone. University libraries are no longer the primary storehouses of an informed society, and professors are no longer the only people capable of specialization. The capabilities of distance learning mean students do not have to leave their dorm rooms to listen or see a lecture. And if they don't need to be in their dorm room, it follows that they need not be on campus at all. Moreover, in the sciences, where application guides discovery, business, not academia takes the lead. Computer scientists now find better opportunities starting up their own businesses, or participating in others, so much so that the field in academia is losing its brightest minds. Those who have traditionally been the medium for the transmission of information — professors —are no longer regarded as the best for the task of representing their field. Some say they are the worst.

The Academy's Response

The academy now responds to the challenge of relevance by adopting the criteria of the critics and therefore surrenders the field before the battle is joined. The most compelling argument most university advocates make for themselves is economic. Salaries for college graduates are always higher than for those who never attended, making it hard to justify not going to college when one possesses the necessary test scores or dollars. But this argument makes two assumptions. One is that those who attend will gain from the experience. Were that consistently so. There is no measurement for such a claim. Colleges and universities need to devise a system to measure the value-added worth of their processing. Even having students retake the verbal part of the SATs would produce some solid facts: do students perform better after four years of higher education? And, more to the point, which colleges add value, which do not?

But short of solid research, all the universities can adduce in evidence is the quality of their alumni — alas! For the evidence of rampant incompetence among college graduates need not be spelled out here. One only needs to seek the resume and letter file of hiring officers for major corporations. The results speak for themselves, but by then, the tuition check has been cashed. Recent college graduates are beginning to wonder about the calculus that feeds this economic argument, since more and more college graduates are entering the work-force, thus watering down any real or perceived benefit to having attended in the first place.

In reality, there is a wide variety of possibilities for economic benefit from college. The surest is to be found in socialization. The university serves as a finishing school for the middle class. (The rich are already done for.) Whether students actually gain from exposure to higher-level thinking is immaterial, and most everybody knows it. The goal is to expose students to adulthood. This view is expressed clearly by Harvard University President Neil Rudenstine: "Such an environment also creates opportunities for people from different backgrounds...to develop forms of tolerance and mutual respect on which the health of our civic life depends." So the gains are not at all academic, mostly personal and psychological, and that is assuming Rudenstine is correct. But surely he is not. For so trivial and instrumental a goal hardly proves commensurate with the cost — both money laid out and money not earned. Rudenstine seems to have in mind the sort of privileged, entitled students that his own university famously values, not people for whom time and money are precious.

The second assumption is just as false: It is that those who earn more after earning a degree would not necessarily have the same success without it. That can't be guaranteed, and those who grew up in the generation immediately before World War II would argue that point. The reality is that a college degree is becoming like a high school degree. It is so ordinary that it fails to confer much status, but is a requirement to entry to the middle class. There are no guarantees however. Meanwhile, honest trades requiring no college degree go begging, including welders, machinists, electricians, and plumbers. But the nation's public school systems emphasize college as a goal above all others. The result now is that college graduates are in overabundance in the labor force. How do we prove this? By the clear need for employers to train workers in their tasks once they're hired, and to hope that the ability to learn has been inculcated by four years (or more) in college. Would that college could guarantee even that, since it can't. Meanwhile, those who are lucky enough not to have false aspirations of college greatness choose a different, and perhaps more successful, path. The argument comes forth that in an age when knowledge and information will create wealth, we need a knowledgeable and informed work force — therefore college-educated. No one has proven that college is the only, or best, way to achieve that kind of work force. It is just one of many ways.

Global Testimony to American Excellence: Where We Do Compete

For a more compelling argument, American universities should consult a different constituency altogether: overseas competition. Foreigners send huge numbers of their young people to American universities, not only to learn English or to explore the possibilities of a green card, but actually to get an education. That is so not in all fields but in the important ones. The world still sends its brightest students here to study diplomacy, economics, engineering, computer science, medicine, and other sciences. This student represents a distinct use of higher education — one that is reserved for building a schooled elite class, a free market economy and the many knowledge-based systems that any developing nation requires. For such skills, American colleges are still the best place to learn and work, and everyone knows it. But those areas that do not make clear their applications or their intrinsic value to improving the mind, are not part of the sought-after curriculum. It is still a sacrifice, even for the wealthy, to send their young to a foreign land. So their time here isn't wasted, and those who are capable of taking advantage of the experience are sent; those who aren't capable aren't sent.

Only in American universities do undergraduates and graduate students engage their professors in some of the debates and research at the very edges of their field. And only American universities produce students capable of self-guided research. Why? For precisely the same reasons that so many foreign students come here to study. American universities, at their best, require students to think for themselves, to study fresh problems and explore unfamiliar territory. It is part of the American model of higher education, and one that has worked for decades. And, we argue, it provides a useful reminder of why American universities achieved so much and can continue to achieve much more — just as we said in chapter 1.

The recreation of a society of scholars, whether in Cambridge or Austin, does not occur by accident. It is a difficult goal to reach, and those who reach it must guard it carefully lest it be lost. Why? Because the excellence that does exist in American universities exists in the most fragile of contexts: that between a teacher and a student. Charles Sykes, one of academia's many gadflies in the 1980s, mocked universities for routinely failing to provide this level of interaction. He was not wrong, and his critics did not prove him wrong. Moreover, Sykes was effective in demonstrating the very low standards most professors met in teaching. An outsider, he did not make the case he ought to have made that the same professors also do not publish much. One-book professors produce one-book students, and this inactivity then serves to explain fifty years of not teaching. Sykes missed that one. But he was right on target elsewhere.

Not wishing to go over this ground, we turn instead to another matter entirely. The very willingness of most students not to consider the potential for interaction with qualified faculty at all, but to seek most knowledge and discovery in self-guided searches through computer software and databases. The growth of distance learning, corporate learning and corporate apprenticeships have all pointed to one major trend: knowledge can be gained nearly anywhere, and practical self-instruction occurs anywhere but on the campus. Students now widely accept the reality of huge lecture halls where information can be ignored until needed, at exam time. That acceptance spells the doom of the university. Students no longer assume that by going to college, they will benefit from the wisdom, or gain an education, from professors. Rather, it is seen as an economic choice, a lifestyle choice, a status choice.

When Lewis Perelman, another insightful critic, suggested in his 1992 book *School's Out*, that technology had superseded the campus, he was only partially correct. His argument rested on the theory that the campus was a storehouse of information no different than a computer. Once the information could be relayed in ways other than a lecture, the destruction of academia was sure to follow, he argued. Perelman expressed something universities must consider, but his is not a vision that is likely to be put into play. Education remains a human process, requiring many participants. While not necessarily a positive indicator, the yearning to go to college as a way to escape parental pressures demonstrates, in itself, an important purpose. If universities could find a way to create a process of intellectual growth equal to the social growth that occurs outside the classroom on many campuses, they would have an answer to Perelman. As is, they have only half the answer, poorly phrased.

That answer, put into words by Neil Rudenstine earlier in this chapter, is simple: that universities serve to inculcate American minds in the many facets of living in a democracy. For Rudenstine, that experience includes the daily consideration of other cultures, races, and so on, which explains his, and other academics', opposition to any reduction in affirmative action programs. Such a mission takes for granted that universities know best what a democracy is all about, and moreover, what is best for it. For the moment, consider only that this is the answer provided to counter Perelman's challenge. The university as defender of democracy is much different than a simple storehouse of information. In it, one assumes, a student can find not only the information, but the wisdom and experience that will make a defender of social and political democracy. That wisdom and experience is derived not only from a set curriculum, although that is clearly important, but by interactions between students, administrators and professors. If universities are living laboratories for democracy, then they by definition must pull together people into common quests for wisdom and knowledge. Clearly, no computer can do that for any person. Stated so, academia has a cogent response to a real challenge.

Now, consider the arguments of Allan Bloom. The philosophy professor and best-selling author wrote his 1987 *The Closing of the American Mind* for many audiences, but especially for academics. He perceived not only a malaise, but a rot in American higher education, and addressed it in the context with which he was most familiar — philosophy. While he embraced the concept of a university as a place where knowledge develops from interactions between students and professors, he did not subscribe to the notion that universities serve democracies. Rather, he argued, universities should "preserve what is most likely to be neglected" in a democracy: those ideas that are universal, immutable, and authoritative (We begin to see why some charged him with elitism). The modern mind, Bloom said, is prone to blocking out authority. In one sense, this is intellectual self-sufficiency, on the other, it is antihistorical and dangerous. Thus, in Bloom's view, the university's mission is to rally against the present dogma of historical revisionism and to imbue democracy with the kind of searching found in thinkers like Aristotle, Plato, and Socrates — who challenged convention, not truth. Not surprisingly, Bloom was a classicist, and embraced the kinds of questions posed by humanists. If universities succeeded in keeping alive the questions of Plato, he argued, they would do more for American democracy than any other institution.

Who will challenge if not Universities?

So we have an alternative mission for the Academy: the impartial questioner. Who, Bloom wonders, will challenge if not universities? Who will provoke the mind to seek answers to unanswered questions of the spirit and the soul? Who will lead science to do good? Who will define good from evil? These are the kinds of questions that had faced universities in Germany in the 1930s, when the answers came back with ambivalence, moral degeneration, and incompetence. That spelled the death of German universities not only then but for decades to follow the debacle, and from which they have never wholly recovered. The tradition of academic excellence and independence that German nationalism under the Nazis dismantled was replaced. Those who succeeded chose their successors, and an unbroken chain links the contemporary German university to its past, if not to the Nazi ideology, still to the totalitarian mentality that was embodied therein.

That is why German students still need to be told what to think, and what the professors want, each one to rule unchallenged in his or her own domain. It would be unfair to characterize the German universities as comprised by little Hitlers indoctrinating their stormtroopers. But for Americans those universities present a strange and puzzling picture, one made all the more incomprehensible by reason of the inhospitality and collective coldness of colleagues there. German universities create an academic Siberia, not only for overseas guests, but for the professors themselves: polar bears with tweed jackets and thick glasses. For our part, we embody the opposite: chaos instead of the redevivus New Order. The American university faced a version of that crisis in the 1960s, when student rebellions laid waste to any authority — bureaucratic, academic or otherwise — that once existed on campuses.

Just as the Germans have yet to recover from the National Socialist debacle, we still work out the aftershocks of the earthquakes of the late 1960s and early 1970s, when the American equivalent of student stormtroopers took over, leaving behind those whom Roger Kimball rightly called tenured radicals. In the wake of those rebellions, resegregation in the form of racial or ethnic dormitories, intellectual anarchy, and ideological fadism took hold of the campus, although Bloom concluded not all is lost. "Our thought and our politics have become inextricably bound up with the universities, and they have served us well, human things being what they are," he wrote in his concluding chapter. And in the de facto recognition that universities are a part of the framework of a democracy, Bloom argued — and we agree — that a university must set an example, uphold standards, and more than anything else, involve the labors and energies of thinking people. He sets high goals for the behavior of academia. Those high goals justify what society gives to these institutions; failing to meet them may be cause for concern, but not setting them is cause for surrender.

In our earlier volume, *The Price of Excellence,* we have documented how American universities served at the very forefront of a national struggle to win a forty-year cold war. In that twilight struggle, fought with ideas more than with guns, no research was unworthy, no student unteachable, no goal pointless. We stood on the walls of the American redoubt, firing books at the enemy — and, more to the point, inspiring the defenders to stand firm for yet another battle. Everyone understood the task, and most did their duty gladly. The mission has ended, the task is done.

What now? Now, universities serve students from the middle and upper classes only, producing research no better and no worse than that created by industry research and development teams. The vast infrastructures of universities are assets, but their colleges of liberal arts go begging. The great colleges of arts and sciences blow in the wind, sustained by the fumes of nostalgia and an occasional multimillion-dollar gift. The meaning of knowledge and serious criticism are in question, and universities have little to say on the issue, having allowed revisionists to rule their roosts. Their defenders recognize only a short-sighted problem, which is whether to teach Marquez or Shakespeare. The bigger problem is whether it matters if universities teach literature or the humanities at all. Should they, as some suggest, go into the business of vocational training? And if not, how can universities make compelling a curriculum and academic experience that fulfills both the minds and careers of professors and students?

Those who have articulated a vision of the future tell only a piece of the story, but that story is made clear throughout: Knowledge does not merely occur when someone declares new information, or looks it up. It inhabits teaching, where it is passed from one generation to the next. Which is why, as most undergraduates will recognize, it is not only the subject that matters, but the professor who delivers it. And in that combination, of timeless knowledge and professional learning, will universities articulate what makes their experience different, and important. Here what is at stake is the very future of humanity, so we claim. Let us say why. In a word, we represent civilization: the increment of human knowledge. We — and no one else in our society — know and can hand on the heritage embodied in the great libraries that contain the treasure.

Can Humanity Forget What It Knows?

What universities owe society is the protection of the heritage of learning that sustains the social order of civilization. That heritage of learning is preserved in books, but is best transmitted in person, from generation to generation. For civilization hangs suspended by the gossamer strand of memory. If only one cohort of mothers and fathers or teachers fails to convey to its children or students what it has learned from its parents and masters then the great chain of learning and wisdom snaps. If the guardians of human knowledge stumble only one time, in their fall collapses the entire edifice of knowledge and understanding. More important, therefore, than finding new things is sifting and refining the received truths. And the generation that will go down through time bearing the burden of disgrace is not the one that has said nothing new — for not much new marks the mind of any age — but the one that has not said what is true.

These self-evident truths concerning the continuity of civilization pertain not alone to wisdom, such as philosophy and religion preserve. They address much more concrete matters than the wise conduct of affairs. There are things that we know because of the hard work of people who have come before, knowledge that we have on account of other peoples' trial and error. And that is knowledge that also hangs in the balance from age to age, and that is knowledge that we can and do forget, with awful consequences for those who will come after us, to whom we for our part are answerable.

The simple fact is that we either remember or recapitulate the work of finding out — one or the other. And now, with 5,000 years of recorded science and philosophy, mathematics, history and social science, literature and music and art, if we lose it all, we probably shall never regain what is gone. It would be too much work, require resources of time and intellect not likely to come to hand. Lest our meaning be lost in abstraction, let us give a single concrete and telling case. When the turret of the battleship USS Iowa blew up, people could not repair it. The reason is that the materials and technological know-how to repair the guns, available when the ship was built in World War II, were lost beyond recovery. That is what we mean when we say civilization hangs suspended by fragile strands. So too, when it was decided to resume construction of the Cathedral of St. John the Divine in New York City, people found out that only a few stone masons were left in the world who could work the giant blocks from which a cathedral is built; they would have to train young apprentices, or the work would not be done. Languages too have come and gone; linguists make haste to preserve what is nearly going to be lost as an example of the potentialities of intelligible speech.

We owe this point to a biologist at Rutgers University, David Ehrenfeld, writing in *Orion* (Autumn, 1989, pp. 5-7), who argues that "loss of knowledge and skills is now a big problem in our universities." That is a problem, he maintains, not in the humanities, which we know are dying in ignorance, but in the natural sciences. His case in point is one that surprised us. He says, "We are on the verge of losing our ability to tell one plant or animal from another and of forgetting how the known species interact among themselves and with their environments." This is because subjects fall out of the curriculum, or are taught piecemeal by people on the periphery of the university. He says, for example, "Classification of Higher Plants," "Marine Invertebrates," "Ornithology," "Mammalogy," "Cryptograms" (ferns and mosses), "Biogeography," "Comparative Physiology" — "students may find some of them in the catalogue, but too often with the notation along side, 'not offered...' "

Ehrenfeld explains: "The features that distinguish lizards from snakes from crocodilians from turtles ...aren't any less accepted or valid than they were twenty-five years ago, nor are they easier than they used to be to learn on students' own from books without hands-on laboratory instruction." But people do not work in those fields. Ehrenfeld further explains why the question is an urgent one. He tells the following story: "One morning last April, at eight o'clock, my phone rang. It was a former student of mine who is now a research endocrinologist at a major teaching hospital in Houston. She had an odd question: at what point in animal evolution was the hemoglobin molecule first adopted for use specifically as an oxygen carrier? It was an essential piece of information for medical research she was planning." The information the student wanted was in an elementary "Introduction to comparative biochemistry." When Ehrenfeld asked colleagues who was working on this sort of thing, he found out, nobody. The graduate students had never even heard of the field of comparative biochemistry.

Now here we have a very concrete case of the loss of knowledge once possessed. Ehrenfeld comments: "not outdated, not superseded, not scientifically or politically controversial, not even merely frivolous: a whole continent of important human knowledge gone." It was not dead, it lived only in books, which no one read or understood or could use in the quest for knowledge. Ehrenfeld draws from this story conclusions that need not detain us. In his view the loss of comparative biochemistry is because of the flow of funds into the wrong hands, into the hands of people who are not "capable of transmitting our assembled knowledge of the natural world to the next generation." So he says, "we fear for conservation when there is no one left in our places of learning who can tell one moth from another, no one who knows the habits of hornbills, no one to puzzle over the diversity of hawthorns."

If we now take the case as exemplary, we may ask ourselves, where, in society, do we assign the task of holding on to what we know and making sure the next generation gains access to that? The stakes are too high for the answer to invoke the episodic and the anecdotal: "Here am I, send me." The accident of individuals finds its match in the uncertainty of books; putting whatever is worth knowing into books, encyclopaedias for example, will not serve, since mere information does not inform, and facts without explanation of what they mean and how they fit together do not bear meaning or serve a purpose. In age succeeding age, in some few places, the mind of humanity in the past is recreated, not preserved inert but actively replicated, reenacted as a model for the mind of humanity to come. We speak of the university as such a place, of teachers as the actors out of knowledge in intellectually replicable form. For to preserve what we know we must repeat the processes of discovery, since the only mode of real learning is our own discovery, which permits us not merely to know things, but to understand something. All the facts in the world about moths and hornbills and hawthorns, left uninterpreted, will not yield comparative biochemistry.

May we point to what an intellectual tradition looks like, when it is written down in a form that permits recapitulation and renewal from age to age — a kind of university in the form of a book? Indeed we may. As it happens, the senior author has spent his life working on a document that was composed in order to present, within a few volumes, the life and structure, the way of life and world view and social theory, of an entire world of humanity: the Jewish people. A few remarkable intellectuals undertook to write a book — the Talmud — that would serve as not a mere source of information but as a handbook of civilization: how to form society, what society had to know to do its work, all of useful knowledge so formed as to yield meaning and order and coherence.

To write a book that would do that, they worked out not an encyclopaedia of information but a guidebook for a journey of mind, of intellect: this is how to think, this is what to think, this is why to think.

They made certain, therefore, that what they knew would be known by coming generations, not because the institutions would endure, nor because the politics would accord to their doctrines priority of place. Indeed, the writers of this document would have found surprising Professor Ehrenfeld's certainty that problems are to be solved by putting money in the right hands, or keeping it out of the wrong ones.

What they did was two things. First, they wrote a book that could be sung. Second, they wrote notes to the music, so that anyone could sing the song. They did not spell out everything, rather, they gave signals of how, if students wanted to spell things out, students could on their own: Again, don't ask, discover. So they opened the doors of learning to make room for all to come, with learning as an active verb, with discovery its synonym. These notes — signals of how a moving argument would be reconstructed, how inexorable reason might be recapitulated — were few, perhaps not so few as the eight notes of our octave that capture most of the sounds we want to sing, but not an infinite repertoire of replicable sounds either. But the medium — notes to the music — is only secondary.

Their primary insight into how civilization as they proposed to frame it should be shaped lay in another matter altogether. It had to do with their insistence upon the urgency of clear and vigorous and rigorous thought, the priority of purpose to argument, the demand for ultimate seriousness about things to be critically examined. Through practical reasoning and applied logic, they formed the chains to link mind to mind, past to future, through a process that anyone could enter — and no one, once in, would leave.

We said they wrote a book that could be sung. We mean that both literally, in that, as for most writing in antiquity, their writing was a document meant to be chanted and hummed and sung out loud, not read silently; it was meant to be studied in community through the reconstitution of the classical debate as in the manner of the dialogues of Plato. Not meditated upon privately and personally, it was writing that was, in the old and classic sense, political, public, shared, subject to coercion, if in the form of reason rather than naked power to be sure. But we mean that in another sense as well. The great author, James Baldwin, said in a short story, every song begins in a cry. So when we say they wrote a book that could be sung, we meant to invoke metaphor of a piece of writing that begins not with the words and the music, but in the guts. We speak of revelation, such as most of us have known and of which all of us have heard: the unearned insight, the unanticipated moment of understanding.

That is what we mean by a book that could be sung, of truth in a form of such art that whoever hears will see and feel, knowing that is visceral.

So to be sure it is possible to forget what we have learned, leaving for a coming generation the task of recapitulating processes of discovery and interpretation. But it also is possible to imagine and even identify the means by which, as a matter of fact, humanity has defended itself from the loss of what it already has in hand. We use the Talmud as a case in point; others may well identify other appropriate cases. Philosophy is one, Confucianism another, mathematics a third. All compare as media of cultural transmission and reconstitution to the Talmud: models of how to think and what to think, transmitting the cumulative learning and wisdom of the long ages. We think of such fields as music and mathematics, philosophy and its offspring in the social sciences, and a variety of the natural sciences as well, as fields of learning that link us to the accumulated treasures of important knowledge and sustaining truth.

What they have in common are rules of right thought, a heritage of conventions to be replicated, retested, and realized from age to age, a process of testing and reevaluation, an endless openness to experiment, whether in the laboratory or in the classroom. Indeed, much that we in universities identify as useful and important knowledge qualifies. For as a matter of fact, so far as the sum of human knowledge is concerned, either we in universities will convey it to the coming generation so they can understand it, or it will be lost for all time.

It is the simple fact that nearly everything that we teach in universities comes to us from somewhere else, and even for the greatest scholars among us, nearly everything comes from someone else as well. And most of it comes to us from many past generations of intellects. Whether philosophy or mathematics or music, whether how we regain the past in history, or how we interpret the facts of the natural world, the treasure and storehouse of human knowledge are realized, today, in the here and now, in universities. Or, those treasures are lost, much as comparative biochemistry formed a threatened species of learning when people lost access to what that field had to tell them. So the task of universities, if not unique then at least distinctive among all of the institutions that preserve and hand on past to future, is to preserve civilization and afford access to civilization. Ours is the task of remembering, recapitulating, reenacting.

And that leads us to the word "re-mind." Ours is the task of reminding, in a very odd sense of the word, that is, to re-gain mind. We form the links in the great chain of learning, and if we prove strong to the task, another generation will know what we do, but if we prove weak, the work of many generations past will be lost, and many generations to come will be the losers. The stakes in universities and what they do therefore are not trivial; we do more than serve, carry out a more than transient or merely useful task. We preserve, but in a very special way: we show the generation to come the "how" of knowledge, not merely the "what"; we show in our time what humanity has done over all time to make sense of the world. That is the how — the what, by comparison, is much easier.

Lest these observations on the danger of forgetting what we know appear mere commonplaces, let us point out alternative views. For we set forth a profoundly conservative theory of universities and their tasks, based on a deeply conservative premise on the character of civilization and society. We do maintain that it is more difficult to keep what we have than to add to what we know. We very much take to heart Professor Ehrenfeld's warning that, if the few old men who know how to work the giant blocks of stone die without heirs, we shall no longer know how to build cathedrals, and, in time to come, when we see them, we shall not even know what they are, the same way, when we see the monstrous statues on Easter Island, we know only to marvel, but at what accomplishment we can not say. Even today, compare the British cathedrals with the towns that they ornament: can these people have built such a thing? Would they imagine such a project, for a thousand years of work? The disjuncture of one civilization, leaving its monuments to another, provokes sad questions indeed.

Then the failure of civilization, the forgetting what we know, looms large in our mind: We can lose what we have but get nothing better. Society defines what is at stake, and risking its slender goods for the main chance threatens utter chaos: "Gone, not outdated, not superseded, not even controversial, not frivolous: a whole continent of important human knowledge gone"! Indeed, so far as civilization finds nourishment in knowledge and understanding — and we can not define civilization without knowledge and understanding — there can be no greater catastrophe than that loss of a continent of human knowledge; that rock that washes out to sea is all the ground we ever had on which to stand.

What, then, we must ask ourselves, does the fact that humanity indeed can forget what it knows dictate for public policy in the here and now? The stakes having been defined in the way we have, the upshot is not to be ignored. And by this point in these pages, readers will know our message: the union of ambitious scholarship with sustaining teaching.

First, our principal task in universities must be the work of rigorous teaching. Make certain the next age can take over what we have learned. At stake in our classroom is the coming generation and its capacity to learn and make sense of knowledge. Therefore, our main effort focuses upon the "how" of learning, by which we mean, upon how our students grasp what we wish to tell them, on the processes by which we turn information into useful knowledge, useful knowledge into understanding -- all through (re)discovery, the recreation of intellect in age succeeding age. That is the hope that sustains us at the beginning of each semester and every course. It is also the hope that, if not wholly realized, also is not entirely disappointed at the end.

The corollary, second, is that the creation of new knowledge is less important than the recapitulation — the retesting, reconstruction, reconstitution — of received knowledge. Most professors most of the time in most universities know little about what it means to create new knowledge. As a matter of fact, it is estimated that two-thirds of all professors have published scarcely a line; of those who publish books, most publish one, few more than one, which means the discovery of new knowledge in the responsible form of a statement for the criticism of others ends with the dissertation; and 95 percent of all scholarly books come from perhaps 5 percent of the scholars. Not only so, but the same studies demonstrate an exact correlation between quantity and quality of publication: those who publish have the good ideas, as the accumulated evidence of influence and agenda-setting the humanities and in the sciences alike demonstrates, and those who do not publish have no ideas worth publishing; *if they did, they would* — harsh, true words.

What this means is that most professors most of the time in most universities find themselves expected to do what few of them have ever done, and fewer still have done more than once. We have therefore to reconsider the entire structure of higher education, and our task is to re-frame our work in such a way that the work people really do — and want to do and often do supremely well — is valued, and that that work is done. Most professors should teach more than they now do; but they also should study more than they now do in order to teach what they themselves must make their own.

Which brings us to three, which is that the recapitulation of received knowledge is not the same thing as the mere repetition of things people think they know, or have heard from others assumed to know what they are talking about. Teaching is now defined in some few, conventional ways. For example, the teacher talks, the students listen. The teacher is the authority, the students inert and passive respondents thereto. Or opinions are exchanged, so that no one is authority, and there is no task but to say what one thinks. For another example, students listen to professors but not to one another, and professors listen to no one but themselves. For a third example, writing lots of things down on paper is taken to demonstrate knowledge and understanding.

But what if teaching is understood in other terms altogether, as engagement in a shared task of learning and understanding and explanation? What if teaching is a form of leading, specifically, of leading by example — follow me! That is, to be sure, a risky path, and it is a way of teaching that fails much more often than it succeeds. For it makes the teacher into the model, rather than the authority, and models are there to be examined and criticized. And that mode of teaching makes the classroom into a laboratory in which mental experiments are undertaken. Since, in this reading of the act of teaching, the professors turns out to be the guinea pig, our call is for us to play a not very inviting role. But it is an honest one, and it is one that serves the best interests of the students.

Fourth and last, if as we claim our task is to echo the natural sounds of knowledge which constitute learning, then some sounds will resonate, others not. Today we make a cacophony of noise; most of what we teach is mere facts, about this and that, and no theory instructs us on what takes precedence, and why some facts are trivial or merely particular. For example, entire areas of learning even now turn out to be made up of an endless series of case studies, yielding no theory, generated by no theory. One such field is ethics; students can study journalistic ethics, medical ethics, legal ethics, universities can even raise money for professorships in all of these subjects. And students can make themselves into an expert in some field of ethics, medical ethics having attracted more than its share of failed careerists and bright-eyed opportunists than any other field of learning in the 1980s, much the counterpart of social science in the 1950s, or computer science in the 1970s.

But these entrepreneurs of learning make things up as they go along. What sounds right to them can be right; there is no theory of the thing they study, because there is no principled inquiry into the foundations of analysis and criticism. Yet we in the West have inherited a tradition of philosophical ethics that comes to us from the Greeks and a tradition of theological ethics that comes to us from ancient Israel through Christianity and Judaism; we have those theories, those principles of decision making, that have laid the foundations for coherent thinking about a cogent subject. When a field can give only examples and cases, its casuistry attests to its intellectual bankruptcy.

The field of medical ethics as currently practiced exemplifies better than any other presently current why charlatans prosper when civilization perishes. One of the great figures in the study of religion in America lectured on medical ethics — not his field of publication — at the University of South Florida. The lecture consisted of stories about tough decisions. A man I like and respect, he got from the senior author a letter saying he had violated the pure food and drug and truth in advertising acts — all in one forty-five minute lecture. He dispensed untested medicine, and he represented himself as knowing what he only intuits from ad hoc impressions — the opposite of knowledge. But the casuistry serves because philosophy is not studied, and by reinventing the wheel, hospital ethicists unwittingly teach a dreadful lesson indeed: what it means to lose the heritage of learning.

So yes, humanity can forget what it knows, and that is so in biology and philosophy, and the costs are there to see at Easter Island, in the ancient glyphs we no longer can read, the languages we cannot speak, and in the areas of learning that are true and useful but no longer accessible. The task of nearly all scholars — for few contribute weighty new truth in any generation — is rarely new knowledge but always the reconsideration of knowledge. When we succeed — and we in universities are the only ones who can do the work — we shall hold on to what we have received, because we shall have made it our own. And that is what we conceive to be the principal work of any generation: to make what has come to us as a gift into something that is our own, that is, something that we too can use: We mean, in our own case, to make learning our own in such a way that we too can learn.

Does Higher Education Have a Future in the American University?

So much for the task of the future and why universities by right claim for themselves the highest priority for public policy in the U.S.A. But what about the prognosis of the future?

Matters clearly have deteriorated so that the very future of universities as they have served is in question. In addressing the future, what concerns us is a more fundamental question than that of the future of universities as we know them. Rather, we take up the future of education, aware that education now and throughout the whole of recorded history has chosen for itself a variety of institutional forms. Of these many possibilities, universities in this country form a rather odd, particular, and special model, not at all commonplace either today or ever before. Let us once more stress: universities as they now flourish are only one institutional form that the higher education has adopted for itself, and it is not the preferred one. Most countries today cannot afford to accord the leisure to study full time to young people from eighteen to twenty-two or three; they are required for the work force, the army, or are expected to support themselves and their families. Those countries that do invest in higher education focus upon technical or scientific learning, for which an immediate vocational purpose is accomplished: pre-vocational training in a sophisticated form, to be sure, but surely, in most areas of higher learning, with a particular job in mind (including that of a schoolteacher).

In fact, most cultures, over most of recorded history, have conducted the tasks of higher education in other ways than we now do. They did not take mature young people and set them apart in colleges organized for the purpose of teaching them outside of the framework of home, family, and the workaday world. Apprenticeship provides a more suitable model than ours in many ways. And in the world today, few nations send for full-time university-level (tertiary) education so high a proportion of their young people of university age. Not only so, but the conception of a university devoted to generalist concerns — the liberal arts B.A. that we take to be the norm — is entirely unknown in most of Europe, which regards university education as specialized and vocational.

So overseas[1] vocationalism defines learning, even if the vocation is merely to become a professor. To take a single example, when religion is studied in the European universities, it is in faculties (that is, departments) of theology, and the students — it is assumed — will go on to become pastors or religion-teachers in secondary schools. Some theology faculties automatically certify their students for Church service, and at least one of them — Göttingen — can appoint only Lutherans on that account (so when the senior writer served as a visiting research professor, he was designated an honorary Lutheran, much as the Japanese in South Africa were classified as honorary whites.) The Churches control theology (as they should), but then, for other than theological purposes, no one studies religion. But in the U.S.A and Canada, religion, a discipline that straddles humanistic and social scientific approaches, flourishes, preparing students for no particular career, but affording them access to a critical component of the social order. Useful knowledge, but not very practical, the study of religion lays the foundation for no career, in the way in which, in European universities, theology does. And when religion, not theology and not holy scripture and its philology, is studied, it is by few students, with scarcely a handful of professors. We excel in the absence of serious competition.

For Western civilization, which alone recognizes the university as a medium for the organization of higher education, and for the imitators of Western civilization, the secondary level of education — the gymnasium or lycée in Germany and France, for instance, and not uncommonly, the "college" in Britain — provides that final layer of general education in the arts and sciences that in this country we apply at the university level. From the perspective of other countries today, ours is a very strange pattern.

We stress that fact so that what is familiar may be seen in a fresh way as a strange and uncommon way of doing things. And that fresh perspective will permit us to consider what it is we think we do when we segregate our young people for four or five years: what goal do we set for their higher education, that we do not set for the main elementary and secondary stages? And only when we have answered that question shall we address the corollary: Are universities as we now know them the best way of accomplishing that goal?

Now what we think students can do in their late teens that they cannot do in their younger years is to transform mere information into real learning, and real learning into understanding. That is, a deeper grasp of the order and structure of information into an enduring mode of thought and reflection. In the primary grades they acquire information and those skills needed for learning: reading, grammar, basic science, and mathematics, for example. In the secondary years they learn how to organize what they know into intelligible patterns and to draw conclusions, to derive propositions, from those patterns. What we can help people do in higher education, then, is make the move from knowing things to grasping what they mean.

By their nature, these observations tend to seem highly abstract, and we immediately offer a concrete statement of the same matter, now in terms of an ordinary experience in the university. We look for our model of authentic higher education to the world of Classical and Christian antiquity, that is, the earliest centuries of the Christian or Common Era. That is for several reasons. First, it is because the educational program of

Classical Christianity defines the institutions and the curricula of Western civilization. Those educational institutions — the universities, from Bologna nine hundred years ago onward — form along with the Catholic Church, on the one side, and the institutions of Judaic learning, on the other, the oldest enduring, continuing institutions of the West and of the world. We turn to Classical Christianity, second, because Christianity defines matters for the largest sector of the world's population today, being the single most numerous religion (Islam is second, and no other organized religion comes close to either). And, third, we ask the Classical tradition of learning to guide us to a statement of why we do what we do, because that tradition has, on its own, made its way to our own times through philosophy and through natural science, not only through faith. Much that we define as culture, therefore, took shape in the age of Classical Christianity, and most of the rest reaches us through that same age.

How, in Classical and Classical-Christian writing, did education for mature people, such as we teach in universities, make its mark? What purpose did it serve, and what did people expect to gain from it? Education sustained life — much as, for religious people, religion does. We find a poignant and affecting answer in the way in which a pagan, an enemy of Christianity, drew upon his education: the uses to which he put his learning. It is the Emperor Julian, who came to the throne of the Roman Empire a Christian but threw off the pretense and reestablished Classical learning in its pagan form as the official cult and culture of Rome. In the fourth century of Christianity, he came to power. Describing his inner feelings at that time, the great Greek historian, Polymnia Athanassiadis, in her presentation of the Emperor Julian's "Letter to Themistius," which she describes as "very much the product of Julian's particular education," states:

> After the long inner struggle in Gaul and all the uncertainties that had beset him during the march to Constantinople, Julian arrived in the capital as sole emperor, and at last found that there was no longer any external force that could prevent him from beginning to fulfil his mission....Alone, free, and responsible, this sudden realization of his position momentarily frightened him; it was only natural that he should seek to reassert his identity by invoking his only inalienable possession - his education and cultural background. In the midst of despair and loneliness he was thus enabled to feel a strong bond of solidarity with the endless generations of men who, like himself, had had recourse to

Homer and Plato to express their own emotions more fully, and to acquire a deeper consciousness of the conditions of their actual lives...Themistius [to whom Julian wrote]...felt and believed that in a world whose material condition was so exclusively governed by fortune, the only sure possessions that anyone could lay claim to were of either a spiritual or an intellectual order...[2]

Ascending the throne, Julian carried with him models of action in Homer and analytical thought in Plato, to which he could refer in addressing the world before him. He could find his own feelings in the feelings of those classics, he could identify with the attitudes and emotions of men (today we would rightly say men and women) who defined the good life, the truthful thought, the beautiful outcome. They asked tough questions — in the dialogues of Plato, for example — and so he was learned in how to think vigorously and responsibly. They recorded great moments, deep feelings, profound emotions. So he could find in them the precedents he required, not to legitimize but to amplify and deepen, the attitudes and emotions that he felt. He was not the first, nor, for that reason, would he be the last. He formed a link in a chain of mature, wise, and public-spirited persons, who had not to reinvent but to renew the ancient tradition of wisdom and justice and goodness that nourished human civilization.

We refer, then, to that tradition of classicism that the Classics, inclusive of philosophy and natural science, and Christianity and Judaism and Islam (to name the four enduring traditions of intellect that reach us from antiquity and govern our lives today) represent. Those media for the formation of the bond of solidarity with endless generations endow us with what we ourselves cannot invent and do not have to: the way of expressing our own emotions more fully, to form a deeper consciousness of the conditions of our actual lives. We take the conception of classicism to be the notion that we have at our disposal models and examples, and choices others have taken up, moments at which others have endured what we now endure, felt what we feel, hoped for what we hope — and left us the record for our edification and enlightenment. Classicism means we are not the first, therefore we also will not be the last.

What justifies higher education as we pursue it in America is the correspondence between the mature age of our students, the kinds of choices of life and career that rightly occupy them, with the mature character of those classical records of human experience, preserved in philosophy and science, in literature and history, in religion and in the arts, in every corner of the curriculum of the liberal arts. What we teach in Miss Athanasiadis's words is how through the received records of human experience we and our students may learn "to express their own emotions more fully, and to acquire a deeper consciousness of the conditions of their actual lives." That forms a profoundly constructive conception of higher education. It is a conception that, at its foundations, insists learning must change the learner — a conception worthy of the Great Tradition formed of philosophy, Judaism, Christianity, Islam, and Buddhism, with their rich experience of learning aimed at personal transformation (and illumination or salvation). Because of what we know, we must be different from what we were before we knew it, from what we might have been if we did not know. That forms a conception of knowledge as not information alone, but information as a tool for reform and renewal: knowledge as a medium of transformation. It is an enormous and surprising conception of what it means to know. And it also forms the definition of what we we do when we teach.

What We Mean by the Classics of Learning

Having described this notion — the classicism of higher education as the medium for the transmission of civilization's entire heritage of intellect and learning — as we have, we may well be asked whether in insisting upon the classical character of learning, we impose also a more specific sense of that same word. Do we mean, Classical as limited to Greek and Latin writings? or perhaps we mean to eliminate from the curriculum those new humanities and new social sciences for which a place has been found only just now; namely humanities represented by the Afro-American heritage or the heritage of Israel, the Jewish people; the social sciences recast to encompass women as well as men? In other words, does classical encompass the advent of perspectives upon human experience other than those deemed normative and exclusive a generation ago? Should not the old canon take its leave, the new books take over?

Political convention demands the answer, "yes indeed." But academic discipline requires the answer, "it depends." The academy bears responsibility to its own deepest convictions, which encompass old and new alike and call all to judgment before a single standard. Dead white European males, as much as living African-American females, gain a hearing only if they deserve it, and vice versa. By what criteria?

Afrocentrists, Jewish or feminist studies (to name three prominent representatives of the new humanities and the new social sciences) bring into the curriculum the classical records of a different heritage from the familiar one, they provide a wider range of models, a broader selection of experience, to which we may refer in deepening our own. That opening represents a natural step within the classical philosophy of education. It is not a merely political decision, forced upon an unwilling university; it is not a mere accommodation to the advent of new voices. As our received curriculum at its best replicated that sense for "a strong bond of solidarity with the endless generations of men who, like himself, had had recourse to Homer and Plato to express their own emotions more fully, and to acquire a deeper consciousness of the conditions of their actual lives," so our opening curriculum, properly formulated, may realize in new ways an ancient and established ideal.

To be sure, all recognize, and many deplore, that the advent of new traditions of learning now suffer from the formation of special truths for different sectors. In place of integration, comes self-segregation for blacks — and at the intellectual level at that. In place of a free, wholly accessible society, universities find themselves asked to sponsor self-celebration amid self-ghettoization for the Jews. And, rolling in endowment money for chairs in Jewish studies (defined by the donors in ethnic, not cultural, terms to begin with), university administrations can't say no. In place of advancing propositions of general intelligibility relevant to all, the claim for women, for example, of a special perspective that only insiders can appreciate corrupts academic discourse. These common results of the advent of the new humanities contradict our thesis. But they do not have to. By the nature of what is taught, they ought to enrich, not impoverish; include, not exclude; celebrate the possibilities of us all, rather than indulge the sensibilities of only a few.

So much for higher education. How about the American university? Does higher education as we have defined it — an institution which changes people, giving students the power to enrich successive decades of their lives — have a future in the university as we know it? The conventional answer, we reckon, is no, for it is now easy to dismiss universities as corrupted by special pleading, attenuated by the sloth of professors, and irreparably damaged by the politicization of entire fields of learning. Universities face the consequences of the demand that they take upon themselves tasks of social engineering, with professors to serve as highly paid (but untrained) social workers. In such a system, education is set aside in favor of good feeling, and the desired emotions are given priority over rigorous demands for accuracy, erudition, and clarity. Those antiintellectual, deeply political forces have taken over the elite sector of the American campus and have destroyed the usefulness of universities as we know them.

Surrendering Classicism

Entire fields of learning have given up classicism in their own subjects and adopted the style of the moment. How can we insist, as we do, that higher education (in the terms we have defined) looks forward to a solid and distinguished future in our universities when fields of learning have themselves abandoned all that was enduring in their own traditions? Certainly the obvious example, in the context of this argument, comes to us from the study of literature. It is no caricature to claim that in literature courses, the style of the day rules. The field now cannot distinguish literature from other writing; it cannot define the excellent from the ordinary; it cannot even say what it conceives beautiful writing to be. Everybody's opinion is as good as everyone else's, and no one can define a thing. Now, one may ask, if the professor of literature cannot tell us what literature is, or why one thing is art and another is not, or what a poem means, or why a novel works, then what has that professor to teach? And what has that field — English, for example — to say to the future? The answer is nothing. Some fields at this time have lost all claim upon the future, having announced they have nothing to say. When professors of literature deny there is any such thing as literature, even no such thing as an author's purpose, students hear their message and make their choices — and in the end, so will the consensus of the academy, and those who support it.

The very notion of classicism insists upon the possibility of learning from others; the conception that in Plato or Homer (for the Emperor, Julian) we find models for ourselves rests upon the insistence, that there is something to be taught, and something to be learned from the past, that transcends the here and now and takes priority over the subjective and the personal. That is the very essence of the classical ideal of learning: words available from some other time and some other place can make sense of the here and now. We revert to Athanasiadis's statement, "In the midst of despair and loneliness he was thus enabled to feel a strong bond of solidarity with the endless generations of men who, like himself, had had recourse to Homer and Plato to express their own emotions more fully, and to acquire a deeper consciousness of the conditions of their actual lives." Now some fields of learning have declared themselves bankrupt — both intellectually and morally — by denying the enduring heritage of wisdom and learning that has been theirs to inherit. They say, in the trenches in World War I, educated British officers recited Shakespeare to their troops. They say, in the foxholes of World War II, learned Christians recited the Bible. From day to day, Torah-sayings illumine the everyday for literate Jews. That is what it means to inherit a classical tradition and find nourishment in it. It is one way; to be sure, there are many others.

Literature now gives up the conception of art that can be defined; today's philosophy for a time abandons the perennial issues, the very continuity of thought, that marked the field as the glory of learning; even history is itself unable to explain to itself why anyone should want to know what historians work so hard to find out and to tell us. So these fields in the humanities give up their ancient vocation, but find no enduring new one. And, like the once-influential universities that today become a chorus of hissing cynics about truth, the Stanfords and Dukes and Browns, once-prominent places lose their sense of purposefulness for teaching something. The required courses of Stanford match the weird innovations of postmodernism at Brown: they form an antieducation and inculcate in students contempt for learning.

And yet, people will learn. And they will draw conclusions. The curriculum evolves, and subjects come and go. There was a time in which geography was not a university subject, though in a still earlier age it had been; today it moves once more to the center of things, having found urgent questions to explore. History was once the single most popular major of the humanities and social sciences. Today it meets competition, and historians lose their grasp upon their work, failing to explain its value. Universities close departments of sociology, Afro-American studies, anthropology, religion; but they open departments too; molecular biology and computer science, for instance. So just as once prestigious universities have lost their way, so once central fields in the liberal arts curriculum lose their claim.

And there is a reason for the rise and fall of universities and of fields of learning in universities. What is at stake in higher education proves too weighty to allow self-celebration without solid achievement. What is at stake in higher education proves too urgent to allow self-indulgence, descent into triviality and subjectivity that have made a public mockery of once august fields of learning, English and history, for instance. What is at stake in learning is the power of humanity to draw upon not only its own experience but the accumulated wisdom of the ages — all for support in facing its every day and its here and now. We have too deep a need to know to allow institutions to keep us ignorant, or fields of learning to impose falsehoods onto fact. Anyone who wants to dismiss classicism — broadly construed, widely defined — better have something of value to put in its place.

And, so far, it is clear, few fields of learning and few universities find themselves persuaded to give up the traditions of higher learning and are compelled to adopt what many now find shrill and trivial. Feminist critiques of the sciences have yet to make a plausible case amongst scientists, and feminist physics shows how silly these idealogues can get. As long as most fields of learning and most universities stand their ground and keep their sense, higher education can look toward a long future in the American university. And, therefore, the American university may look forward to a long and influential future for itself, both here at home and throughout the world. The silliness will cease, the great work will endure. In the half-century of the Cold War, nothing, really, has changed all that much. That is because, in the end, people really are not stupid. They are smart. That is what it means to be made in the image of God, "in our image, after our likeness," the very model of the holy intellect.

Why Universities Are Distinct from All Other Centers of Learning—and the Difference a Distinction Makes

Now, as we draw our argument to a conclusion, we turn to the basic definition of the institution — as distinct from the function: What exactly do we mean by a university? And how is a university different from every other type of learning? The answer to these questions will sustain the optimistic convictions — the map of the middle of the road that has just been set forth.

Now defining universities presents difficulties, even though we argue that its indicative trait flourishes in the forms of research, publication, and teaching. For universities are old, and having changed many times, have to reflect on what has lasted. To define a university we obviously cannot point to the buildings, or even the place on which they stand. For the university originally had no fixed location, and few buildings stand for the entire history of a university, from the beginning to the present. So a university is not a place. Lectures were given wherever they were given. Nor do we point to what was taught over time. For the content of learning changed, in the nature of things, and so too did the categories. So a university is not a particular set of subjects that are studied, or that are studied in one way rather than in some other. The issue of distinction now stands forth in stark clarity. To define a university we do not point to a place, however old. We do not invoke a single tradition of learning, however deeply rooted in generations of successive masters and disciples. Nor do we even mark a long-enduring subject, whether law, or religion, though both law and religion form foci for distinguished intellectual effort in universities over a long period of time.

The senior author has spent his life trying to bring to the university curriculum books that formed the curriculum of ancient and enduring centers of learning long before universities came into being at all, those of Judaism, with its canon, curriculum, and corps of teachers and students. He brought the old and established Judaic canon to the new and still problematical. In 1088, when the University of Bologna, began as the West's oldest university, the Mishnah, a philosophical statement in the form of a law code that bears comparison to Plato's Republic and Aristotle's Politics, was approximately 900 years old, having taken shape toward the end of the second century, and the Talmud half a millennium in antiquity. What this indicates is that humanity puts forward examples of traditions of learning and modes of education that vastly exceed in age and temporal success the age of the university's most ancient foundation. Not only so, but institutions in which the literature of ancient Judaism, beginning with the Mishnah, were studied enjoy a continuous history, if not in one place. The subject for the academy is a very new one. But to that subject and its institutions, even the University of Bologna in its nine hundred years, is very new too, if no longer a mere parvenu.

Nor is the story told by the Mishnah and its successor-writings, the only ongoing tradition of learning that preceded universities. Philosophy, mathematics, music — these unbroken traditions exceed in antiquity the holy books of Judaism. The classics of ancient Greece and Rome may make the same statements in Greek and in Latin as writings in Hebrew and in Aramaic. Most of what we study in universities will see this new, this young, this scarcely-tried institution as a temporary home. And every professor of every subject may find roots to his or her subject of learning, however recent in its contemporary formulation, in the soil of remote antiquity. For mathematics, we now know, dictated the arrangement of the stones at Stonehenge, and the cave drawings in France and Spain, the aboriginal wall-scratchings in Australia, the ruins of the old cities of Africa, the remarkable Mayan monuments of the Yucatan and Aztecs of Middle America and of the Incas of the Andes. These legacies show reflection, judgment, proportion, taste, composition: philosophy and the art of science. And all these traditions of learning, each with its precision and its canons of rationality, every one of them flourished in intellect and in heart, but, for most of the history of humanity, not in universities.

When, therefore, we contemplate the future of the academy our task is to remember not how old, but how new, this sort of place really is: A river always flowing, always changing. Take the water out of the river and you have the banks, and they are, more or less, permanent. But then you have no river anymore. Everyone here, in every tradition of human knowledge, stands for something that was pursued in other contexts than the university, under other circumstances than this one, and in the service of different needs from the ones that sustain and support universities as we know them. If, as humanity can forget what it knows, still, knowledge transcends institutions of a temporal character, and all learning transcends its auspices. Learning recognizes no limitations of an institutional sort. Learning is so natural to humanity that, in the end, it requires nothing more than intellect driven by curiosity and sustained by speculation. Accordingly, we have to ask ourselves what it is that marks as distinctive and as valuable the university as we have known it for the brief spell commencing nine hundred years ago in this place, among the ancestors of this people.

The university is unique not because it is old, for it is young. It is not because the program of learning, the curriculum, is stable, because it proves to be ephemeral, subject to change that, against the backdrop of the hundred-thousand-year history of humanity, happens routinely. And it is not because the university is the best place in which to pursue curiosity and to sort things out, for that remains to be demonstrated, especially when we consider that nearly all of the great intellectual achievements in the history of humanity took place outside of universities and were the accomplishments of persons who were not professors.

If we point to the formative intellects of the world as we know it, Darwin, Freud, Marx — none of them professors — to name only three, we must wonder who needs universities at all. For clearly, the great intellectual steps forward in the natural and social sciences were taken somewhere else, on the *Beagle*, or in the imagination of a despised Viennese

Jew, or in the hall of the British Museum, open to a lowly foreign journalist. Not only so, but one of the most ancient and continuous traditions of learning in humanity, Talmud study, was carried to levels of intellectual sophistication by men who suffered privation in all ways but one, the intellectual, and who were supported by their wives — clearly not the model of the modern-day university. And, to take a contrary case, until two generations ago, American universities formed bastions of special privilege and class interest, conferring not so much learning as status. Today it honors not so much wisdom and intelligence as correct gender, skin tone, and religion.

What makes the distinction of universities, and confers upon them purpose is this: We assemble in universities to treat learning as shared, plural, open, and diverse. What we institutionalize in universities is the possibility of shared discourse and public exchange of knowledge among different people who know different things and who seek to find a language common to those different things. What it means to study, in some one place, mathematics and botany, or sociology and religion, is that we judge it better to study these things in one place than in many places. And in the end, though not every day, that judgment releases the power to explain many things in a few ways. If chemistry did not speak to geology, or physics to mathematics, or economics to political science, then the premise of the university that learning many things helps us to understand them all in some cogent way would prove flawed. But it is not flawed, for, as we know, economics without mathematics, and political science without history, and anthropology without psychology, are not possible. Learning flows across disciplinary lines, to the discomfort of the limited and the specialized, because humanity will not stay within bounds. The analytical mind in mathematics, in times past turned to measure the dimensions of God. For some generations the pursuit of a unique truth requires the diversity of knowledge. And so throughout: there are no limits to mind and imagination.

It is this same quest to understand and make sense of things that is natural to our condition as human beings. And understanding means putting many things together in some few ways. The mathematicians at Stonehenge had to make many observations, gather accurate facts beyond number, to know how, at just one moment in the cycle of the solar year, light would enter one space of the temple, and not some other, and continue in one line, though not in any other. And those same mathematicians at Stonehenge had also to want to mark that moment, had to believe it mattered in so profound a way that the energies of an entire society, over a long period of time, could be invested in nothing better than the realization of that magic circle of stones that embodied the facts they put together. When we consider the caves in Ireland, the temples in Middle America, where, at some solar moment, a sliver of light strikes some one point on a flat rock, then but at no other time, when we contemplate the calculations in mathematics, the engineering skills, required to make a temple or dig a hole in such a way that, just then, things would be this way, we realize what has always been at stake in learning. It is not the fact naked and celebrated in its raw state, but the fact ennobled by a sense of its universality and by its implicit reference to many other facts.

In universities we draw together many disciplines or fields of learning, in quest not for information but explanation and understanding. What this means for those of us who study the particularities of a single human group, the Jews through time, or the Classics, or the anthropology of a tribe or the sociology of a class, is simple. We all learn a great deal about some one thing. But only when we can intelligibly address others, who know a great deal about something else, are we able to join in that mode of discourse that marks the university as singular and unique. It is when we aim to face problems in common, and try to explain many things using some few facts, that we join universities and belong nowhere but in universities. There we find our distinction, or unique purpose.

And how are we to do this? It is by treating the particular as exemplary, the unique as typical. When we see knowledge as suggestive, as information that can be explored in diverse ways, and then offer useful examples for the testing of hypotheses of common interest, then we form universities. For how we treat knowledge indicates where we are. If we learn only for ourselves, we may be wise, but that is not the mark of those who should, or do, spend their lives in a university.

For the senior author this task has not been accomplished without difficulty. The history and literature and religion of the Jews lay no credible claim to uniqueness in telling the story of humanity under stress, for Jews are not unique in suffering, nor in loyalty, nor in endurance, nor in hope, though they have special lessons to teach about the power of humanity to endure despite and against great adversity indeed. But there is something characteristic of the intellectual tradition of the Jews, the particular tradition to which he has devoted his life, that he thinks does have a distinctive contribution to make to public discourse in the university. It is an example of that very activity that the university is meant to nurture, seeing things whole, all together, and within a single, unifying theory of explanation.

All forms of learning display a quest for connections, an explanation of many things. In the canon of Judaism, that quest is shared. For that canon makes the effort to put together everything worth knowing and to explain it all in some one way. Providing an account of the formation of the world and the history of humanity, telling the story of everything, that remarkable canon, represented by the culminating statement of the Talmud of Babylonia, provides us with an example of what a university can comprise and compose: Everything put together, all at once, in a cogent way, in a single intelligible statement. In its odd context, that document and the writings it holds together form a singular instance of what it means for learning to come together into a single system of understanding, for facts to yield a rationality, and for data all together and all at once to make sense.

Our work of learning in the particular kind of institution that we form in universities is different from others: the intent is not merely to describe but to explain, and to explain a fact not on its own, but in relationship to everything else. True, appeals to perennial philosophy and to encompassing explanations differ from here to there, with the result that there are, after all, diverse disciplines within the university. The diversity of the university is as critical to the definition as the unity of learning in cogent explanation that marks the academic intellect but no other. No one can imagine — although we in the university try — a single inherited system that holds things all together all at once and can make sense of everything.

The framers of the Talmudic canon put together all knowledge, as they identified worthwhile knowledge, and they explained everything they knew in some one way. They produced not an encyclopaedia of knowledge but a single coherent and cogent statement of what they knew, set forth in a cogent and proportioned way. It was their theory of the whole, all together and all at once. When we in the university can do that, we shall also have founded a tradition of learning that will endure, as theirs has endured. That is our task, and failing to succeed completely, in trying to meet the goal, we do something few have ever done.

Epilogue: To Generation XIII

With so vivid a faith in the academy's enduring value to our country, we turn toward the future. For we have no doubt that universities will take a critical place in American civilization for the long age to come — if it knows its role. If the senior author could come back to life to celebrate the nation's tricentennial and could speak to the college students of that generation, what would he offer? Here is a message that at once recapitulates what from the wisdom of the centuries teaches us, and also what the senior author has learned out of the long career as a teacher and publishing scholar.

In fact he should repeat precisely what he said to the freshman class at Brown University in freshman week, September, 1972, addressing the class of 1976, the beginning of America's tenth generation of freedom. The message took up the issues burning at the height of the cultural revolution in American higher education. To him that opening week of classes joins all the power and promise of youth with the aspirations and ambitions of age: the students and professors take a long look at what is coming. The promise and the power of that hour, when everything seems new to freshmen and all things seem possible in an American college, set the task at hand.

The very foundations of the university had just then come under assault. Events took place on campus that no one could have anticipated — buildings occupied, libraries and laboratories vandalized, professors and students intimidated. Some thought back to besieged Britain in September, 1940, and wondered what would endure. So, reflecting upon how Churchill saved Britain — rearmed the British spirit — by what he said about blood and sweat, toil and tears, and through the language in which he said it, the senior author wondered what sentences might say all that needed to be said at a difficult time. To counsel beginning students at a ruined university, he sought words to turn crisis into opportunity. He looked to plain words for simple truths in a difficult hour. He had to explain to a new generation what aspects of the worthy past had lasted and what would last — and to define for that new generation a worthy, consequential place in the ongoing work of tradition.

The explanation required not defense, but advocacy, of ideals. For the past dies unless the generation that follows takes up what it considers worthwhile and adopts and makes its own what others have learned. The message of that unsettling time frames what he conceives to be the goal of learning even in more placid times.

The students were many and ready to listen for at least twenty minutes — but no more than that. The room was bright, the sun was in the speaker's eyes; he could scarcely make out faces in the glare. It was just as well. He meant to speak impersonally, with a message of an ancient, ever-renewed world merely to whom it may concern. This is what he said to freshmen as they began their higher education when no one knew for certain the worth of that education. Hear it in the same words he used on that day in 1972, for this is his message, from the end of this difficult century, to the coming age, one that all hope will prove an easier age than ours:

* * *

This week marks the commencement of your four years at this university. My purpose is to introduce those four years.

You come to take your places in an ongoing enterprise, a university. It was here before you came. It probably will be here after you leave. But you can and will make your mark upon it. You can enhance its life, or blight its future. Each generation of faculty, students, and administrators has that power. For universities are fragile. They rise and fall, through periods of excellence and mediocrity. This you already know, for you applied to many universities and colleges and chose the best for you, so you realize that significant differences separate one university from another. We have no truth-in-advertising law to cover universities; they all call themselves by the same name. But the differences are there, and in the next four years, you are one of the givens, one of the data, that will characterize and distinguish this university from others.

But your first impression must be different. As you enter this university, you must perceive yourselves to be the last and least in a long procession of men and women. You see buildings you did not build, a library, carefully nurtured for two hundred years, that you did not create, a faculty you did not assemble, a community you did not form. Everything seems so well established, so permanent. But that impression is illusory.

Just a few years ago students in universities burned and ravaged the buildings designed for their use, closed the libraries, shut down the classrooms. Clearly students have the power to destroy.

By their excellence students also have the power to build. Faculties come to teach the best students they can find; high salaries and pleasant working conditions alone do not suffice to keep talented men and women in universities composed of bored and sullen students. If you are purposeful, if you are mindful, if you are critical, thoughtful, interested students, you will give the university the good name of a place where the life of thought and ideas is fully and richly lived. And within my experience, our university's greatest asset is its students. I cannot exaggerate the excellence, the charm, of the students I have known here, and I do not speak for myself alone.

So do not see yourselves as unimportant. Your coming is important; it is the decisive event of the present. What other generations have created, the wealth they have lavished on this place, the care and concern they have given it, the endowment of centuries, are opportunities now fallen into your hands. Do not waste what other men and women have made. Do not take for granted the unearned increment of the ages. For four years you live on the labor of other, earlier generations, who gave to the future what they in turn had received from the past.

What happens in this university? First, let me say what does not happen. The problems of the world are not going to be solved by you. You are not coming here to make a better world, to improve the condition of humankind, or to solve the problem of poverty. Indeed, the money that society (not to mention your parents) spends on you here is diverted from other worthwhile projects. The endowment of this university could purchase better housing for many of the poor or raise the welfare benefits for many of the needy. But it is set aside so that you, mature men and women perfectly capable of working at some useful and remunerative task, may remain idle. You are kept unemployed, and others have to pay for your keep, so that you may read books, work in labs, listen and talk, write and think.

A university is an expression of a highly aristocratic, anti-egalitarian ideal; It stands for the opposite of the equality of all men and women, for there are inequalities in matters of the mind and spirit. A great many people past and present have set aside their wealth and their energies for the aristocratic ideal that excellent minds have the opportunity for growth and improvement, that the intellect be cultivated. Your years here could just as easily be spent on more socially relevant purposes. You could, after all, take a job and earn a living for yourselves. But you sacrifice that income. Your four years of apparent idleness represent a joint decision, by you and your family and "society," that at the moment it is better to think so that later you may do; it is wiser now to hold back so that later you may go much farther on-ward.

Yet the activity that will not take place at this university — your im-mediate engagement with the great tasks of society — imposes on you an extraordinary struggle: the struggle to postpone easy accomplish-ment and quick distinction. True achievement depends on depth of learn-ing, on capacity for clear thinking, on ability to pursue knowledge where curiosity leads, above all on implacable criticism of all givens. True achievement depends on these things, rather than on the prema-ture acceptance of public responsibility. Young men and women want to go forth, to do great things. We keep you here to study, to think about things. You come full of energy. You would find it natural to take on great tasks. You want nothing less than to sit long hours in the discipline of the mind. To read and write, to argue and expound, to confront the various claims to truth in a sophisticated, critical spirit — these represent stern tests for men and women at your age (or any other). You are called to an unnatural repression of your personal selves, to overcome the natural instincts of your age.

Nothing is so hard as seeing your contemporaries at their life's work and postponing your own. You represent only a small proportion of your age group. The majority will not be with you this fall; many are at work, or at considerably less demanding universities than this one. Nothing is so inviting as picking up the burdens of the world and enter-ing the workaday life, nor so demanding of self-discipline as denying them. You come to learn, not with the curious but empty minds of preteens, but the strength of maturing, able men and women. The con-quest of the self — by overcoming ambition, distraction, and sheer laziness, and by bringing your best abilities to the service of the mind — will prove most satisfying of all conquests for those of you who achieve it. Later on no enemy will prove so difficult as the enemy within. No challenge will prove harder to meet than the one you now meet within yourself. In the university you have now to vanquish the undisciplined impulse to ready yourself for struggle with, for service to, the world.

Above all, if you succeed in acquiring the critical mode of thought that is our ware, you will have the one thing you will need to become im-portant people: the capacity to stand firm in what you think right, in what you propose to accomplish in life. Today you have to postpone the quest for worldly success. Later on that success may not come; you may have to walk quite by yourself. When the world is against you, you will have to rely for strength only upon your own convictions. I speak from experience: The world is not going to give you many satisfactions, especially if you propose to change it. For if you do, you thereby claim things are not yet perfect. What everybody thinks is true really is not so. What everybody wants to do, thinks it right and best to do, is not the best way at all. Great men and women achieve their greatness above the mob, not within it. And they cannot be loved on that account.

The world will love its own, those who tell and do the things reassuring to the mediocre. Here you begin to struggle with the given, with the natural, with how you feel and how your friends feel. Do not expect the success that comes from easy accomplishment and ready recognition. What will justify the effort if all there is before you is defeat and renewed struggle? You must not learn to expect success in order to justify your efforts. You must learn to need only to think the effort necessary, whatever the outcome. Great things are not accomplished by the shouters but by the workers. But to learn to work — that is a hard task indeed.

I have said what will not happen here. What then does happen here? Only one achievement makes worthwhile the years and money you devote to your university education: You should learn to ask questions and to find the answers to them. Everything else is frivolous, peripheral, for the shouters and the headline chasers. And a great many of the questions you will ask and learn to answer are irrelevant to shouting and to headlines.

Now, what are these questions? They are not the generalities but the specificities, not the abstractions but the concrete and detailed matters that delimit the frontiers of knowledge. Do not ask, what is a human being? or What is truth? or What is history? or What is biology? Your teachers may give you answers to these great questions, but the answers are routine. And your teachers cannot tell you the value of the answer. What we want is only to know: not necessarily how to harness atomic energy, but about energy and matter, not necessarily how to "cure cancer," but about the nature of living matter. Notice I did not say we seek the truth but only the truth about . . . I mean to emphasize the tentativeness, the modesty, the austerity of our work. I begin, after all, as a critic of my own perceptions; only then do I criticize those of others. In what I do I seek to know the limits of knowledge, to define just what is factual about the facts purportedly in my hands. For the asking of questions, the seeking of answers, begins in a deep skepticism. If I thought we knew all we need to know, what should I find to ask? The asking of questions is a subversive activity. It subverts accepted truths, the status quo.

Your teachers here do not propose to tell you what is generally agreed upon as the truth about this or that subject. In this regard you must not assume they are like your teachers in high school or prep school, teachers who were responsible for communicating established knowledge, for teaching you what is already agreed upon. Your teachers in college are different because they are actively engaged in the disciplined study and questioning of the given. They are trying to find out new things, trying to reassess the truth of the old. The high school teacher you already know tends to take for granted the correctness of what he or she tells you. The teachers here are going to ask whether what they tell you is so, how they claim to know it, and, above all, how they have found it out. They are active participants in learning, not passive recipients and transmitters of other people's facts. How they think, how they analyze a problem, therefore, is what you have to learn from them. It is all they have to teach you. What they think you probably can find out in books, mine or someone else's. Why they think so — this alone they can tell you. Before now, in high school, the result of learning was central. Here, in college, the modes and procedures of thinking are at issue.

I said earlier that what makes your years here important is the asking of questions and the finding of answers. But there is a second important process, flowing from the first, in which you must learn to participate: the process of communication It is not enough to have found ways of thought. One has to express them as well. As the great Yale historian, Edmund S. Morgan, says, "scholarship begins in curiosity, but it ends in communication." You do not need to justify asking questions. But if you think you have found answers, you do not have the right to remain silent. I do not guarantee people will listen to you. The greater likelihood is that they will ignore what they do not understand or vilify what they do not like. Nevertheless, you are not free from the task of saying what you think. This will take two forms, and you must master both writing and speaking. You must learn to express your ideas in a clear and vigorous way. You must do this both in writing and in discussions in the classroom (and outside as well). I promise you that your teachers will give you many opportunities to exercise and improve your skills at both.

On the importance of communicating ideas as the center of the educational experience, let me again quote Edmund Morgan:

> Communication is not merely the desire and responsibility of the scholar; it is his discipline....Without communication his pursuit of truth withers into eccentricity. He necessarily spends much of his time alone.... But he needs to be rubbing constantly against other minds.... He needs to be made to explain himself.... The scholar... needs company to keep him making sense... people to challenge him at every step, who will take nothing for granted.

> Morgan said these words to a freshman class at Yale, and he ended, "In short, he needs you."

And this brings me back to where I started, your importance to this university. You are our reason for being, not because you will listen passively and write down uncritically, but because without you there is no reason to speak or to write. What happens in the classroom is not the impersonal delivery of facts, but the analysis of possibilities and probabilities by concerned people, teacher and student alike. Learning is not a passive process. A timid person cannot learn. An impatient person cannot teach. Learning is a shared experience. Without students, who is a teacher? More than the calf wants to suck the mother's milk, the cow wants to suckle that calf. I do not mean to suggest you have nothing to do but sit back, hear what a teacher has to say, and announce why he or she is wrong or why you do not agree. That childish conception bears slight resemblance to what is to be done. I mean you have to learn things for your part, and ask questions of your own perceptions, as much as of your teacher's: It is a shared quest, a collective skepticism.

What is the measure of success? How will you know, in four years, whether or not you have wisely spent your time here? First, you should have a good grasp of one specific field of learning, not solely the data of such a field, though they are important, but the way that field works, how specialists think within it, and why.

Second, you should have mastered three skills that mark the educated man and woman: how to listen attentively, how to think clearly, and how to write accurately. To be sure, the modes of thought and the means of writing or other forms of expression will differ from one field to the next. But in general all modes of thought and expression will exhibit a concern for accuracy, clarity, precision, order, lucid argumentation.

Third, you should feel slightly discontented, discontented with yourselves and therefore capable of continued growth; discontented with your field at work and therefore capable of critical judgement and improvement; discontented with the world at large and therefore capable of taking up the world's task as a personal and individual challenge.

You come not merely to spend four years in a world you have not made and for which you therefore do not bear responsibility. You come to join and build a community, a community of scholars. If the experience of community is meaningful to you, you will, wherever you may be, never really leave it. You will continue to participate in the scholarly enterprise — asking questions, finding answers, telling people about them.

* * *

If the two authors of this book had to summarize our notion of how learning takes place in the academy in a few words, these are the words that, predictably, we should choose to say to students, conventional and otherwise: (1) don't ask, discover, therefore (2) take responsibility for your life and your mind, so that (3) you will live a well-examined life.

Other institutions in society set for themselves the goal of turning out better or healthier human beings, churches and synagogues and hospitals for example. Some do a better job of helping people die, hospices, for instance. But none takes responsibility for the heritage of learning that the West has stored up, nor does any other insist on its unique duty to educate, that is, in the formal classroom, laboratory, and library, to transmit that treasure to the coming generation. We of the academy do that best, and no one else does it at all. No one.

True, no other enduring institution of the social order fails to realize its ideals so commonly or so miserably as we have in the past decades and even now. But, over time, think too of the successes!

Notes

1. We do not claim to know the situation in Latin America or in Africa apart from South Africa or in Asia. We speak from direct knowledge of the Antipodes (Australia, New Zealand), North America, and Western Europe. But apart from local conditions and local traditions, for example, ethnography of Indian village life or Hindu religious texts and Sanskrit in India, who goes to India to study anything at all? And apart from Hebrew language and archaeology, why should anybody pursue an advanced degree in the state of Israel? Even in Jewish studies, where they are supposed to excel, they staff their university faculties with Americans and Canadians. To take an example out of the mainstream, Americans rarely go to business school in Japan, but for that schooling Japanese gladly come to MIT and Harvard. So, as we argued just now, the world makes its judgment that, for all our failures, we succeed at our fundamental task. Would that our critics, Sykes, Kimball, D'Souza, had taken note of that fact and asked, not only when we fail why we fail, but also when we succeed, why we succeed.

2. Athanassiadi, Polymnia. *Julian, An Intellectual Biography* (Rutledge, 1992), pp. 94-5.

Epilogue

The Major Matters Most of All

Scholarship: Intellectual Specialization in Higher Education

In the view of contemporary critics, the intellectual specialization represented by disciplinary study is the source of higher education's shortcomings—the academy's equivalent of original sin. Critics complain that American college curricula have become diffuse and aimless, that colleges lack a sense of community, and that professors teach neglectfully and too little (Kimball). They blame scholarly specialization for the disciplinary loyalties, cloistered departmentalism, and fragmented curricula that allegedly rob college learning of shared goals, values, and meaning. They charge that specialized knowledge creates a culture of limited expertise, which artificially constricts the curriculum, suppresses diversity and alternate ways of knowing, and produces authoritarian and impersonal teaching. The critique of specialization carries with it a deep suspicion of the faculty's professionalization, particularly as it is manifest in the culture, and perhaps the practice, of research. In 1985, the Association of American Colleges' report, Integrity in the Undergraduate Curriculum, summed up all these concerns most succinctly: "the development that overwhelmed the old curriculum and changed the entire nature of higher education was the transformation of the professors from teachers concerned with the characters and minds of their students to professionals, scholars with Ph.D. degrees with an allegiance to academic disciplines stronger than their commitment to teaching or to the life of the institutions where they are employed" (p. 6).

On the grounds that specialization is the root of our educational ills, many reform proposals in the eighties advanced structured core curricula or programs of general education as primary ways to integrate under-graduate learning and thereby develop and nurture community. For example, Lynne V. Cheney's *50 Hours: A Core Curriculum for College Students* (1989) recommended a required program of sixteen semester courses, extending through the junior year, with the claim that, among other benefits, a required core brings "needed order and coherence" to undergraduate learning (p. 2) and "provides a context for forming the parts of education into a whole" (p. 12). Likewise, Ernest Boyer's *College: The Undergraduate Experience in America* (1997) advocated an "integrated core," extending over four years to give students "a more integrated view of knowledge and a more authentic view of life" by over-coming "the fragmentation and specialization of the academy" (pp. 90-91).

This volume takes a different approach to the problem of liberal education at the turn of the millennium. The writers maintain that what matters in higher learning is learning. They deny that scholarship detracts from teaching, or that good teaching can go forward without scholarly substance. In taking that view, they deal with the realities of the campus. Since World War II, academic disciplines have become "the principal, even exclusive way, to organize legitimate curricula and faculty professional work" (Weaver, 1991, p. 25). Whether we like it or not, the professional mission of most contemporary faculty members is shaped largely by a field of knowledge, an area of study. Whether we like it or not, disciplinary professionalism, more than any other factor, fixes the divisions within contemporary college curricula, programs, and courses. To be sure, the professoriate created these conditions and could move to change them. But such pervasive undoing of the world's most ambitious and successful system of higher learning seems unlikely, surely for the near term. Instead of trying to dismantle the foundations of the faculty's professionalism, this volume asks what will happen if we build on them. Instead of devising programs that countervail against intellectual specialization, it explores if, and how, the college faculty's disciplinary professionalism can become a vehicle to achieve educational goals traditionally associated with liberal learning. Hence, instead of addressing the curriculum in general, the authors focus on the learning in particular that distinguish college from high school.

The difference lies in particular in the concentrated study in and of a field of knowledge, the major. So my contribution to the discussion inaugurated here concerns the major in particular: what would it mean to make the major into a primary - perhaps the primary - path to a liberal education? At least three basic changes in the accepted practice and purpose of college study would result. First, placing the major at the center of liberal education calls into question the established categories of general and specialized learning in college study. Second, a focus on the major shifts the center of curricular and educational change from the college to the department. Finally, from the standpoint of the major, the distinctive mark of liberal education is less the study of many subjects than an attitude about learning, a resourcefulness grounded in awareness of where knowledge comes from and how it is made. These themes inform the arguments that follow.

Why General Education Isn't

The move to reconceive the major rather than to rejuvenate (yet again!) general education is not merely a concession to the faculty's disciplinary professionalism. Rather, general education, as conventionally understood, can neither theoretically nor practically address the problems of intellectual fragmentation, the lack of community, and neglectful teaching that critics think afflict American higher education. There are reasons that general studies cannot make college learning whole.

To begin, consider how disparate from one another the fields of learning really are. A review of Stephen Toulmin's nearly classic theoretical description of "the variety of rational enterprises," which covers most of the fields and subjects typically taught and studied in college, makes the divisions plain (1972, pp. 359-411). Toulmin explains that a "rationally developed 'discipline'" emerges when a "shared commitment to a sufficiently agreed set of ideas leads to the development of an isolable and self-defining repertory of procedures; and where those procedures are open to further modification, so as to deal with problems arising from the incomplete fulfillment of those disciplinary ideals." Toulmin trenchantly distinguishes among "compact disciplines," "diffuse disciplines," "would-be disciplines," and "non-disciplinary activities." Compact disciplines, such as atomic physics, are methodologically and institutionally coherent. They exhibit a high level of agreement about collective ideals, procedures, modes of argument, and criteria of adequacy, and they have efficient professional meetings and organizations. Sub-fields within compact disciplines are likely to be pragmatic and procedural, and specialized journals contain a "substantial amount of cross-citation." In contrast, diffuse and would-be disciplines, which include most of the social sciences and humanities, often are loosely organized professionally and lack "a clearly defined, generally agreed reservoir of disciplinary problems." These characteristics thwart consistent critical testing of new concepts and procedures. Diffuse and would-be disciplines may "even lack common standards for deciding what constitutes a genuine problem, a valid explanation, or sound theory." In these fields, Toulmin argues, theoretical debate is "largely...methodological or philosophical...directed less at interpreting particular empirical findings than at debating the general acceptability (or unacceptability) of rival approaches, patterns of explanation, and standards of judgment." Subdisciplines in these areas tend to be ideological, even sectarian, and cross-citation is relatively infrequent.

In non-disciplinary activities, where Toulmin classifies such fields as fine arts and ethics, "the very questions at issue are liable to be more complex, changeable, or even personal, than in a normal discipline. As a result, both the ecological demands of the particular situation and the criteria for judging conceptual novelties will be that much the less well-defined, settled, or agreed."

The most common model of general education offers students experience in a number of fields across the disciplinary spectrum, but Toulmin's analysis shows why this approach is an unlikely vehicle for integrated learning. How could a wide and necessarily superficial sampling among disciplines so disparate in intellectual endeavor, requirement, and habit produce intellectual unity, especially at the beginning of a college education? Many institutions recently have addressed this difficulty by developing integrated core courses designed to generate an intellectual commonality by supplying students with a shared set of learned references. But such commonality, a faculty's considered but unavoidably arbitrary construction, hardly qualifies as integrated learning for the student. It builds on faculty expertise in discrete fields, on precisely what students do not know and cannot know from a small sample of courses. A general problem in such programs is that the discrete pieces do not connect with one another. More important, they rarely connect with programs of specialized study, the one thing the students come to know well. General education cannot supply comprehensive coherence to an entire college education. It can produce order, but not meaning.

Moreover, general education is only general with respect to some particular. The very meaning of general is relative. Prescribed general education programs typically are no less restrictive than are programs of study in discrete fields. They are just restrictive in different ways. A "great books" curriculum may seem "general" with respect to literature or history, but it also seems narrow and specialized with respect to physics or computer science. General education can be broadening in the best sense (captured by an alumna at the University of Rochester, where I teach, who wrote, "That poetry course I had to take showed me a part of myself I didn't know was there"), but it also can be limiting and dulling (a current Rochester student complained, "I had to take a French course to satisfy my language requirement, and that made me put off an economics course that really interested me. I'm turned off to French for good!").

Even if general education does provide a common set of references for students and faculty - and only the most structured, and thus restrictive, programs do - it is a cumbersome vehicle for the development of community. Because general studies does not reflect the faculty's own graduate education, the institutional effort necessary to develop and maintain a general education program is disproportionate to the program's impact on students' learning. Often, faculty who work to develop or substantially revise general education requirements and programs are enervated by the process, and the task of sustaining the program over time falls to the administration, the campus unit least well equipped for it. A field of knowledge represents a cluster of problems, a set of data, and a heritage of curiosity that can form a discourse and define a community of inquiry. General education cannot constitute an area of knowledge because it was invented as an antidote to specialized study - that is, general education is cast only in terms of what it is not. As conventionally practiced, general education can provide students essential, valuable, and enriching exposure to unfamiliar fields and methods, and it can lead students to subjects they otherwise might have bypassed, but it can neither anchor a curriculum nor secure its overall coherence. Our preoccupation with general education has distracted us from the real foundation of undergraduate study - the major.

From College to Department

The limitations of general education as a solution to the problems of fragmentation and diminished community justify a new look at departments as centers of learning. The conception of the major as participation in a knowledge community and its discourse forces fresh attention on the faculty groups that constitute the actual community and the concrete discourse that students encounter.

Typically, though not always, academic departments reflect scholarly disciplines and the purpose of disciplinary professionalism is to foster and facilitate research. Hence, a department's intellectual mission is likely to be shaped heavily, if not primarily, by its field's research agenda. If the major is to become a foundation of liberal education, the department's intellectual mission must be transformed into an educational one. But such a transformation requires understanding the department as more than a gathering of scholars and researchers and conceiving the major as more than a set of up-to-date courses. It means reinventing the department as a teaching and learning collective, in which the faculty, through collaboration with one another and with students, creates programs of study that draw students into learning both within and about a field of knowledge. If we are to use the major as a path to liberal learning, we need to realize the educational potential of disciplinary professionalism.

Hostility to disciplinary professionalism has obscured the contribution of specialized study to the goals of liberal education. An academic discipline forms the intellectual setting that nurtures a lifetime of learning, and it constitutes the forum in which new thinking is tested and assessed. Disciplines are loci of both criticism and self-criticism. They provide the context of public accountability for analysis, research, and interpretation, a framework of thought and knowledge essential for the crucial task of distinguishing insight from idiosyncrasy. Disciplines represent heritages of curiosity, and they are the concrete manifestations of shared interests. As they appear on discrete campuses in the form of departments, programs, committees, or the equivalent, the disciplines offer precisely the ingredients of intellectual community that American college education is now widely believed to lack.

Disciplinary professionalism also is essential to good teaching. Many traits make for good college teaching, but primary among them is knowing something very well. The current preoccupation with enrollments and retention - the consequence of severe market pressures - has led to a widespread confusion between instruction and student-centeredness, between teaching well and paying attention to (and spending time with) undergraduates. These activities are not the same. The professoriate is more than a helping profession, and college teachers are not mere facilitators. Professing implies expertise. Only by knowing something very well can we convey to students its force and appeal. We cannot represent the power of the varied realms of inquiry and discourse we want students to encounter unless we are deeply engaged with those realms ourselves. We cannot show them how knowledge is discovered, invented, constructed, and evaluated without laboring at it ourselves. In teaching, there is a small distance but a world of difference between critically passing on the work of others, which is most of what we do in the classroom, and passing critical opinions about work we have not done and could not do. Only the former teaches respect for learning. Thus, even the ever-popular interdisciplinary studies assume disciplinary competence as their foundation. The scholarship required for effective teaching is discipline-based and therefore departmentally centered.

As a practical matter, reform of the college major depends on the ability of thousands of discrete academic departments to rethink the way they do business. Departmental cultures powerfully shape the aims and practice of teaching, and departmental curricula are far more capable than collegiate ones of reasonably rapid change . Too often administrators and faculty see departments as bureaucratic or intellectual units rather than pedagogical ones. Too often, departments take corporate responsibility for everything but teaching. And too often, the result is insular and parochial learning that commits the errors the critics condemn. Disciplinary faculty members conceive themselves to inhabit a national or international realm of learning, a kind of intellectual heaven, in which disciplinary discourse and course content transcend campus boundaries. For students, however, the campus is not a transient, earthly prelude to the sphere of celestial conversation. For students, the major is local. Committees of the guild - with scholarly input from around the globe - can devise learned curricula in their varied subjects, but the students' major is comprised of eighteen to twenty-four months of partial, though fairly intense, study with a small number of teachers on a particular campus, and what students know of a field and how it works is a consequence of their experience with that group of teachers. To place the college major at the center of a liberal education shifts the focus of curricular change from the collegiate to the departmental faculty.

In American higher education, academic departments are less than a century old, and their definition and institutional purpose are far from uniform. Departments vary in character and strength, even on a single campus, and their roles differ in disparate institutions. Some liberal arts colleges, particularly where departments are small, discourage departmental identity in favor of an institutional one. In research universities, where departments are the centers of graduate education, departmental boundaries tend to be high. The conventional university or college reward structure does not encourage the development of a corporate departmental ideology. When funds are short, administrations typically withdraw resources from the collective; that is, they cut departments and their budgets. Conversely, when resources are strong, administrations tend to disburse rewards to individuals, to the discrete faculty member. This sort of policy obscures departmental purpose. It discourages truly collective educational work and offers colleagues little reason to have a stake in one another's teaching.   If departments are to be a center for curricular change, positive rewards will need to flow to the department as a whole, rather than only to individual members.

In principle, nothing about disciplinary teaching and learning obstructs the generalizing and critical perspective of liberal education. General learning is not learned generalization, and being able to generalize does not mean being a generalist. Thus, it is a common administrative wish, particularly for technical and scientific subjects, to assign introductory courses to the most senior and accomplished members of a field precisely because their deep understanding, achieved from within the discipline, allows them to generalize about and explain their field to beginners. Recent proposals for revising college learning implicitly equate the outlook of liberal learning with educational breadth. But critical perspective on knowledge requires more than peripheral vision, more than multiple outlooks. The self-consciousness about knowledge that truly distinguishes liberal education from both high school learning and technical training - the awareness, for instance, that knowledge is constructed, tentative, limited, and interpretive - is ineluctably a matter of depth. Meaningful and revealing perspective cannot be imposed on a field from without and is not achieved by adding yet another point of view. Rather, it emerges from within, from thinking one's way to the edge of a field, asking questions a discipline provokes but cannot answer, and moving outward to make connections. A generalizing perspective is grounded in experience and hard work in a field, not in an opinion about it. Liberal learning builds on the disciplines. It is not their antithesis.

Departmental Learning: Collectivity and Collaboration

Despite what critics have claimed, the current apparently poor fit between disciplinary professionalism and liberal learning does not result from overly limited subject matter or analytical focus. The issue is not specialization but narrowness: the intellectual selfishness that makes us disciplinary professionals poor and indifferent translators of what we know. To place the major at the center of liberal learning requires us to solve not a problem of restricted subject matter but a problem of restrictive and insular teaching. Despite our concern to maintain fresh and contemporary course offerings, in our departments and our majors we keep too many of our interesting questions to ourselves. Within the major, students too infrequently are exposed to the reasons we, their teachers, find our fields compelling. We all too rarely share with students why our work is fun. In other words, we have not allowed our own disciplinary professionalism to serve as a model for education. We have not drawn our undergraduate majors in as colleagues so that they might, in ways appropriate for them, learn as we learn.

Our failure to do this regularly and systematically in the liberal arts major is largely the consequence of the separation between research and teaching and our tendency to identify disciplinary professionalism only with research. This separation of research from teaching, which bounds off the work faculty do with one another from work they do with their students, has roots deep in the history of higher education. The two institutional models from which American higher education derives are the English college and the German research university. Although these institutions are very different in function and design, in both the work of learning is exam driven. In both, students' knowledge - their acquisition of education, so to speak - is certified by success on an examination. In both, teachers prepare students for tests only students will take, for work only students will do.

This division between the faculty's work and the students' work is the basis for the broadly held, but often unstated, conception of teaching as epiphenomenal rather than foundational. The separation undergirds the view of teaching is something distinct, even divergent, from research, of teaching as derivative intellectual work. Such a conception of teaching builds barriers between teachers and students. If teaching is secondary activity, and it is something we do only to (or with) students, we will never be able to take students as seriously as we take ourselves, or their learning as seriously as our own. It is a short hop from secondary to second-rate. The sharp distinction between teaching and research carries with it a conception of the student as other, as someone whose intellectual life is somehow fundamentally different from, and fundamentally less than, our own.

One way to break the barrier between teaching and research, and the barrier between teacher and student that comes in its wake, is to re-conceive the liberal arts major as a curriculum that employs the professional practices of a discipline to create a continuum of learning that draws students and faculty into one another's work. It is in the major that the heavenly realm of faculty discourse and the earthly arena of students' discovery should merge. A major conceived along these lines will help students develop a self-consciousness about how a field of learning works and will draw faculty into collective work that gives them a stake in one another's teaching.

Let me illustrate with a concrete example. In 1983, the administration of the College of Arts and Science at the University of Rochester transformed an interdepartmental program of religious studies into the Department of Religion and Classics. The department began its history with a dozen student majors. By 1993, that number had grown to over 120, in an undergraduate student body of fewer than 4,000. One reason for the department's success, in addition to good teaching, is that its programs of study are designed to encourage collective work among faculty, faculty and students, and students.

The department's major in religion requires ten courses: one introductory course in the Bible (Hebrew Bible or New Testament); one introductory course in the history of a religion (Judaism, Christianity, Islam, Religions of South Asia, or Religions of East Asia); one intermediate level course in the nature of the field (Theories of Religion), required of all junior majors, with any course in religion as a prerequisite; six additional religion courses, no more than three of which can be in a single religion; a senior seminar or senior tutorial in the field. The major has a structure, but not a rigid one. The introductory courses ensure that students have some capacity for critical use of the Bible, because of its importance in U.S. cultural and political life, and that they are familiar with the history and morphology of one major literate religion. The course in theories of religion supplies all religion majors with a common set of theoretical readings and a common frame of intellectual reference. The work of the senior year, whether as a seminar or a tutorial, draws upon and develops the work of the theories course.

Perhaps the most distinctive feature of the department's work is the way it systematically engages advanced majors in the education of beginning students. Junior and senior majors who did well in a required course (introductory and theories) work with (not for) the faculty in teaching that course. The theories course epitomizes this feature of the department's work. Typically, Theories of Religion has an enrollment of between fifty and sixty students, most of them junior majors or minors in the department. The course is taught by a faculty member and two teaching fellows, senior majors who did well in the course in the previous year. They receive academic credit, not money, for their work as fellows. The faculty member and the teaching fellows prepare the syllabus together and work collaboratively throughout the course.

The theories course requires roughly 200 pages of reading per week in primary scholarly works that have given the study of religion its disciplinary contours. The focus of the course is the quality of the argument in each work and the way each scholar conceives the subject of religion. Readings come from such fields as phenomenology, history of religion, psychology, anthropology, sociology, theology, and literary theory. Students are asked to explain how each writer distinguishes between religion and not-religion and how he or she defends that position. The course aims to help students understand that what appeared in some earlier course as a matter of fact about either religion in general or a particular religion actually depends on a theoretical argument, that is, on disciplined intellect and imagination. The course stresses the problem of generalization and asks students to use theoretical works to think about religion as an analytical category, to think about religion in general.

Each class is divided into three groups of approximately twenty students apiece, and each group meets with the teaching fellows, who work as a team, in a ninety-minute preparation section one or two days before the class meets as a whole. In these sections, students review the reading they will discuss in class later in the larger class, and they are required to bring with them a two-page restatement of the argument. The teaching fellows evaluate, but do not grade, these restatements and return them in the next class. The fellows also bring deficient restatements to the faculty member, who typically asks students having difficulties to rewrite their statements.

The work of the class itself consists of small group presentations on the readings of the week. These presentations work as follows. Each week, a different team of two to four students presents a five-to-ten page critical analysis of the reading the class has done. These teams review their analyses with the faculty member several days before the class meets as a whole, and they normally rewrite the paper twice before they present it. Thus, all students, even in a fairly large class, have the opportunity for small group work with a faculty member. Students do most of the talking in the classes. Each class begins with a presentation of the team's collective paper, which is distributed to all, and a discussion follows. Since all the students in principle (though not always in fact!) have previously read and discussed the reading, discussion usually moves at a fairly high level, and students have the chance to challenge one another's readings, interpretations, and thinking and to assess differences of opinion and judgment in a public forum with other knowledgeable readers. The teacher's role is to keep the discussion focused and to help bring conversation to closure. But, for the most part, the teacher sits on the sidelines, like a coach rather than a judge.

Although one faculty member is responsible for this course, all departmental faculty have either co-taught the course or taken it. The course varies slightly from year to year but is built around a stable set of readings, so it has continuity over time. It also is typical for departmental faculty to drop in on the course for a session or two. Thus, the course provides a common frame of reference for faculty and majors alike and set an intellectual agenda for the department's educational work.

I am convinced that the course is effective because its structure allows students to replicate modes of faculty learning in their own studies. The teaching fellows have the opportunity to reread a semester's worth of books and to think about how to explain them to their peers. By the end of the course they know these works extremely well. In their small groups, students learn how to negotiate their differences to produce a collective paper. They are rarely unprepared for group meetings, because each will receive the grade the paper earns. Their learning takes place largely as the faculty's learning does, in conversation that results from disagreement and strives for clarity. Students learn something about making an argument to people who know what they know, and about what it takes to be persuasive.

The traits of the theories course illustrate the potential of the major as a vehicle for liberal learning. Although offered only to majors and minors, the course supplies critical perspective by focusing on how the field structures arguments, how it makes its case, and how it persuades itself. By showing that core arguments of the field can be assessed (and how they can be assessed), the course demystifies such arguments and shows their constructed, tentative, character. By having students learn as faculty do, teaching one another through conversation, rereading, argument, and public writing, the course illustrates how scholarship works. Exchanges among students are much more intense than those between students and faculty. Although the course employs a highly discipline-specific set of readings, it draws students into problems of inference and generalization and helps them see both the limitations and power of specialized knowledge. Most important, the course exposes students to the field as both an intellectual and social construction. Students directly experience the complex relationship between thought and discourse, between ideas and the communities that hold them. On the basis of a course such as this, students can see the field of religion in relation to other fields. Because they have labored together to understand how their own subject works, they can begin to understand how other subjects work.

In the final analysis, the issue of the place of the major in liberal education is less a question of specialized versus general learning than of reflective and thoughtful teaching. If we draw students into the questions and problems that make a field compelling, and into the modes of argument and communication that give a field its vitality, these students can learn to be critical of their own knowledge and to understand their role in constructing what they know. If departments become educationally thoughtful about how they engage students with their field's subjects and procedures, and if faculty become collectively responsible for the educational coherence of departmental offerings, we can have our disciplinary professionalism and liberal learning too.[1]

Works Cited

Association of American Colleges. *Integrity in the College Curriculum* (Washington, D.C,., 1985)

Ernest Boyer, College: *The Undergraduate Experience in America* (New York: Harper & Row, 1987)

Lynne V. Cheney, *50 Hours: A Core Curriculum for College Students* (Washington, D.C.: National Endowment for the Humanities, 1989)

Bruce A. Kimball, "The Historical and Cultural Dimensions of the Recent Reports on Undergraduate Education," in *ASHE Reader on The History of Higher Education,* L.F. Goodchild and H.S. Weschler, eds., (Needham Heights, Mass: Ginn Press, 1989):592-615

Stephen Toulmin, *Human Understanding: The Collective Use and Evolution of Concepts* (Princeton: Princeton University Press, 1972)

F.S. Weaver, *Liberal Education* (New York and London: Teachers College, Columbia University Press, 1991)

Notes

1. My gratitude goes to Deborah Derylak, who helped enormously with the research for this article, and to my colleagues Celia Applegate, Suzanne O'Brien, Dale McAdam, and Douglas Brooks for constructive critical readings.

Bibliography

Association of American Colleges. 1985. Integrity in the College Curriculum *Washington, D.C.*

Athanassiadi, Polymnia. 1992. Julian, An Intellectual Biography. London: Routledge.

Baker, Liva. 1976. I'm Radcliffe! Fly Me! The Seven Sisters and the Failure of Women's Education. New York: Macmillan Publishing Co., Inc.

Barzun, Jacques. 1968. The American University. New York: Harper & Row.

Bloom, Allan D. 1987. The Closing of the American Mind: How Higher Education has failed democracy and impoverished the souls of today's students. New York: Simon and Schuster.

Bowles, Frank and Frank A. DeCosta. 1971. Between Two Worlds: A Profile of Negro Higher Education. New York: McGraw Hill Book Company.

Boyer, Ernest. 1987. College: The Undergraduate Experience in America. *New York: Harper & Row.*

Brint, Steven and Jerome Karabel. 1989. The Diverted Dream.: Community Colleges and the Promise of Educational Opportunity in America, 1900-1985. New York: Oxford University Press.

Brubacher, John S. and Willis Rudy. 1976. Higher Education In Transition. New York: Harper & Row Publishers.

Carnochan, W.B. 1993. The Battleground of the Curriculum: Liberal Education and American Experience. Stanford, Calif.: Stanford University Press.

Cheit, Earl F. 1971. The New Depression in Higher Education . The Carnegie Commission on Higher Education. New York: McGraw-Hill Book Company.

Cheit, Earl F. 1973. The New Depression in Higher Education — Two Years Later. The Carnegie Commission on Higher Education.

Cheney, Lynne V. 1989. 50 Hours: A Core Curriculum for College Students. Washington, D.C.: National Endowment for the Humanities.

Clark, Burton R., ed. 1984. Perspectives on Higher Education. Berkeley, Ca.: University of California Press.

Conant, James B. 1948. Education In A Divided World. Cambridge, Ma.: Harvard University Press.

Coyne, John R. Jr. 1970. The Kumquat Statement. New York: College Notes & Texts, Inc.

Curran, Charles E. 1990. Catholic Higher Education, Theology, and Academic Freedom. Notre Dame, Ind.: University of Notre Dame Press.

Digest of Education Statistics. 1993. National Center for Educational Statistics. U.S. Department of Education.

D'Souza, Dinesh. 1991. Illiberal Education: The Politics of Race and Sex on Campus. New York: Vintage Books.

Ehrenfeld, David. 1989. Orion Nature Quarterly. August issue. Myrin Institute, New York.

Erikson, Erik. 1968. Identity, Youth and Crisis. New York: W.W. Norton.

Feynman, Richard. The Meaning of It All; Thoughts of a Citizen Scientist. Helix Books, 1998.

Freeland, Richard M. 1992. Academia's Golden Age: Universities in Massachusetts 1945-1970. New York: Oxford University Press.

Gates, Henry Louis. 1992. Loose Cannons: Notes on the Culture Wars. New York: Oxford University Press.

Greeley, Andrew M. 1969. From Backwater to Mainstream: A Profile of Catholic Higher Education. New York: McGraw Hill Book Company.

Gross, Theodore L. 1980. Academic Turmoil: The Reality and Promise of Open Education. Garden City, N.Y.: Anchor Press/Doubleday.

Hall, James W., ed. With Barbara L. Kevles. 1982. In Opposition to Core Curriculum: Alternative Models for Undergraduate Education. Westport, Ct.: Greenwood Press.

Hirsch, E.D. Jr. 1987. *Cultural Literacy: What Every American Needs to Know.* Boston: Houghton Mifflin Co.

Jencks, Christopher and David Riesman. 1968. *The Academic Revolution.* Garden City, N.Y.: Doubleday & Co., Inc.

Kaiser, Charles. 1988. *1968 In America: Music, Politics, Chaos, Countercul- ture, and the Shaping of a Generation.* New York: Weidenfeld & Nicolson.

Kaysen, Carl, ed. 1973. *Content and Context: Essays on College Education.* New York: McGraw Hill Book Company.

Kerr, Clark. 1991. *The Great Transformation in Higher Education 1960-1980.* Albany, N.Y.: State University of New York Press.

Kimball, Bruce A. 1989. *"The Historical and Cultural Dimensions of the Re- cent Reports on Undergraduate Education,"* in ASHE Reader on The His- tory of Higher Education, *L.F. Goodchild and H.S. Weschler, eds., 592-615. Needham Heights, Mass: Ginn Press.*

Kimball, Roger. 1990. *Tenured Radicals: How politics has corrupted our higher education.* New York: Harper & Row.

Lavin, David E., Richard D. Alba and Richard A. Silberstein. 1981. *Right Versus Privilege: The Open-Admissions Experiment at the City University of New York.* New York: The Free Press.

Lagemann, Ellen Condliffe. 1989. *The Politics of Knowledge.* Middletown, Conn.: Wesleyan University Press.

Magat, Richard. 1979. *The Ford Foundation At Work.* New York: Plenum Press.

Marsden, George M. 1994. *The Soul of the American University: From Prot- estant establishment to established non-belief.* New York: Oxford Univer- sity Press.

McGill, William J. 1982. *The Year of the Monkey: Revolt on Campus, 1968- 1969.* New York: McGraw-Hill Book Company.

Morison, Robert S., ed. 1966. *The Contemporary University: U.S.A.* Boston: Houghton Mifflin Co.

Neusner, Jacob, and Noam M. M. Neusner, *The Price of Excellence. Universi- ties in Conflict during the Cold War Era. New York, 1995: Continuum.*

Neusner, Jacob. How To Grade Your Professors and Other Unexpected Advice. Boston, 1984: Beacon.

Penick, James. L., Carroll W. Pursell, Jr., Morgan B. Sherwood and Donald C. Swain, eds. 1972. The Politics of American Science, 1939 to the Present. Cambridge, Ma.: The MIT Press.

Perelman, Lewis J. 1992. School's Out: Hyperlearning, the New Technology, and the End of Education. New York: William Morrow and Company, Inc.

Riesman, David. 1980. On Higher Education. San Francisco: Jossey-Bass Inc.

Roebuck, Julian B. and Komanduri S. Murty. 1993. Historically Black Colleges and Universities: Their Place in American Higher Education. Westport, Ct.: Praeger.

Sacks, David and Peter Thiel. 1995. The Diversity Myth; Multiculturalism and the politics of intolerance at Stanford. Oakland, California: Independent Institute.

Smith, G. Kerry, ed. 1970. 1945 1970 Twenty-five years. San Francisco: Jossey-Bass Inc.

Steinberg, Stephen. 1974. The Academic Melting Pot. New York: McGraw-Hill Book Company.

Stone, Joseph and Joseph Church. 1984, 5th edition. Childhood and Adolescence: A Psychology of the Growing Person. New York: Random House.

Sykes, Charles J. 1988 ProfScam: Professors and the demise of higher education.Washington D.C.: Regnery Gateway.

Sykes, Charles J. 1990. The Hollow Men: Politics and Corruption in Higher Education. Washington D.C.: Regnery Gateway.

Toulmin, Stephen. 1972. Human Understanding: The Collective Use and Evolution of Concepts. *Princeton, N.J.: Princeton University Press.*

Wallerstein, Immanuel and Paul Starr, eds.1971. The University Crisis Reader: The Liberal University Under Attack, Volume One. New York: Random House.

Weaver, F.S. 1991. Liberal Education. *New York and London: Teachers College, Columbia University Press.*

Wechsler, Harold S. 1977. *The Qualified Student: A History of Selective College Admission in America.* New York: John Wiley & Sons.

Newspapers and Magazines

Chicago Tribune
Christian Science Monitor
Chronicle of Higher Education
Denver Post
Governing
The Nation
National Review
New Republic
New York Times
Newsweek
Phi Beta Kappan
Philadelphia Inquirer
St. Petersburg Times
Tampa Tribune
Time
Wall Street Journal
Washington Post

Index

Learning:
    classics of learning defined, 167-69,
    distinctions in centers of learning,
        171-6
    don't ask, discover, 138;
    and growing up, 129-36
    how to discover things on their own,
        136-42;
    in the public interest, 117-20
    surrendering classicism, 169-71

Marx or Marxism, 9; affecting univer-
    sity curriculum, 66-72, and politics
    of, 72-80
McClintick, William, 105
Morgan, Edmund S.,182-8
Multiculturalism, affecting university
    curriculum, 66-80

National Association of Admission
    Counselors, 105

Ozick, Cynthia, 22

Pattison, Robert, 80
Perelmnan, Lewis, 107-8, 150
Polymnia Athanassiadis,165-66
Princeton University, 35
Professors
    ability to convey useful knowledge,
        1-4
    attributes of a good teacher, 24-29
    combining teaching with research,
        15, 21-24, 47-50
    extra-curricular activities, 33-39
    grading of, 18-20
    making a difference, 1-4
    professionalism, 23-29
    research without students, 8-10
    sophisticated or arcane language,
        use of, 9
    usefulness of lecture system ques-
        tioned, 2-4
    who should teach, 15-18

Reagan Ronald, 110
Research, combining scholarship, re-
    search and teaching, 15, 21-24, 47-50
Rudenstine, Neil, 148

Sachar, Abram, 35
Sacks, David, 73

Scholarship
    combining scholarship, research and
        teaching, 15, 21-24, 47-50
    defining authentic scholar, 51
        graduate education and the scholars'
        apprentice, 86-91
    intellectual specialization in
        higher education, 187-99
    personal identity replacing intellec-
        tual merit, reducing status of
        scholarship, 72-81
Silber, John, 36
Sommers, Christina Hoff, 76
Stecklow, Steve, 103
Stone, Joseph, 134
Students
    ability to succeed in college, 125-26
    adolescents and higher education,
        99-103
    assessing status of alumni, 99-100
    best time to go to college, 122-3
        at age of maturity, 126-36
    evaluating reputation of institution,
        95-9
    exploring new areas for study, 120-21
    motivation and responsibility for
        study, 123-29
    professionalism of institution,
        99-103
    purpose for attending college, 113
    selecting courses of study, 120-22
    significance of college diploma,107-
        108
    who should go to college, 95-143
Swearer, Howard, 31
Sykes, Charles, 8, 78, 149

Teaching
    and apprenticeship, 52-57
    canon of what is to be taught, 60-62
    combining scholarship, research and
        teaching, 15, 21-24, 47-50
    dialogue, value in teaching, 49
    humanities, the new humanities for
        good and ill, 57-60
    meaning of, 81-82
    what should universities teach,2-3,
        23-45, 47-93
    what teachers want, 82-85
Tenure,
    input from graduate students and pur-
        suit of scholarship, 11